MIND DUST AND WHITE CROWS

MIND DUST AND WHITE CROWS

THE PSYCHICAL RESEARCH OF WILLIAM JAMES

EDITED BY

GREGORY SHUSHAN

INTRODUCTION BY

ANDREAS SOMMER

www.whitecrowbooks.com

Mind Dust and White Crows

Copyright © 2023 by Gregory Shushan. All rights reserved.
Introduction: Copyright © 2023 by Andreas Sommer. All rights reserved.
Published by White Crow Books, an imprint of White Crow Productions Ltd.

The right of the authors to be identified as the author of this work has been asserted by them in accordance with the Copyright, Design and Patents act 1988.

No part of this book may be reproduced, copied, or used in any form or manner whatsoever without written permission, except in the case of brief quotations in reviews and critical articles.

A CIP catalogue record for this book is available from the British Library.

For information, contact White Crow Productions Ltd.
by e-mail: info@whitecrowbooks.com

Cover Design by Astrid@Astridpaints.com
Interior design by Velin@Perseus-Design.com

ISBN: Paperback: 978-1-78677-204-6
ISBN: eBook: 978-1-78677-205-3

Non-Fiction / Body, Mind & Spirit / Parapsychology / Philosophy

www.whitecrowbooks.com

William James sitting in a séance with the medium
Mrs. Walden, sometime before 1910.

MS Am 1092 (1185), Houghton Library, Harvard University

WILLIAM JAMES
For thirty-five years Professor of Philosophy at Harvard College. One of the greatest living psychologists

Portrait of William James by William Oberhardt, illustrating the 1909 article "The Confidences of a 'Psychical Researcher'" (see Chapter 20)

CONTENTS

INTRODUCTION: WILLIAM JAMES AND THE RIGHT TO INVESTIGATE BY ANDREAS SOMMER 1
A NOTE ON THE TEXTS 25

PART I: PSYCHOLOGY AND PSYCHICAL RESEARCH 27
1. THE HIDDEN SELF 29
2. WHAT PSYCHICAL RESEARCH HAS ACCOMPLISHED 51
3. ADDRESS OF THE PRESIDENT BEFORE THE SOCIETY FOR PSYCHICAL RESEARCH 69
4. PSYCHICAL RESEARCH 81
5. SENSE OF PRESENCE 87
6. TWO REVIEWS: *COCK-LANE AND COMMON SENSE* BY ANDREW LANG AND *DIE ENTDECKUNG DER SEELE DUREH DIE GEHEIMWISSENSCHAFTEN* BY CARL DU PREL. 93

PART II: TELEPATHY, AUTOMATISM, AND EXTENDED CONSCIOUSNESS 97
7. TELEPATHY 99
8. NOTES ON AUTOMATIC WRITING 107
9. REPORT OF THE COMMITTEE ON HYPNOTISM (EXCERPT) 127
10. THE CONSCIOUSNESS OF LOST LIMBS (EXCERPT) 131
11. REVIEW OF *TELEPATHIC DREAMS EXPERIMENTALLY INDUCED* BY G. B. ERMACORA 133
12. REVIEW OF *PHANTASMS OF THE LIVING* BY EDMUND GURNEY, FREDERIC W. H. MYERS, AND FRANK PODMORE 137
13. A SUGGESTION ABOUT MYSTICISM 143

PART III: MEDIUMSHIP 153

14. REPORT OF THE COMMITTEE ON MEDIUMISTIC PHENOMENA ... 155
15. A RECORD OF OBSERVATIONS OF CERTAIN
    PHENOMENA OF TRANCE 161
16. REVIEW OF *A FURTHER RECORD OF OBSERVATIONS OF
    CERTAIN PHENOMENA OF TRANCE* BY RICHARD HODGSON 171
17. MRS. PIPER, "THE MEDIUM" (WITH A LETTER TO
    J. MCKEEN CATTELL) 177
18. REPORT ON MRS. PIPER'S HODGSON-CONTROL (EXCERPTS) 181
19. PHYSICAL PHENOMENA AT A PRIVATE CIRCLE 199
20. THE CONFIDENCES OF A "PSYCHICAL RESEARCHER" 205

PART IV: POSSESSION 223

21. MEDIUMSHIPS OR POSSESSIONS 225
22. TWO REVIEWS OF *DEMON-POSSESSION AND ALLIED
    THEMES* BY REV. JOHN L. NEVIUS 233
23. DEMONIACAL POSSESSION (LECTURE SUMMARY, NOTES,
    AND CORRESPONDENCE) 239

PART V: THE METAPHYSICS OF LIFE AFTER DEATH 251

24. MIND, SOUL, AND CONSCIOUSNESS 253
25. REVIEW OF *HUMAN PERSONALITY AND ITS SURVIVAL OF
    BODILY DEATH* BY FREDERIC MYERS 267
26. HUMAN IMMORTALITY 281
27. POSTSCRIPT 313

APPENDICES 320

APPENDIX A: EXPERIMENTS SINCE THE DEATH OF PROFESSOR
    JAMES BY JAMES H. HYSLOP (EXCERPTS) 321
APPENDIX B: FROM WILLIAM JAMES? BY E.F. FRIEND (EXCERPTS) 325

SOURCES 331
FURTHER READING 335
INDEX 337

INTRODUCTION

WILLIAM JAMES AND THE RIGHT TO INVESTIGATE

Andreas Sommer[1]

Between Naturalism and Pragmatism

"Men," celebrity biologist Thomas H. Huxley once wrote, "make their gods after their own likeness, in their own image make they them."[2] A nearly identical verdict has been attributed more prominently to Huxley's German contemporary, noted atheist philosopher and advocate of "scientific materialism," Ludwig Feuerbach. Like Huxley, Feuerbach and his followers held that supernaturalism sprang from an unchecked human impulse which anthropomorphized nature by populating it with gods, spirits and occult forces, often in the service of an unconscious drive to make the world conform to our metaphysical biases and emotional needs. The

---

[1] *Acknowledgements*: My research has been made possible by support from the Wellcome Trust, London, a Junior Research Fellowship at Churchill College, Cambridge, and funding by the Perrott-Warrick Trust at Trinity College, Cambridge University.

[2] T.H. Huxley, (1892) *Essays upon Some Controverted Questions*. London: Macmillan and Co., p. 188.

problem of unconscious metaphysical bias also lay at the foundation of the work of the founder of the American psychological profession and major proponent of philosophical pragmatism, William James.

Secular reformers like Huxley and Feuerbach argued from their rather understandable positions as critics of orthodox Christian theologies and their immense stranglehold on nineteenth-century politics, education and intellectual freedom[3]. James, on the other hand, developed a far more symmetrical and thoroughgoing approach. Acknowledging the harmful social, educational and political effects of theological bigotry and censorship, he fully conceded that religious faith, especially its institutionalized and dogmatic forms, was often a product of cultural conditioning and expression of anti-scientific temperament. Yet, throughout his career James launched frontal attacks on what he considered blatantly one-sided wholesale dismissals of any belief in the "supernatural" as self-evident childish wishful thinking, a view relentlessly propounded by Huxley and countless other popularizers of scientific naturalism.

James was, and continues to be, admired as a rigorous, critical, progressive, and fair-minded thinker. But unlike most of his academic peers, he felt the programmatic anti-supernaturalism of contemporary science popularizers like Huxley was ultimately no less removed from concrete human experience as was fundamentalist religion, and hardly more rational or scientific. James moreover thought it especially problematic if science was tacitly portrayed, as pioneering science popularizers were wont to do, as a unified body of static and irreversible knowledge rather than an open-ended project of enquiry marked by sometimes foundational revisions and changes.

If there was something that irked James in particular, it was a somewhat disingenuous exploitation by celebrity scientists of their audiences' sense of moral duty. The "ethics of belief" popularized by Huxley and allies like the mathematician William K. Clifford, after all, left absolutely no wiggle room by postulating that it was "wrong in all cases to believe on insufficient evidence."[4] In Huxley's words, to violate

---

[3] See, for example, Frederick Gregory (1977) *Scientific Materialism in Nineteenth Century Germany (Studies in the History of Modern Science 1)*. Dordrecht: Springer; and Bernard Lightman (1987) *The Origins of Agnosticism. Victorian Unbelief and the Limits of Knowledge*. Baltimore, ML: Johns Hopkins University Press.

[4] William Kingdon Clifford (1879) "The Ethics of Belief." In *Lectures and Essays by the Late William Kingdon Clifford*, edited by Leslie Stephen and Frederick Pollock, 2:177–211. London: Macmillan. p. 211)

"the plain rule of not pretending to believe" what we "have no reason to believe" just because a belief served our individual advantage, was to sink to "the lowest depths of immorality."[5]

In a text first published in 1879, James took issue with these writers' strategy to "use the conjuring spell of the name of Science, and to harp on Reverence for Truth as means whereby to force them on the minds of simple public listeners."[6] Profound discontent with Huxley's and Clifford's one-dimensional ethics of belief grounded in scientism would form the central theme of essays later collated in James's *The Will to Believe*. The rule of rejecting belief unsupported by robust evidence no doubt performed useful functions if applied as a flexible rule of thumb, James recognized. Instead of warranting rigid application to all spheres of life, however, it needed to be soundly qualified according to specific contexts. While being critical of the kinds of religious faith that engendered intolerance or were too abstract to serve healthy ends, in *The Will to Believe* and other works James therefore defended the individual's right to believe in transcendental realities – as long as grounds for such belief were not conclusively refuted and, most importantly, if faith served health-preserving or constructive functions.

Having himself undergone severe struggles of faith in his youth, James was rather well aware of the fundamental clash of any belief in a hidden ultimate benevolence of the cosmos with the brutal and merciless appearance of physical nature as revealed by then established facts of science. Such faith may rest on mere instinct or intuition, while in other cases it might be the result of totally subjective but measurably transformative transcendental experiences – the kinds of which were to form the subject of his classic study, *The Varieties of Religious Experience* (1902). No matter if faith was based on intuition or on full-blown transcendental experiences with dramatic after-effects, James argued that it could make a real and important difference in human life. For a sizeable part of the general population, he believed, trust

---

[5] Thomas H. Huxley (1878) "The Influence upon Morality of a Decline in Religious Belief." In *A Modern Symposium. Subjects: The Soul and Future Life. The Influence Upon Morality of a Decline in Religious Belief*, 247–52. Detroit, MI: Rose-Belford. p. 252)

[6] William James (1920) "Review of W. K. Clifford, Lectures and Essays, and Seeing and Thinking." In *Collected Essays and Reviews by William James*, edited by Henry James, 137–46 (original publication 1879). New York & London: Longmans, Green and Co.

in divine benevolence and a spiritual kinship of souls transcending earthly categories like sex, race and social class provided considerable motivations for the cultivation of genuine altruism, empathy and compassion.

Of particular interest to James was the practical utility of spiritual belief when it harbored the potential to sustain the necessary strength to carry on in the face of devastating experiences of tragedy and loss. The cash-value of faith as a powerful tool to cope with the very real tragedies and hardships of life, he suggested, was sometimes indistinguishable from functions of unsubstantiated prior belief in perfectly mundane do-or-die situations. James illustrated this with examples like the following:

> If I refuse to bale out a boat because I am in doubt whether my efforts will keep her afloat, I am really helping to sink her. If in the mountain precipice I doubt my right to risk a leap, I actively connive at my destruction.[7]

But even in the realm of science, James argued, Huxley's command of heroically suppressing belief in the absence of solid evidence was in fact rarely obeyed. On the contrary, rather than forestalling progress, subjective prior belief was typically a basic precondition for the very making of scientific knowledge. Scientists, after all, usually – and often rather tenaciously – swore on the truth of their pet theories and hypotheses *before* they were put to the empirical test: "Hardly a law has been established in science, hardly a fact ascertained, which was not first sought after, often with sweat and blood, to gratify an inner need."[8] Hence, for James the "most useful investigator, because the most sensitive observer" was "always he whose eager interest in one side of the question is balanced by an equally keen nervousness lest he become deceived."[9] Human life in both the scientific and non-scientific domains was therefore replete with cases

> where a fact cannot come at all unless a preliminary faith exists in its coming. *And where faith in a fact can help create the fact*, that would be an insane logic which should say that faith running ahead

---

[7] William James (1897) *The Will to Believe and Other Essays in Popular Philosophy*. London: Longmans Green and Co., p. 109)

[8] Ibid., p. 55.

[9] Ibid., p. 21.

of scientific evidence is the 'lowest kind of immorality' into which a thinking being can fall. Yet such is the logic by which our scientific absolutists pretend to regulate our lives![10]

James and the Society for Psychical Research

One of the essays in *The Will to Believe*, entitled "What Psychical Research Has Accomplished" appears to be something of an outlier in that it is not directly concerned with the overall theme of the book. In essence a defense of the British Society for Psychical Research (SPR) against polemical attacks by journalists and several fellow psychologists, the essay – all of whose three different versions are for the first time published in the present volume – stressed the scientific rigor which characterized the work conducted by the SPR, of which James was President in 1894 and 1895. Founded in 1882 in London, the SPR was the first major body formed by elite intellectuals with the explicit goal of studying alleged phenomena associated with mesmerism, spiritualism and other hotly contested occult beliefs and practices in an open-minded yet scientifically thorough manner. The first generations of SPR members included various giants of British and international science, such as physics Nobel laureates J. J. Thompson and Lord Rayleigh, and later Madame Curie.[11] The most active early representatives of the SPR, however, were figures who ambitiously strove to integrate the study of reported marvels as a legitimate branch of the fledgling discipline of experimental psychology.[12]

Leading amongst those were friends of the SPR's founding President, the noted Cambridge philosopher and educational reformer Henry Sidgwick, and his wife, mathematician Eleanor Sidgwick. The closest allies of the Sidgwicks, and most industrious investigators in the SPR, were philosopher of music and psychological writer Edmund Gurney, as well as the inventor of the term "telepathy," the classicist and pioneering theorist of the subconscious mind, Frederic W. H.

---

[10] Ibid., p. 25.

[11] See, e.g., Richard Noakes (2019) *Physics and Psychics: The Occult and the Sciences in Modern Britain.* Cambridge: Cambridge University Press.

[12] Andreas Sommer (2013) *Crossing the Boundaries of Mind and Body. Psychical Research and the Origins of Modern Psychology.* PhD thesis, London: University College London.

Myers. By far the most active American member and collaborator of the SPR was William James, who was also a close co-worker and personal friend of Gurney and, following Gurney's death in 1888, of Myers, too. Working with James and the future Nobel Prize winner, French physiologist Charles Richet, the Sidgwicks and Myers became prominently involved in the first International Congresses of Psychology from its first session in 1889 to Henry Sidgwick's death in 1900 and Myers's death the following year. In 1892, Henry Sidgwick even served as president of the second congress which took place in London, with Myers (together with the more orthodox psychologist James Sully) acting as congress secretary.

A major joint project of the SPR and James, which was commissioned by a committee of the first psychology congress in Paris, was an international census of so-called veridical hallucinations.[13] This was a replication of a previous survey conducted in England by the SPR with the late Gurney as the principal investigator[14]. The objective of both endeavors was twofold: Hardly uncontroversial at the time, they provided the first substantial evidence that hallucinations – i.e. clear and distinct sensory impressions that did not seem to correspond with physical reality – occurred in many mentally heathy persons. The second but far more contested innovation was the use of fledgling statistical methods to assess whether unexpected and usually dramatic quasi-hallucinations of friends and family members at the time of their suffering an unexpected death, accident or other crisis at a distance, reported by reputable persons without plausible knowledge of the "hallucinated" event, could be explained by mere chance coincidence. The results of both research projects strongly suggested that coincidence and other ordinary explanations were insufficient to account for a significant portion of the investigated veridical impressions.[15]

---

[13] Henry Sidgwick, Eleanor Sidgwick, and Alice Johnson (1894) "Report on the Census of Hallucinations." *Proceedings of the Society for Psychical Research*, vol. 10, pp. 25-422.

[14] Edmund Gurney, Frederic William Henry Myers, and Frank Podmore (1886) *Phantasms of the Living*. 2 vols. London: Trübner.

[15] See, e.g., Alan Gauld (1968) *The Founders of Psychical Research*. London: Routledge & Kegan Paul, chapter 7; Pascal Le Maléfan and Andreas Sommer (2015) "Léon Marillier and the Veridical Hallucination in Late-Nineteenth and Early-Twentieth Century French Psychology and Psychopathology." *History of Psychiatry* 26: 418–32.

The most enduring collaboration of James with the SPR, however, were investigations of the trance medium Leonora Piper. An ordinary Boston housewife, Mrs. Piper was discovered by James just when she was about to embark, somewhat reluctantly, on a career as a professional medium after she experienced spontaneous states of trance. During many of these sleep-like states, which she soon learned to control and self-induce, Piper was said to convincingly impersonate recently deceased individuals, including many whom she could not have plausibly met when they were alive. Investigations of Piper covered a span of about four decades of painstaking experiments, which continued after James's death in 1910. Initially, James and his colleagues at the SPR deployed thoroughgoing if not ethically questionable safeguards against fraud, such as the employment of detectives who shadowed Piper's whole household, as well as invasive and painful measures to test if Piper might feign her trances. James and other initially skeptical investigators quickly convinced themselves that not only her trance states were genuine, but that she regularly made highly specific and idiosyncratic statements concerning the lives of impersonated individuals, which included intimate details about the supposed spirit's personal relationship with sitters. James and practically all long-term Piper investigators agreed that such statements and impersonations often exceeded the possible use of information that could be acquired by fraudulent means such as snooping, or the ingenious reading of subtle clues given away by sitters which could be used by clever cheats to gradually construct a convincing but fake spirit impersonation.

After publishing initial experimental observations concerning Piper in the *Proceedings* of the short-lived first incarnation of the American SPR (which he had helped form in 1884), James was one of several contributors to the first of several major reports of her trance phenomena by the SPR in England,[16] which was issued in the same year as his famous textbook, *The Principles of Psychology*. Without naming Mrs. Piper, the founder of experimental psychology in America briefly referred in the *Principles* to his initial tests with her, putting his convictions on record that she was indeed capable of producing veridical statements in her sleep-like states, and that "a serious study

---

[16] Frederic William Henry Myers, Oliver Lodge, Walter Leaf, and William James (1890) "A Record of Observations of Certain Phenomena of Trance." *Proceedings of the Society for Psychical Research* 6: 436–659.

of these trance-phenomena is one of the greatest needs of psychology"[17] (see Chapter 21 of the present volume).

Candid statements by James regarding his belief in the authenticity of Piper's anomalous knowledge of facts other than through the recognized channels of the senses, however, were no embrace of the spiritualist faith, according to which veridical impersonations of the dead by mediums provided sufficient if not conclusive proof for human survival of bodily death. As James freely acknowledged, the approach taken in canonical psychological texts like the *Principles* and later the *Varieties* was the more cautious methodology developed by his friend Frederic Myers. Grounded in the scientific ideal of establishing continuities between the best data of conventional mental and life sciences and the fundamental but increasingly well-established anomalies investigated by the SPR and similar associations on the continent, Myers's research programme differed markedly from ordinary spiritualist modes of reasoning: Rather than studying occult effects as isolated rogue phenomena, Myers and fellow workers at the SPR attempted to bridge the gulf between conventional scientific knowledge and the seemingly marvelous. The main objective was to obtain solid knowledge of ordinary and extraordinary capacities of the incarnate mind, and to merge these data into a synthesis that made sense of all its functions and capacities – as a necessary step before evaluating their relevance for the bigger question of the persistence of consciousness after death.

Both Myers and James conceived of telepathy as an influx of information from a cosmic nexus of interconnected minds. Perpetually occurring *beneath* the threshold of conscious awareness, telepathic connections were held to occasionally make uprushes *into* conscious awareness through the subconscious or subliminal partitions of the mind. In altered states like mediumistic and hypnotic trance, during which inhibiting and controlling functions of conscious awareness were bypassed or suppressed, the external setting was thought significantly to shape the form of manifestations. With Myers, James proposed that a more parsimonious interpretation even of strikingly veridical trance readings by mediums than the "spirit hypothesis" was to think of mediumistic trance impersonations as a benign form of split personality plus telepathy, shaped to a considerable degree by expectations and other suggestive influences from sitters and experimenters.

---

[17] William James (1890) *The Principles of Psychology*, Vol. I. New York: Henry Holt, p. 396.

What set James and Myers apart was their personal attitude to the question of post-mortem survival. James was no doubt open-minded regarding the problem, actively supported research on survival, and respected grounds which had convinced some of his fellow psychical researchers that Mrs. Piper and other mediums indeed at least occasionally channeled spirits of the dead. However, while James had only a mild personal interest in the problem and was to remain on the fence regarding the "spirit hypothesis," it is fair to say that Myers was downright obsessed with the problem of survival. Yet, contrary to Myers's portrayal as a self-deluded fanatic by Wikipedia editors and certain writers today, a perusal of his writings and private correspondence strongly suggests that his methodological and empirical approach was overwhelmingly self-disciplined.[18] This was also stressed by James, who compared Myers's integrative method in psychology to the general methodology applied by Darwin in biology in several letters to friends and colleagues as well as in print. Moreover, in his obituary of Myers in 1901, which he wrote as an explicit appraisal of Myers's work as a psychologist, James addressed the great question of the hereafter as the driving engine of Myers's work, but stated:

> His contributions to psychology were incidental to that research, and would probably never have been made had he not entered on it. But they have a value for Science entirely independent of the light they shed upon that problem; and it is quite apart from it that I shall venture to consider them.[19]

The research program of Myers and allies in the early SPR including James, with its focus on altered states and the psychology of mediumistic impersonations, confronted head-on one of the great fundamental questions of the psychological sciences and what is now called the philosophy of mind: Is the self-unified, or is it inherently fragmented

---

[18] See Gauld, *Founders*; Frank M. Turner (1974) *Between Science and Religion. The Reaction to Scientific Naturalism in Late Victorian England*. New Haven, CT: Yale University Press, chapter 5; John P. Williams (1984) "The Making of Victorian Psychical Research: An Intellectual Elite's Approach to the Spiritual World." PhD thesis, Cambridge: University of Cambridge; and Trevor Hamilton (2009) *Immortal Longings: F.W.H. Myers and the Victorian Search for Life After Death*. Exeter: Imprint Academic.

[19] William James (1901) "Frederic Myers's Service to Psychology." *Proceedings of the Society for Psychical Research* 17, p. 14.

and divided? It is therefore no accident that the early SPR contributed significantly to modern studies of multiple personality disorder, and related benign and non-pathological divisions of the self, occurring in states ranging from dreams and trances in mentally healthy persons to disruptive fugue states in full-fledged multiple personality disorder.[20] One classical case in the history of multiple personality disorder, that of Ansel Bourne, was investigated and treated by James in collaboration with another leading SPR researcher and close friend, Richard Hodgson.

Wills to Believe: Materialistic Science vs. Religious Superstition?

Hodgson was also the originator of the first experimental study demonstrating the rather disconcerting fallibilities of eyewitness testimony by using a blind design.[21] Along with the aforementioned use of statistical and probabilistic methods,[22] problems of memory and fallibilities of perception were another area of more conventional psychological research pioneered by the SPR. Prior to Hodgson's experiments, for example, by far the most searching survey of the literature on problems of eyewitness testimony at the time could be found dispersed throughout the two bulky volumes of Gurney's study of veridical hallucinations, and lessons from insights regarding the pitfalls of human perception and memory were evidently taken to heart by Gurney and fellow investigators in their cross-examinations of psychic claimants and witnesses.

Today, Hodgson is mostly remembered as the principal investigator of Mrs. Piper, whose trance phenomena eventually bowled him over

---

[20] E.g., Henri F. Ellenberger (1970) *The Discovery of the Unconscious: The History and Evolution of Dynamic Psychiatry.* New York: Basic Books; Adam Crabtree (1993) *From Mesmer to Freud. Magnetic Sleep and the Roots of Psychological Healing.* New Haven, CT: Yale University Press; Carlos S. Alvarado (2002) "Dissociation in Britain during the Late Nineteenth Century: The Society for Psychical Research, 1882-1900." *Journal of Trauma & Dissociation* 3: 9–33.

[21] Richard Hodgson and S. J. Davey (1887) "The Possibilities of Mal-Observation and Lapse of Memory from a Practical Point of View. Experimental Investigations." *Proceedings of the Society for Psychical Research* 4: 381–495.

[22] See also, Ian Hacking (1988) "Telepathy: Origins of Randomization in Experimental Design." *Isis* 79: 427–51.

to accept the spirit hypothesis to account for some of them. To say that this conversion came as a shock to both skeptics and spiritualists would be an understatement. After all, Hodgson had previously earned a reputation as a zealous debunker of mediums and dogmatic opponent of spiritualism, and spiritualist magazines had printed occasional notes of warning to mediums to steer clear of him. Indeed, the first seven years of the SPR work had overall frustrated expectations by spiritualists in- and outside the Society to have their beliefs confirmed, as its first investigations of mediums (who, unlike Mrs. Piper, specialized in producing predominantly physical rather than mental anomalies) had failed to yield encouraging results. This critical approach had caused several clashes between members of the "Sidgwick group," including Hodgson and devout spiritualists. Many accused the SPR, moreover, of pathologizing veridical visions of the dying and departed because of its (albeit expressly provisional) use of the term "hallucinations," and of deliberately undermining the evidential basis for spiritualism by interpreting veridical mediumship in terms of benign multiple personality plus telepathy from the living.[23]

One of the most scientifically accomplished spiritualist members of the SPR unhappy with its uncompromising standards of investigation was Darwin's co-discoverer of evolution through natural selection, Alfred Russel Wallace. Whereas Darwin and his famed "bulldog" Huxley were biased by deep hostility to psychic matters from the outset, the example of Wallace serves as a counter-reminder that we should not simply rest our conviction regarding any controversy on the scientific standing of a proponent or opponent alone. In fact, while Wallace's work as a naturalist rightly warrants him to be named in one breath with Darwin, the critical faculties displayed by him in these controversial matters left much to be desired. Debates especially with the Sidgwicks and Hodgson in the periodicals of the SPR in the mid-1880s reveal Wallace's almost complete disregard for ordinary explanations of psychic phenomena including conscious and unconscious fraud, and the pitfalls of eyewitness testimony especially under unfavorable conditions of observation such as in (usually darkened) séance rooms.

This lack of scientific rigor concerning spiritualist phenomena displayed by Wallace in fact once brought William James into the unfortunate situation of having to publicly distance himself from the

---

[23] E.g. Hamilton, *Immortal Longings*; Gauld, *Founders*; Sommer, *Crossing the Boundaries*.

great naturalist. During a visit of Wallace to the US in 1886, he and James attended a séance in Boston by a medium who specialized in the supposed materialization of spirit forms. When a leading spiritualist magazine later touted the news that both Wallace and James had been impressed by the medium's performances, James saw himself forced to issue a correction: Not only had he failed to witness anything that convinced him of the medium's occult capacities, he also observed how Wallace was haplessly taken in by fairly obvious trickery carried out with the help of the medium's accomplices.[24]

If spiritualists were overall unsupportive of the rigorous research of James and the SPR, allergic responses by Wallace and others to approaches which at first glance bordered on mental pathology – such as the SPR's provisional use of the term "hallucinations" as a label even for veridical, i.e. telepathically induced, visions – may have been somewhat understandable. After all, whereas writers like Huxley mostly claimed that fraud and wishful thinking were sufficient explanations of all and any belief in psychic phenomena while simply ignoring the voluminous and painstaking research publications of the SPR, several of James's colleagues in fledgling university psychology went much further. Prominent psychologists such as James's own first doctoral student G. Stanley Hall (the founder of the American Psychological Association and the *American Journal of Psychology*), Hall's crusading henchman Joseph Jastrow in the US, W. B. Carpenter in England, and not least the creator of the psychological profession in Germany, Wilhelm Wundt, all proposed that belief in occult phenomena constituted clear-cut evidence of mental degeneration. Sweepingly dismissing reports of their occurrence as indications of an epidemic delusion, these critics practically declared any open-mindedness to reported psychic phenomena as obvious pathological relapses into primitive stages of mental and racial development.[25]

This hardly differentiating approach – dominated as it was by ridicule and blanket pathologization – allowed such critics, who

---

[24] William James (1887) "Letter from Professor James." *Banner of Light* 60: 4.
[25] E.g., John P. Williams (1985) "Psychical Research and Psychiatry in Late Victorian Britain: Trance as Ecstasy or Trance as Insanity." In *The Anatomy of Madness. Essays in the History of Psychiatry. Volume I*, edited by W. F. Bynum, R. Porter, and M. Shepherd, 233–54. London: Tavistock; Andreas Sommer (2020) "James and Psychical Research in Context." In *The Oxford Handbook of William James*, edited by Alexander Klein. Oxford: Oxford University Press. DOI: 10.1093/oxfordhb/9780199395699.013.37 (Epub ahead of print).

zealously took it on themselves to shape public opinion and academic curricula regarding science and the occult, to lump in actual cases of mentally disturbed claimants of the occult with reported psychic experiences by both uncritical and more discerning believers, along with scientifically rigorous long-term collaborative efforts by James and the SPR to separate the wheat from the chaff. Usually attacking their targets from a safe distance and without making any sustained efforts to investigate claimed marvels first-hand, prominent critics overwhelmingly limited their activities to polemical attacks in popular media and well-attended public lectures.

Strategies of rather questionable scientific value included occasional staged debunking exercises, as in the case of the widely celebrated supposed demolition of Mrs. Piper's mediumship by G. Stanley Hall and his assistant, psychologist Amy Tanner. Based on just six sittings and a complete misrepresentation of previous decades of research published by the SPR and American investigators including Hall's former student, James Hyslop, Hall and Tanner touted the initial SPR consensus that Piper was a case of multiple personality as their own discovery. Moreover, applying physiological and mental tests which seemed to have little purpose other than causing Piper discomfort and embarrassment, the authors stated they did not observe the remotest trace of anomalous knowledge during her trances.[26]

Hall had delayed the publication of Tanner's book until after James's death, but Hyslop was one of several surviving Piper investigators who tried in vain to put the record straight when he published a detailed demonstration of numerous and severe misrepresentations by Hall and Tanner of his own published experiments.[27] Jastrow and other self-appointed border guards of fledgling scientific psychology, however, praised the book in Hall's *American Journal of Psychology* as the "verdict of a patient investigation sustained by a scientific conscience and enthusiasm," which had once again proven that "the 'psychic research' platform is not only logically inadequate but psychologically perverse."[28] More recently, a historian with no discernible sympathies

---

[26] Amy E. Tanner (1910) *Studies in Spiritism*. New York: D. Appleton.

[27] Hyslop, James H. (1911) "President G. Stanley Hall's and Dr. Amy E. Tanner's Studies in Spiritualism." *Journal of the American Society for Psychical Research* 5: 1–98.

[28] Joseph Jastrow (1911) "Studies in Spiritism by Amy E. Tanner." *American Journal of Psychology* 22, p. 122)

for the occult has argued that "Hall and Tanner proved little with their tests except that they could do physical damage to Mrs. Piper."[29] Yet, perhaps needless to say, it is verdicts like Jastrow's which continue to dominate public opinion regarding mediumship up to the present day.

Hall may have been inspired in his debunking efforts by another celebrity psychologist close to James's academic stable, Hugo Münsterberg, whom James had recruited from Germany to run the Harvard laboratory of experimental psychology. Münsterberg is still widely celebrated for his alleged exposure of the Italian celebrity medium, Eusapia Palladino. Following previous reports of fraud committed by Palladino, she had recently been rehabilitated through investigations by notable European scientific figures, including physics Nobel Laureates Marie and Pierre Curie.[30] After a series of prolonged tests using automated controls and recording devices, most of Pierre Curie's fellow investigators shared his conviction that Palladino's reported physical phenomena, which included levitations and movements of objects at a distance, were genuine scientific anomalies – which, they believed, provided no evidence for spirits, but for new psychophysical forces of nature.

Outraged by such reports published or signed by a growing number of scientists of eminent standing, Münsterberg suddenly changed his tune. Previously satisfied to publicly declare any and all psychic phenomenon simply impossible and to scoff at both spiritualists and SPR researchers as self-evident fools, he saw his chance to use his prestige as Harvard's new celebrity psychologist when he accepted an invitation to attend séances with Palladino in late 1909. In a popular article published in the following year, Münsterberg claimed responsibility for the discovery of fraud allegedly committed by Palladino during a sitting he attended, and lumped in elite psychical researchers with uncritical spiritualists, insinuating that they were all disciples of James's pragmatist philosophy.[31] Evidence such as private correspondence, and

---

[29] Coon, Deborah J. (1992) "Testing the Limits of Sense and Science. American Experimental Psychologists Combat Spiritualism." *American Psychologist* 47, p. 149.

[30] E.g., Jules Courtier (1908) "Rapport sur les séances d'Eusapia Palladino." *Bulletin de l'Institut Général Psychologique* 8: 407–578.

[31] Hugo Münsterberg (1910) "My Friends the Spiritualists: Some Theories and Conclusions Concerning Eusapia Palladino." *Metropolitan Magazine* 31: 559–72.

not least the minutes of the séance in question which Münsterberg had signed, suggests that he took considerable license with basic truth in his published version of events. James, who had warned the organizer of Palladino's American sittings to invite hardliners like Münsterberg, was outraged if unsurprised of his colleague's dishonesty, including his deliberate conflation of spiritualism with psychical research and even with James's philosophical pragmatism.[32]

Modern writers with sympathies for spiritualism and other forms of unchurched spirituality have framed these controversies almost consistently in terms of dogmatic materialism battling spiritual truth. On the other end of the belief spectrum, figures usually affiliated with militant secular "Skeptics" associations have by implication appropriated men like Carpenter, Jastrow, Hall and Münsterberg as apostles of scientific materialism.[33] Never mind that practically all psychological opponents of James and the SPR were actually outspoken opponents of materialism. Most of them – especially Carpenter, Wundt and the ordained minister Hall – in fact held deep religious convictions, which opposed them to materialism perhaps as vehemently as to the occult, while others like Münsterberg were vocal advocates of philosophical idealism.[34]

---

[32] Andreas Sommer (2012) "Psychical Research and the Origins of American Psychology: Hugo Münsterberg, William James and Eusapia Palladino." *History of the Human Sciences* 25: 23–44.

[33] Writers and activists affiliated with the "Skeptics" movement have been highly successful in influencing public opinion through popularization and journalism since about the early 1980s and, more recently, by controlling pertinent contents on Wikipedia. See Trevor J. Pinch, and Harry M. Collins (1984) "Private Science and Public Knowledge: The Committee for the Scientific Investigation of the Claims of the Paranormal and Its Use of the Literature." *Social Studies of Science* 14: 521–46; and Martin, Brian (2021) "Policing Orthodoxy on Wikipedia: Skeptics in Action?" *Journal of Science Communication* 20 (02): https://doi.org/10.22323/2.20020209. On Huxley and precursors of the Skeptics movement in the UK see, e.g., Peter J. Bowler (2014) "From Agnosticism to Rationalism: Evolutionary Biologists, the Rationalist Press Association, and Early Twentieth-Century Scientific Naturalism." In *Victorian Scientific Naturalism. Community, Identity, Continuity*, edited by Gowan Dawson and Bernard Lightman, 309–26. Chicago, IL: University of Chicago Press.

[34] See, e.g., Sommer, *Crossing the Boundaries*; and "James and Psychical Research."

Likewise, Huxley and most of his allies in the cause of radically purging modern culture from the "supernatural" were as hostile to any belief in occult phenomena as anyone could well be. Yet, ongoing portrayals of Huxley as a materialist and atheist also do not stand up to scrutiny. His published writings and private correspondence show that his coinage of "agnosticism" in 1869, and lifelong critique of writers claiming that science had proven the truth of materialism, were sincere expressions of his position. Huxley's fervent anti-clericalism and open clashes with representatives of orthodox Christianity, moreover, were part of his intent to demolish theological orthodoxy not to get rid of religion as such. As is now recognized, Huxley first and foremost wanted to make room for a new, anti-supernaturalist and quasi-pantheistic faith that worshipped a forever unknowable divine principle manifesting itself in nature. Hardly an outlier, Huxley shared these intents and metaphysical commitments with major allies in the cause of popularizing agnosticism and scientific naturalism in Britain, such as his friends, the physicist John Tyndall and the philosopher Herbert Spencer.[35]

If readers have been accustomed to view any opposition to the "empirical occult" as evidence for sympathies with materialism on the one hand, and to popular conflations of psychical research with spiritualism and religion on the other, it is also not often acknowledged that most leading investigators and scientific spokespersons for the existence of "paranormal" phenomena in continental Europe were devout positivists if not materialists. For instance, the longest-standing doyen of an unrestrictedly empirical psychical research in France, Charles Richet, was a dye-in-the-wool atheist whose belief that mind was nothing but a byproduct of brain processes and therefore incapable of surviving death was near absolute.[36] Other important investigators of Palladino such as the Curies, and celebrity psychiatrist Enrico Morselli and physiologist Filippo Bottazzi, were likewise committed to naturalistic if not materialist ontologies and worldviews. Still, their

---

[35] Lightman, *Origins of Agnosticism*; Ruth Barton (1987) "John Tyndall, Pantheist. A Rereading of the Belfast Address." *Osiris* 3: 111–34; William J. Mander (2020) *The Unknowable. A Study in Nineteenth-Century British Metaphysics*. Oxford: Oxford University Press.

[36] Charles Richet (1924) "The Difficulty of Survival from the Scientific Point of View." *Proceedings of the Society for Psychical Research* 34: 107–13; Sommer, *Crossing the Boundaries*, chapter 2.

metaphysical convictions and antipathies with spiritualism did not prevent them from publishing empirical findings in support of occult phenomena.[37]

As regards to James, his life-long interest in psychic phenomena and mystical experiences may invoke the assumption that he was little more than a religious apologist. Yet, his open doubts concerning theism in general, and Christian theology in particular, deeply upset many of his devoutly religious scientific and philosophical colleagues. Moreover, as James briefly confessed in "The Confidences of a 'Psychical Researcher'" (his final popular defense of psychical research in 1909 – see Chapter 20 of the present volume) and in private correspondence earlier, he was perfectly willing to consider that certain occult phenomena may be genuine scientific anomalies, but may not reveal any hint as to a hidden spiritual, divine or moral order of the cosmos whatsoever.

James's critique of Huxley and fellow popularizers of scientific naturalism might obscure the fact that he shared important basic premises with them. Indeed, primary sources overwhelmingly suggest that James's personal religious convictions were no more definite or pronounced than Huxley's, and probably less so. Perhaps most significantly, his whole project of philosophical pragmatism was grounded in a radically agnostic and philosophically skeptical position which was at least as heartfelt as Huxley's, but incomparably more even-handed: Both Huxley and James recognized that neither philosophy nor science were intrinsically capable of conclusively settling metaphysical core questions, such as the existence let alone nature of God. But while Huxley was content to overwhelmingly scoff reports of occult phenomena out of intellectual discourse, James maintained an ultimately agnostic stance regarding metaphysical interpretations while advocating research on the occurrence of reported psychic phenomena and on tangible repercussions especially of transformative experiences.

---

[37] Sommer, *Crossing the Boundaries*, chapter 2; Andreas Sommer (2014) "Psychical Research in the History and Philosophy of Science. An Introduction and Review." *Studies in History and Philosophy of Biological and Biomedical Sciences* 48: 38–45; and Brancaccio, Maria Teresa (2014) "Enrico Morselli's Psychology of 'Spiritism': Psychiatry, Psychology and Psychical Research in Italy around 1900." *Studies in History and Philosophy of Biological and Biomedical Sciences* 48: 75–84.

Conclusion: William James Contested

Nowhere did James's open disdain for both traditional and new conventions of thought assert itself as when he likely became the first noted intellectual to stress the need of impartial empirical approaches to mystical and other contested experiences with a focus on their measurable results. The very point of his *Varieties of Religious Experience*, after all, was to stress the clinical and social rather than theological significance of veritable personality transformations to the better, in persons reported to be overcome by typically unsought, spontaneous encounters with the perceived divine: Over a century after the publication of the *Varieties*, it can no longer be doubted that James was on to something when he called attention to the fact that, often in an instant, people from all walks of life holding all sorts of prior beliefs have come away from such experiences with a newfound mental resilience and strength in the face of life's great challenges, and, equally importantly, a heightened sense of compassion for others.[38]

Communities of mainstream mental health professionals only began adopting a more pragmatic approach to such experiences since the concluding decades of the twentieth century.[39] Almost completely unacknowledged by other sections of medical and scientific communities, the upshot of the growing body of the clinical literature has refuted nineteenth-century views of the inherent pathology of certain transformative spiritual experiences, and has on the contrary acknowledged their salutary if not therapeutic effects. By leaving metaphysical and theological interpretations aside, the overall ethos directing most of this modern research may well be expressed in James's own words: "If the *fruits for life* of the state of conversion are good, we ought to idealize and venerate it, even though it be a piece of natural

---

[38] E.g., Bruce Greyson (1983) "Near-Death Experiences and Personal Values." *American Journal of Psychiatry* 140: 618–20; Etzel Cardeña, S. J. Lynn, and Stanley Krippner, eds. (2014) *Varieties of Anomalous Experience: Examining the Scientific Evidence*. Second edition. Washington, DC: American Psychological Association.

[39] For a historical sketch of these revisions in medical practice, see Andreas Sommer (2021) "Conflicts and Complexities: Medical Science, Exceptional Experiences, and the Perils of Simplistic History." In *Spirituality and Mental Health Across Cultures (Oxford Cultural Psychiatry)*, edited by Alexander Moreira-Almeida, Bruno Paz Mosqueiro, and Dinesh Bhugra, 47–59. Oxford: Oxford University Press.

psychology; if not, we ought to make short work with it, no matter what supernatural being may have infused it."[40]

The tropes of conversion and transformation bring us back to the influential modernist sentiment by writers like Huxley and Feuerbach, which we encountered in the beginning of this introduction: Belief in gods and spirits was to be explained in terms of an infantile projective drive, stemming from an all-too human desire to see sentient beings like ourselves at work in inanimate nature. A related urge to project our own personalities upon the world might be visible in the habit of modern writers not so much to create gods in their own image, but notable historical figures – to "transform" them, as it were, so they fall in line with a writer's own beliefs and agendas, however much contrary to concrete historical evidence.

For example, historians of science now widely acknowledge that, belying twentieth-century standard assumptions of the inherent "naturalism" let alone "materialism" of science, virtually all figureheads of the Scientific Revolution such as Copernicus, Kepler, Galileo, Francis Bacon, Robert Boyle and Isaac Newton were no prototypes of the modern naturalistic scientist, but held rather strong magical beliefs and engaged in practices including alchemy, astrology and other occult sciences of the day. Moreover, far from ceasing during the Enlightenment, open-minded engagement with the occult by scientific, medical and philosophical elites continued until at least the twentieth century.[41] On the other hand, trying to understand the concrete means by which educated westerners became "disenchanted" since the Enlightenment, leading historians of science and medicine have found that these continuities were squarely written out of history, for religious and political rather than properly scientific reasons. Magic and the occult have been exorcised not by impartial, dispassionate test and experiment, but overwhelmingly through polemics, ridicule and pathologization.[42]

---

[40] William James (1902) *The Varieties of Religious Experience. A Study in Human Nature. Being the Gifford Lectures on Natural Religion Delivered at Edinburgh in 1901-1902*. London: Longmans Green & Co., p. 237.

[41] See, e.g., Jason Ānanda Josephson-Storm, (2017) *The Myth of Disenchantment: Magic, Modernity, and the Birth of the Human Sciences*. Chicago, IL: University of Chicago Press; Noakes, *Physics and Psychics*; Sommer "Psychical Research."

[42] E.g., Roy Porter (1999) "Witchcraft and Magic in Enlightenment, Romantic and Liberal Thought." In *Witchcraft and Magic in Europe. Volume 5. The Eighteenth and Nineteenth Centuries*, edited by Bengt Ankarloo and Stuart

Together with revisions concerning the prevalence, pathology and therapeutic value of transformative mystical and other transcendental experiences in medicine, this consensus in the history of science could well be called a minor revolution in mainstream academia. And yet, although this revolution occurred several decades ago, expert opinion has practically failed to inform general intellectual opinion let alone public education, and has done little to introduce much-needed balance into ongoing public debates on science and the "supernatural." Indeed, in the face of such stubborn academic resistance to acknowledge these revisions, it seems that standard explanations of persisting *belief* in the occult in terms of self-evident wishful thinking and bias requires a more balanced perspective. Whereas instances of wishful thinking as a motivator for belief in all sorts of occult phenomena are easy enough to come by, it is time that some of the rather obvious motivations for programmatic *disbelief* are acknowledged as well.[43]

Unsurprisingly, in the case of James scholarship it has almost been customary for biographers to omit, downplay, or outright deny the central place of psychical research in the overall opus of the founder of modern American experimental psychology and pioneering pragmatist philosopher.[44] The only monograph specifically dedicated to James's psychical research to date has acknowledged this historiographical mess, but hardly improved the state of the art. After explicitly denying the significance of psychical research for James's work in philosophy, its author misrepresents methods and attitudes of James and fellow

---

Clark, 191–282. Philadelphia, PA: University of Pennsylvania Press; Lorraine Daston and Katharine Park (1998) *Wonders and the Order of Nature, 1150-1750*. New York: Zone Books; Michael Hunter (2020) *The Decline of Magic: Britain in the Enlightenment*. New Haven, CT: Yale University Press. For a constantly updated list of pertinent books in mainstream history of science and medicine, see https://www.forbiddenhistories.com/key-readings.

[43] On this theme see, e.g., Michael Grosso (1990) "Fear of Life after Death." In *What Survives? Contemporary Explorations of Life After Death*, edited by G. Doore, 241–54. Los Angeles: Jeremy Tarcher; Andreas Sommer (2016) "Are You Afraid of the Dark? Notes on the Psychology of Belief in Histories of Science and the Occult." *European Journal of Psychotherapy & Counselling* 18: 105–22.

[44] For reviews of the literature, see Eugene Taylor (1996) *William James: On Consciousness Beyond the Margin*. Princeton, NJ: Princeton University Press; Marcus Ford (1998) "William James's Psychical Research and Its Philosophical Implications." *Transactions of the Charles S. Peirce Society* 34: 605–26; and the introduction to Sommer, *Crossing the Boundaries*.

workers at the SPR and on the continent, shows a complete unawareness of basic historical contexts regarding crucial religious and political underpinnings of the making of "naturalistic" modernity, and engages in name-calling, e.g. by terming James's refusal to explain mediumistic phenomena by deliberate fraud "foolish."[45] On the other end of the spectrum of belief, certain spiritualist writers have openly accused James of intellectual cowardice, as payback for his inability to share their absolute faith in the conclusiveness of the spirit hypothesis following research with Mrs. Piper.[46]

All this is obviously not to say James should be placed on a pedestal or was inherently beyond reproach. And like James, we can and should acknowledge that holding fast to Huxley's rule of never believing without supporting evidence is a major safeguard in the avoidance of harmful error. But we should still heed James's warning that, if applied inflexibly as an iron rule and to all areas of life, Huxley's command dangerously obscures the vastly complex functions of individual beliefs in every-day life as well as in standard scientific practice, and is bound to backfire and cause substantial damage as well.

I for one strongly believe that it's high time that our focus on harm caused by evident occult quacks and preachers of QAnon-style conspiracy theories should be complemented by the overdue admission of the suffering caused by centuries of pathologization of individuals reporting psychic and transcendental experiences. Moreover, we need to ask ourselves to which extent the western intellectual taboo regarding occult beliefs and experiences has actually created the void of solid, evidence-based knowledge regarding these things – the very vacuum which has been exploited by ruthless con-men as well as by certain self-styled New Age gurus who may be well-meaning enough, but might ultimately be duping themselves along with their followers.

As with any new book, the question of readership may be useful to address. Who is most likely to benefit from reading this volume? Given the hopelessly polarized and divided nature of discourse on the "paranormal," it can be expected that most readers of this book are roughly affiliated with parapsychological, transpersonal or other

---

[45] Krister Dylan Knapp (2017) *William James: Psychical Research and the Challenge of Modernity*. Chapel Hill, NC: University of North Carolina Press, p. 289.

[46] E.g., Michael Tymn (2013) "Questioning the Courage of William James [Letter to the Editor]." *Journal of the Society for Psychical Research* 77: 264–66.

marginalized quarters of modern intellectual life. If you belong to these traditions and if you haven't already, I suggest you also familiarize yourself with some of James's works in philosophy, e.g., the already mentioned *The Will to Believe* (1897) and especially his *Pragmatism* (1907)[47], which will facilitate understanding of the wider contexts in which to read James's psychical research writings. Other readers may belong to more mainstream academic circles such as philosophy and religious studies, and may already be familiar with James's philosophical and perhaps even psychological work. But regardless of your intellectual kinship, I believe it is necessary for a full appreciation of James's unorthodox work to obtain basic familiarity with some of the many primary sources on psychical research to which he refers.[48]

Readers already familiar with all these sources may agree that James's writings on psychical research cannot be viewed as a project standing isolated from his canonical output – and vice versa, as the present book seeks to highlight. Expressing the same deep-seated aversion to metaphysical absolutism in its most predominant kinds, James's multi-faceted project was nothing short of an attempt to revolutionize philosophy and fledgling scientific psychology from the bottom up. Rather than being just another partisan in a timeless metaphysical battle, James fought for the right to come to rigorously scientific and philosophical grips with individual beliefs and experiences – especially those which had been mutually suppressed and marginalized by the opposing quarters of supernaturalist theological orthodoxy on the one hand, and by the dawning orthodoxy of (agnostic as well as properly materialistic) "naturalism" on the other.

It would be too convenient to state that James's attempted revolution has failed, and to simply leave it at that. Most of the work began by James remains to be done, and I strongly feel that empirical research needs to be grounded in a qualified understanding of the historical contexts and the mechanisms by which public opinion on the subject

---

[47] William James (1907) *Pragmatism. A New Name for Some Old Ways of Thinking.* London: Longmans, Green, and Co.

[48] Readers mainly interested in the more recent *scientific* cash-value of Myers/James-type frameworks should study essays in Edward Francis Kelly, Emily Williams Kelly, Adam Crabtree, Alan Gauld, Michael Grosso, and Bruce Greyson (2007) *Irreducible Mind. Toward a Psychology for the 21st Century.* Lanham, MD: Rowman & Littlefield – a rigorous evaluation of their ideas in the light of data from modern psychological and biomedical sciences.

matter of psychical research has been created. Only then can we begin to collectively cultivate another emotional drive apart from the will to believe or disbelieve, which I pragmatically propose must be present in each of us: the will to recognize and remedy our most detrimental personal biases.

A NOTE ON THE TEXTS

This book contains William James's most significant writings on psychical research together with his thematically related writings on the nature of the soul, the afterlife, and immortality. Excluded are a few pieces that were primarily verbatim reports from individuals who wrote to James about their psychical experiences, which were printed under James's name with only minimal input or assessment from him. Also excluded are technical apparatus relating to research protocol, some shorter or redundant reviews, and a number of letters and debates with critics.

While not strictly complete, however, this volume contains material never before published in book form, as well as some more obscure pieces that have been neglected or have not been published in the context of psychical research. Section IV on Possession, for example, will likely be unfamiliar to most readers. It highlights a theme that was obviously of more interest to James than is widely recognized.

Because James often integrated various types of phenomena and theories about them into his discussions, there is some overlap between the sections. Thus, while automatic writing is usually seen in the context of mediumship, his article on the subject focuses on telepathy rather than spirit communication. As such, it has been included in the section I've called Telepathy, Automatism, and Extended Consciousness. Likewise, the piece on "Mediumships or Possessions" sees the former in terms of the latter, and has been here included in the section on Possession. Despite its somewhat general title and theme, "The Confidences of a 'Psychical Researcher'" is predominately concerned with the evidence for survival from mediumship, and has thus been included in the Mediumship section. In any case, the organization of the chapters has been designed to help readers explore James's complex, diverse thinking on psychical research per se, as well as how the subject flowed into his more abstract conceptualizations of what the various kinds of evidence implied on philosophical and metaphysical levels.

The texts in this book have all been transcribed from their earliest – and sometimes only – appearances in original journals, popular magazines, and books dating as far back as 1886. Idiosyncratic or archaic punctuation and spelling have been standardized to modern conventions. In rare cases, brief, irrelevant or repetitive material has been deleted, such as passages pertaining to business matters of the Society for Psychical Research, or paragraphs reused by James in more than one article. The excerpts from James's books have been edited to provide the most relevant passages, though his words have not been altered in any way. Any such lacunae have been designated thus: [...]. Full references for all original sources will be found at the back of the book along with suggestions for further reading. Foreign language terms used casually by James have been translated alongside the original for ease of reading.

Gregory Shushan

PART I

PSYCHOLOGY AND PSYCHICAL RESEARCH

1

THE HIDDEN SELF

This essay originally appeared in 1890 in *Scribner's Magazine*, an upmarket general interest publication covering culture, society, literature, and science. It is an excellent early example of James's integration of psychical research with mainstream psychology in his treatment of trance and other altered states of consciousness. Indeed, as with some of James's other early writings, this chapter reveals that the distinction often made by academics between James's "serious" philosophical and psychological work, and his psychical research was, to James himself, somewhat nonexistent.

His argument for taking seriously "wild facts" and "mystical phenomena" is almost Fortean in tone and message. Charles Fort (1874-1920) was a researcher into extraordinary and anomalous events of all kinds, well known for his vocal and rather sensationalist critiques of *de facto* scientific materialist assumptions about such phenomena.[1] Like Fort, parts of James's piece read as something of a manifesto, not only justifying and promoting the study of such "damned" subjects (as Fort would put it), but also criticizing the kind of science that would deny their existence in the face of all evidence to the contrary.

---

[1] Fort's four main works on the subject were reprinted in a single volume: Charles Fort (1975) *The Complete Books of Charles Fort: The Book of the Damned / Lo! / Wild Talents / New Lands* (first published 1919, 1923, 1931, 1932). New York: Dover.

Indeed, as the American philosopher Ralph Barton Perry stated it (or perhaps overstated it) in 1935, James "not only tolerated, but *preferred*, the despised and rejected – in movements as well as in men. Orthodox science was a symbol of arrogance and vulgar success, disposed to exaggerate its claims and to abuse its power."[2]

That James reused some of the contents of this essay both in his landmark book *Principles of Psychology* and in an article called "What Psychical Research Has Accomplished" (see Chapter 2 of the present volume) shows the importance it held for him in the development of his thoughts and theories on extraordinary experiences.

The focus on the psychological (as opposed to parapsychological) aspects of these cases, involving dissociative identity disorder ("multiple personalities") and hypnosis, prefigures his analyses of the mediumship of Leonora Piper (to whom he alludes towards the end). As with his research on phantom limbs and automatic writing (Chapters 8 and 9), it also reminds us that yesterday's psychical research is often tomorrow's mainstream science.

"The great field for new discoveries," said a scientific friend to me the other day, "is always the Unclassified Residuum." Round about the accredited and orderly facts of every science there ever floats a sort of dust-cloud of exceptional observations, of occurrences minute and irregular, and seldom met with, which it always proves less easy to attend to than to ignore. The ideal of every science is that of a closed and completed system of truth. The charm of most sciences to their more passive disciples consists in their appearing, in fact, to wear just this ideal form. Each one of our various *ologies* seems to offer a definite head of classification for every possible phenomenon of the sort which it professes to cover; and, so far from free is most men's fancy, that when a consistent and organized scheme of this sort has once been comprehended and assimilated, a different scheme is unimaginable. No alternative, whether to whole or parts, can any longer be conceived as possible. Phenomena unclassifiable within the system are therefore paradoxical absurdities, and must be held untrue. When, moreover, as so often happens, the reports of them are vague and indirect, when they come as mere marvels and oddities rather than as things of serious moment, one neglects or denies them with the best of scientific

---

[2] Ralph Barton Perry (1935) *The Thought and Character of William James*, Vol. II. Boston: Little Brown, 155-56.

consciences. Only the born geniuses let themselves be worried and fascinated by these outstanding exceptions, and get no peace till they are brought within the fold. Your Galileos, Galvanis, Fresnels, Purkinjes, and Darwins are always getting confounded and troubled by insignificant things. *Anyone* will renovate his science who will steadily look after the irregular phenomena. And when the science is renewed, its new formulas often have more of the voice of the exceptions in them than of what were supposed to be the rules.

No part of the unclassed residuum has usually been treated with a more contemptuous scientific disregard than the mass of phenomena generally called *mystical*. Physiology will have nothing to do with them. Orthodox psychology turns its back upon them. Medicine sweeps them out; or, at most, when in an anecdotal vein, records a few of them as "effects of the imagination," a phrase of mere dismissal whose meaning, in this connection, it is impossible to make precise. All the while, however, the phenomena are there, lying broadcast over the surface of history. No matter where you open its pages, you find things recorded under the name of divinations, inspirations, demoniacal possessions, apparitions, trances, ecstasies, miraculous healings and productions of disease, and occult powers possessed by peculiar individuals over persons and things in their neighborhood. We suppose that mediumship originated in Rochester, N. Y., and animal magnetism with Mesmer; but once look behind the pages of official history, in personal memoirs, legal documents, and popular narratives and books of anecdote, and you will find that there never was a time when these things were not reported just as abundantly as now. We college-bred gentry, who follow the stream of cosmopolitan culture exclusively, not infrequently stumble upon some old-established journal, or some voluminous native author, whose names are never heard of in *our* circle, but who number their readers by the quarter-million. It always gives us a little shock to find this mass of human beings not only living and ignoring us and all our gods, but actually reading and writing and cogitating without ever a thought of our canons, standards, and authorities. Well, a public no less large keeps and transmits from generation to generation the traditions and practices of the occult; but academic science cares as little for its beliefs and opinions as you, gentle subscriber to this Magazine, care for those of the readers of the *Waverley* and the *Fireside Companion*. To no one type of mind is it given to discern the totality of Truth. Something escapes the best of us, not accidentally, but systematically, and because we have a twist. The scientific-academic mind and the feminine-mystical mind shy from each other's facts, just as they fly from each other's temper and spirit. Facts are there only for those who have a mental affinity with them. When once they are indisputably ascertained and admitted, the academic and critical minds are by far the best fitted ones to interpret and discuss them—for surely to pass from mystical to scientific speculations is like passing from lunacy to sanity; but on the other hand if there is anything which human history demonstrates, it is the extreme slowness with which the ordinary academic and critical mind acknowledges facts to exist which present themselves as *wild* facts with no stall or pigeon-hole, or as facts which threaten to break up the accepted system. In psychology, physiology, and medicine, wherever a debate between the Mystics and the Scientifics has been once for all decided, it is the Mystics who have usually proved to be right about the *facts*, while the Scientifics had the better of it in respect to the theories. The most recent and flagrant example of this is "animal magnetism," whose facts were stoutly dismissed as a pack of lies by academic medical science the world over, until the non-mystical theory of "hypnotic suggestion" was found for them, when they were admitted to be so excessively and dangerously common that special penal laws, forsooth, must be passed to keep all persons unequipped with medical diplomas from taking part in their production. Just so stigmatizations, invulnerabilities, instantaneous cures, inspired discourses, and demoniacal possessions, the records of which were shelved in our libraries but yesterday in the alcove headed "Superstitions," now, under the brand-new title of "Cases of hystero-epilepsy," are republished, reobserved, and reported with an even too credulous avidity.

Repugnant as the mystical style of philosophizing may be (especially when self-complacent), there is no sort of doubt that it goes with a gift for meeting with certain kinds of phenomenal experience. The writer has been forced in the past few years to this admission; and he now believes that he who will pay attention to facts of the sort dear to mystics, while reflecting upon them in academic-scientific ways, will be in the best possible position to help philosophy. It is a circumstance of good augury, that scientifically trained minds in all countries seem drifting to the same conclusion. Nowhere is this the case more than in France. France always was the home of the study of character. French literature is one long loving commentary on the variations of which individual human nature is capable. It seems fitting, therefore, that where minute and faithful observation of abnormal personal peculiarities is the order of the day, French science should take the lead. The work done at Paris and Nancy on the hypnotic trance is well known. Grant any amount of imperfection, still the essential thing remains, that here we have a mass of phenomena, hitherto outlawed, brought within the pale of sober investigation—the rest is only an affair of time. Last summer there appeared a record of observations made at Havre on certain hysterical somnambulists, by M. Pierre Janet, Professor of Philosophy in the Lycée of that town, and published in a volume of five hundred pages, entitled *De l'Automatisme Psychologique* (Paris, Alcan), which, serving as the author's thesis for the Doctorate of Science in Paris, made quite a commotion in the world to which such things pertain.

The new light which this book throws on what has long been vaguely talked about as unconscious mental life seems so important that I propose to entertain the readers of *Scribner's* with some account of its contents, as an example of the sort of "psychical research" which a shrewd man with good opportunities may now achieve. The work bristles with facts, and is rather deficient in form. The author aims, moreover, at generalizing only where the phenomena force him to, and abstract statements are more embedded, and, as it were, interstitial, than is the case in most Gallic performances. In all this M. Janet's mind has an English flavor about it which it is pleasant to meet with in one otherwise so good a Frenchman. I shall also quote some of the observations of M. Binet,[3] the most ingenious and original member of the Salpêtrière school [of hypnosis], as these two gentlemen, working independently and with different subjects, come to conclusions which are strikingly in accord.

Both may be called contributors to the comparative science of trance-states. The "Subjects" studied by both are sufferers from the most aggravated forms of hysteria, and both authors, I fancy, are consequently led to exaggerate the dependence of the trance-conditions upon this kind of disease. M. Janet's subjects, whom he calls Léonie, Lucie, Rose, Marie, etc., were patients at the Havre Hospital, in charge of doctors who were his friends, and who allowed him to make observations on them to his heart's content. One of the most constant symptoms in persons suffering from hysteric disease in its extreme forms consists in alterations of the natural sensibility of various parts and organs of the body. Usually the alteration is in the direction of defect, or anesthesia. One or both eyes are blind, or blind over one half of the field of vision,

---

[3] M. Binet has contributed some of his facts to the Chicago Open Court for 1889.

or the latter is extremely contracted, so that its margins appear dark, or else the patient has lost all sense for color. Hearing, taste, smell may similarly disappear, in part or in totality. Still more striking are the cutaneous anesthesias. The old witch-finders, looking for the "devil's seals," well learned the existence of those insensible patches on the skin of their victims, to which the minute physical examinations of recent medicine have but lately attracted attention again. They may be scattered anywhere, but are very apt to affect one side of the body. Not infrequently they affect an entire lateral half, from head to foot, and the insensible skin of, say the left side, will then be found separated from the naturally sensitive skin of the right by a perfectly sharp line of demarcation down the middle of the front and back. Sometimes, most remarkable of all, the entire skin, hands, feet, face, everything, and the mucous membranes, muscles, and joints, so far as they can be explored, become *completely* insensible without the other vital functions being gravely disturbed. These anesthesias and hemianesthesias, in all their various grades, form the nucleus of M. Janet's observations and hypotheses. And, first of all, he has an hypothesis about the anesthesia itself, which, like all provisional hypotheses, may do excellent service while awaiting the day when a better one shall take its place.

The original sin of the hysteric mind, he thinks, is the *contractions of the field of consciousness*. The attention has not sufficient strength to take in the normal number of sensations or ideas at once. If an ordinary person can feel ten things at a time, an hysteric can feel but five. Our minds are all of them like vessels full of water, and taking in a new drop makes another drop fall out; only the hysteric mental vessel is preternaturally small. The unifying or synthetizing power which the Ego exerts over the manifold facts which are offered to it is insufficient to do its full amount of work, and an ingrained habit is formed of neglecting or overlooking certain determinate portions of the mass. Thus one eye will be ignored, one arm and hand, or one-half of the body. And apart from anesthesia, hysterics are often extremely *distraites* [distracted], and unable to attend to two things at once. When talking with you they forget everything else. When Lucie stopped conversing directly with anyone, she ceased to be able to hear anyone else. You might stand behind her, call her by name, shout abuse into her ears, without making her turn round; or place yourself before her, show her objects, touch her, etc., without attracting her notice. When finally she becomes aware of you, she thinks you have just come into the room again, and greets you accordingly. This singular forgetfulness makes her liable to tell all her secrets aloud, unrestrained by the presence of unsuitable auditors. This contracted mental field (or state of monoideism, as it has been called) characterizes also the hypnotic state of normal persons, so that in this important respect a waking hysteric is like a well person in the hypnotic trance. Both are wholly lost in their present idea, its normal "reductives" and correctives having lapsed from view.

The anesthesias of the class of patients we are considering can be made to disappear more or less completely by various odd processes. It has been recently found that magnets, plates of metal, the electrodes of a battery, placed against the skin, have this peculiar power. And when one side is relieved in this way, the anesthesia is often found to have transferred itself to the opposite side, which, until then, was well. Whether these strange effects of magnets and metals be due to their direct physiological action, or to a prior effect on the patient's mind ("expectant attention" or "suggestion") is still a mooted question.[4] A still better awakener of sensibility in most of these subjects is the *hypnotic state*, which M. Janet seems to have most easily induced by the orthodox "magnetic" method of "passes" made over the face and body. It was in making these passes that he first stumbled on one of the most curious facts recorded in his volume. One day, when the subject named Lucie was in the hypnotic state, he made passes over her again for half an hour, just as if she were already "asleep." The result was to throw her into a sort of syncope from which, after another half hour, she revived in a second somnambulic condition entirely unlike that which had characterized her hitherto-different sensibilities, a different memory, a different person, in short. In the waking state the poor young woman was anæsthetic all over, nearly deaf, and with a badly contracted field of vision. Bad as it was, however, sight was her best sense, and she used it as a guide in all her movements. With her eyes bandaged she was entirely helpless, and, like other persons of a similar sort whose cases have been recorded, she almost immediately fell asleep in consequence of the withdrawal of her last sensorial stimulus. M. Janet calls this waking or primary (one can hardly, in such a connection, say "normal") state by the name of Lucie 1. In Lucie 2, her first sort of hypnotic trance, the anesthesias were diminished but not removed. In the deeper trance, "Lucie 3," brought about as just described, no trace of

---

[4] M. Janet seems rather to incline to the former view, though suggestion may at times be exclusively responsible, as when he produced what was essentially the same phenomenon by pointing an orange-peel held out on the end of a long stick at the parts!

them remained. Her sensibility became perfect, and instead of being an extreme example of the "visual" type, she was transformed into what, in Professor Charcot's terminology, is known as a motor. That is to say, that whereas, when awake, she had thought in visual terms exclusively, and could imagine things only by remembering how they *looked*, now, in this deeper trance, her thoughts and memories seemed largely composed of images of movement and of touch—of course I state summarily here what appears in the book as an induction from many facts.

Having discovered this deeper trance in Lucie, M. Janet naturally became eager to find it in his other subjects. He found it in Rose, in Marie, and in Léonie; and, best of all, his brother, Dr. Jules Janet, who was *interne* at the Salpêtrière Hospital, found it in the celebrated subject Witt... whose trances had been studied for years by the various doctors of that institution without any of them having happened to awaken this very peculiar modification of the personality.

With the return of all the sensibilities in the deeper trance, the subjects are transformed, as it were, into normal persons. Their memories, in particular, grow more extensive; and here comes in M. Janet's first great theoretic generalization, which is this: When a certain kind of sensation is abolished in a hysteric patient, there is also abolished along with it all recollection of past sensations of that kind. If, for example, hearing be the anæsthetic sense, the patient becomes unable even to imagine sounds and voices, and has to speak, when speech is still possible, by means of motor or articulatory cues. If the motor sense be abolished, the patient must will the movements of his limbs by first defining them to his mind in visual terms, and must innervate his voice by premonitory ideas of the way in which the words are going to sound. The practical effects of this law of M. Janet's upon the patient's recollections would necessarily be great. Take things touched and handled, for example, and bodily movements. All memories of such things, all records of such experiences, being normally stored away in tactile terms, would have to be incontinently lost and forgotten so soon as the cutaneous and muscular sensibility should come to be cut out in the course of disease. Memory of them would be restored again, on the other hand, so soon as the sense of touch came back. Experiences, again, undergone during an anæsthetic condition of touch (and stored up consequently in visual or auditory terms exclusively), can have contracted no "associations" with tactile ideas, for such ideas are, for the time being, forgotten and practically non-existent. If, however, the touch-sensibilities ever are restored, and their ideas and memories with them, it may easily happen that they, with their clustered associations, may temporarily keep out of consciousness things like the visual and other experiences accumulated during the anæsthetic period which have no connections with them. If touch be the dominant sense in childhood, it would thus be explained why hysterical anæsthetics, whose tactile sensibilities and memories are brought back again by trance, so often assume a childlike deportment, and even call themselves by baby-names. Such, at least, is a suggestion of M. Janet's to explain a not infrequent sort of observation. MM. Bourru and Burot found, for instance, in their extraordinary male somnambulist Louis V., that reviving by suggestion a certain condition of bodily feeling in him would invariably transport him back to the epoch of his life when that condition had prevailed. He forgot the later years, and resumed the character and sort of intellect which had characterized him at the earlier time.

M. Janet's theory will provoke controversy and stimulate observation. You can ask little more than that of any theory. My own impression is that the law that anesthesias carry "amnesias" with them, will not come out distinctly in every individual case. The intricacy of the associative processes, and the fact that comparatively few experiences are stored up in one form of sensibility alone, would be sufficient to prevent this. Perfect illustrations of the law will therefore be met with only in privileged subjects like M. Janet's own. *They* indeed seem to have exemplified it beautifully. M. Janet says:

> It seems to me, that if I were to awake some morning with no muscular or tactile feelings, if, like Rose, I should suddenly lose my sense of color, and distinguish nothing in the universe but black and white, I should be terrified, and instantly appeal for help. These women, on the contrary, find their state so natural that they never even complain. When I, after some trials, proved to Rose that she could perceive no color, I found her ignorant of the fact. When I showed Lucie that she could feel neither pain nor contact, she answered, 'All the better!' When I made her conscious that she never knew where her arms were till she saw them, and that she lost her legs when in bed, she replied, '*C'est tout naturel*, as long as I don't see them; everyone is like that.' In a word, being incapable of comparing their present state of sensibility with a former one of which all memory is lost, they suffer no more than we do at not hearing the 'music of the spheres.'

M. Janet restored their tactile sense temporarily by means of electric currents, passes, etc., and then made them handle various objects, such as keys and pencils, or make particular movements, like the sign of the cross. The moment the anesthesia returned, they found it impossible to recollect the objects or the acts. "They had had nothing in their hands, they had done nothing," etc. The next day, however, sensibility being again restored by similar processes, they remembered perfectly the circumstance, and told what they had handled or had done.

It is in this way that M. Janet explains the general law that persons forget in the waking state what has happened to them in trance. There are differences of sensibility, and consequently breaches in the association of ideas. Certain of his hysterics (as we have seen) regained complete sensibility in their deeper trance. The result was such an enlargement of their power of recollecting that they could then go back and explain the origin of many of their peculiarities which would else be inexplicable. One stage in the great convulsive attack of hystero-epilepsy is what the French writers call *la phase des attitudes passionnelles*, in which the patient, without speaking or giving any account of herself, will go through the outward movements of fear, anger, or some other emotional state of mind. Usually this phase is, with each patient, a thing so stereotyped as to seem automatic, and doubts have even been expressed as to whether any consciousness exists while it lasts. When, however, the patient Lucie's tactile sensibility came back in her state of Lucie 3, she explained the origin of her hysteric crises in a great fright which she had had when a child, on a day when certain men, hid behind the curtains, had jumped out upon her; she told how she went through this scene again in all her crises; she told of her sleep-walking fits through the house when a child, and how, for several months, she had been shut in a dark room because of a disorder of the eyes. All these were things of which she recollects nothing when awake, because they were records of experiences mainly of motion and of touch, and when awake her feelings of touch and movement disappeared.

But the case of Léonie is the most interesting, and shows beautifully how, with the sensibilities and motor impulses, the memories and character will change.

> This woman, whose life sounds more like an improbable romance than a genuine history, has had attacks of natural somnambulism since the age of three years. She has been hypnotized constantly, by all sorts of persons, from the age of sixteen upward, and she is now forty-five.

While her normal life developed in one way in the midst of her poor country surroundings, her second life was passed in drawing-rooms and doctors' offices, and naturally took an entirely different direction. To-day, when in her normal state, this poor peasant-woman is a serious and rather sad person, calm and slow, very mild with everyone, and extremely timid; to look at her one would never suspect the personage which she contains. But hardly is she put to sleep hypnotically than a metamorphosis occurs. Her face is no longer the same. She keeps her eyes closed, it is true, but the acuteness of her other senses supplies their place. She is gay, noisy, restless, sometimes insupportably so. She remains good-natured, but has acquired a singular tendency to irony and sharp jesting. Nothing is more curious than to hear her, after a sitting when she has received a visit from strangers who wished to see her asleep. She gives a word-portrait of them, apes their manners, pretends to know their little ridiculous aspects and passions, and for each invents a romance. To this character must be added the possession of an enormous number of recollections whose existence she does not even suspect when awake, for her amnesia is then complete. . . . She refuses the name of Léonie, and takes that of Léontine (Léonie 2), to which her first magnetizers had accustomed her. 'That good woman is not myself,' she says, 'she is too stupid.' To herself Léontine (or Léonie 2), she attributes all the sensations and all the actions; in a word, all the conscious experiences, which she has undergone *in somnambulism* and knits them together to make the history of her already long life. To Léonie 1, on the other hand, she exclusively ascribes the events lived through in waking hours. I was at first struck by an important exception to the rule, and was disposed to think that there might be something arbitrary in this partition of her recollections. In the normal state Léonie has a husband and children. But Léonie 2, the somnambulist, while acknowledging the children as her own, attributes the husband to 'the other.' This choice was perhaps explicable, but it followed no rule. It was not till later that I learned that her magnetizers in early days, as audacious as certain hypnotizers of recent date, had somnambulized her for her first *accouchements* [childbirth], and that she had lapsed into that state spontaneously in the later ones. Léonie 2 was thus quite right in ascribing to herself the children—since it was she who had had them—and the rule that her first trance-state forms a different personality was not broken. But it is the same with her second state of trance. When after the renewed passes, syncope, etc., she reaches the condition which I have called Léonie 3, she is another person still. Serious and grave, instead of being a restless child, she speaks slowly and moves but little. Again she separates herself from the waking Léonie 1. 'A good but rather stupid woman,' she says, 'and not me.' And she also separates herself from Léonie 2. 'How can you see anything of me in that crazy creature?' she says. 'Fortunately I am nothing for her!'"

Léonie 1 knows only of herself; Léonie 2 of herself and of Léonie 1; Léonie 3 knows of herself and of both the others. Léonie 1 has a visual consciousness; Léonie 2 has one both visual and auditory; in Léonie 3 it is at once visual, auditory, and tactile. Professor Janet thought at first that he was Léonie 3's discoverer. But she told him that she had been frequently in that condition before. Dr. Perrier, a former magnetizer, had hit upon her just as M. Janet had, in seeking by means of passes to deepen the sleep of Léonie 2. "This resurrection of a somnambulic personage, who had been extinct for twenty years, is curious enough; and in speaking to Léonie 3 I naturally now adopt the name of Léonore, which was given her by her first master."

The reader easily sees what surprises the trance-state may prepare, not only for the subject but for the operator. For the subject the surprises are often inconvenient enough, especially when the trance comes and goes spontaneously. Thus Léonie 1 is overwhelmed with embarrassment when, in the street, Léonie 2's gentlemen-friends (who are not hers) accost her. Léonie 2 spontaneously writes letters, which Léonie 1, not understanding, destroys when she finds them. Léonie 2 proceeds to thereupon hide them in a photograph album, into which she knows Léonie 1 will never look, because it contains the portrait of her former magnetizer, the sight of whom may put her to sleep again, which she dislikes. Léonie 1 finds herself in places known only to Léonie 2, to which the latter has led her, and then taken flight, etc. One sees the possibility of a new kind of "Comedy of Errors," to which it would take the skill of a Parisian *vaudevilliste* to do justice.

I fear that the reader unversed in this sort of lore will here let his growing impatience master him, and throw away my article as the work of either a mystifier or a dupe. These facts seem so silly and unreal, these "subjects" so contrary to all that our education has led us to expect our fellow creatures to be! Well, our education has been too narrow, that is all. Let one but once become familiar with the behavior of that not very rare personage, a good hypnotic subject, and the entire class of phenomena which I am recording come to seem not only possible but probable. It is, after all, only the fulfilment of what Locke's speculative genius suggested long ago, when, in that famous chapter on "Identity and Diversity" which occasioned such scandal in its day, after saying that personality extended no farther than consciousness, he went on to affirm that there would be two different selves or persons in one man, if the experiences undergone by that man should fall into two groups, each gathered into a distinct focus of recollection.

But still more remarkable things are to come, so I pray the reader to be patient and hear me a little longer, even if he means to give me up at last. These different personalities, admitted as possible by Locke, which we, under M. Janet's guidance, have seen actually succeeding each other under the names of Lucie 1, 2, and 3; and under those of Léonie 1, 2, and 3 mutually disowning and despising each other; are proved by M. Janet not only to exist in the successive forms in which we have seen them, but to coexist, to exist simultaneously; in such wise that while Lucie 1, for example, is apparently the only Lucie, anæsthetic, helpless, yet absorbed in conversation, that other Lucie—Lucie 3—is all the time "alive and kicking" inside of the same woman, and fully sensible and wide awake, and occupied with her own quite different concerns. This simultaneous coexistence of the different personages into which one human being may be split is the *great* thesis of M. Janet's book. Others, as Edmund Gurney, Bernheim, Binet, and more besides, have had the same idea, and proved it for certain cases; but M. Janet has emphasized and generalized it, and shown it to be true universally. He has been enabled to do this by *tapping* the submerged consciousness and making it respond in certain peculiar ways of which I now proceed to give a brief account. He found in several subjects, when the ordinary or primary consciousness was fully absorbed in conversation with a visitor (and the reader will remember how absolutely these hysterics then lapse into oblivion of surrounding things), that the submerged self would hear his voice if he came up and addressed the subject in a whisper; and would respond either by obeying such orders as he gave, or by gestures, or, finally, by pencil-writing on a sheet of paper placed under the hand. The *ostensible* consciousness, meanwhile, would go on with the conversation, entirely unaware of the gestures, acts, or writing performances of the hand. These latter, in turn, appeared quite as little disturbed by the upper consciousness's concerns. This proof by automatic writing of the secondary consciousness's existence is the most cogent and striking one; but a crowd of other facts prove the same thing. If I run through them all rapidly, the reader will probably be convinced.

The apparently anæsthetic hand of these subjects, for one thing, will often adapt itself discriminatingly to whatever object may be put into it. With a pencil it will make writing movements; into a pair of scissors it will put its fingers, and will open and shut them, etc. The primary consciousness, so to call it, is meanwhile unable to say whether or no *anything* is in the hand, if the latter be hidden from sight. "I put a pair of eye-glasses into Léonie's anæsthetic hand; this hand opens it and raises it toward the nose, but half-way thither it enters the field of vision of Léonie, who sees it and stops stupefied. 'Why,' says she, 'I have an eye-glass in my left hand!'" M. Binet found a very curious sort of connection between the apparently anæsthetic skin and the mind in some Salpêtrière subjects. Things placed in the hand were not felt, but *thought* of (apparently in visual terms), and in nowise referred by the subject to their starting-point in the hand's sensation. A key, a knife, placed in the hand occasioned *ideas* of a key or a knife, but the hand felt nothing. Similarly the subject thought of the number 3, 6, etc., if the hand or finger was bent three or six times by the operator, or if he stroked it three, six, etc., times.

In certain individuals there was found a still odder phenomenon, which reminds one of that curious idiosyncrasy of colored hearing of which a few cases have been lately described with great care by foreign writers. These individuals, namely, saw the impression received by the hand, but could not feel it; and the things seen appeared by no means associated with the hand, but more like an independent vision, which usually interested and surprised the patient. Her hand being hidden by a screen, she was ordered to look at another screen and to tell of any visual image which might project itself thereon. Numbers would then come, corresponding to the number of times the insensible member was raised, touched, etc. Colored lines and figures would come, corresponding to similar ones traced on the palm; the hand itself, or its fingers, would come when manipulated; and, finally, objects placed in it would come; but on the hand itself nothing could ever be felt. Of course, simulation would not be hard here; but M. Binet disbelieves this (usually very shallow) explanation to be a probable one of the cases in question.[5]

---

[5] This whole phenomenon shows how an idea which remains itself below the threshold of a certain conscious self may occasion associative effects therein. The skin-sensations, unfelt by the patient's primary consciousness, awaken, nevertheless, their usual visual associates therein.

The usual way in which doctors measure the delicacy of our touch is by the compass-points. Two points are normally felt as one whenever they are too close together for discrimination; but what is "too close" on one part of the skin may seem very far apart on another. In the middle of the back or on the thigh less than three inches maybe too close; on the fingertip a tenth of an inch is far enough apart. Now, as tested in this way, with the appeal made to the primary consciousness, which talks through the mouth, and seems to hold the field alone, a certain person's skin may be entirely anæsthetic and not feel the compass-points at all; and yet this same skin will prove to have a perfectly normal sensibility if the appeal be made to that other secondary or sub-consciousness which expresses itself automatically by writing or by movements of the hand. M. Binet, M. Pierre Janet, and M. Jules Janet have all found this. The subject, whenever touched, would signify "one point" or "two points," as accurately as if she were a normal person. But she would signify it only by these movements; and of the movements themselves her primary self would be as unconscious as of the facts they signified, for what the submerged consciousness makes the hand do automatically is unknown to the upper consciousness, which uses the mouth.

Messrs. Bernheim and Pitres have also proved, by observations too complicated to be given here, that the hysterical blindness is no real blindness at all. The eye of an hysteric which is totally blind when the other, or seeing eye, is shut, will do its share of vision perfectly well when *both* eyes are open together. But even where both eyes are semi-blind from hysterical disease, the method of automatic writing proves that their perceptions exist, only cut off from communication with the upper consciousness. M. Binet has found the hand of his patients unconsciously writing down words which their eyes were vainly endeavoring to "see," *i.e.*, to bring to the upper consciousness. Their submerged consciousness was, of course, seeing them, or the hand couldn't have written as it did. Similarly the sub-conscious self perfectly well perceives colors which the hysterically color-blind eyes cannot bring to the normal consciousness. Again, pricks, burns, and pinches on the anæsthetic skin, all unnoticed by the upper self, are recollected to have been suffered, and complained of, as soon as the under self gets a chance to express itself by the passage of the subject into hypnotic trance.

It must be admitted therefore that, in certain persons at least, the total possible consciousness may be split into parts which coexist, but mutually ignore each other and share the objects of knowledge between them, and—more remarkable still—are complementary. Give an object to one of the consciousnesses, and by that fact you remove it from the other or others. Barring a certain common fund of information, like the command of language, etc., what the upper self knows, the under self is ignorant of, and *vice versa*. M. Janet has proved this beautifully in his subject Lucie. The following experiment will serve as the type of the rest: In her trance he covered her lap with cards, each bearing a number. He then told her that on waking she should *not see* any card whose number was a multiple of three. This is the ordinary so-called "post-hypnotic suggestion," now well known, and for which Lucie was a well-adapted subject. Accordingly, when she was awakened and asked about the papers on her lap, she counted and picked up only those whose number was not a multiple of 3. To the 12, 18, 9, etc., she was blind. But the hand, when the sub-conscious self was interrogated by the usual method of engrossing the upper self in another conversation, wrote that the only cards in Lucie's lap were those numbered 12, 18, 9, etc., and on being asked to pick up all the cards which were there, picked up these and let the others lie. Similarly, when the sight of certain things was suggested to the sub-conscious Lucie, the normal Lucie suddenly became partially or totally blind. "What is the matter? I can't see!" the normal personage suddenly cried out in the midst of her conversation, when M. Janet whispered to the secondary personage to make use of her eyes. The anesthesias, paralyses, contractions, and other irregularities from which hysterics suffer seem, then, to be due to the fact that their secondary personage has enriched itself by robbing the primary one of a function which the latter ought to have retained. The curative indication is evident: Get at the secondary personage by hypnotization, or in whatever other way, and make her *give up* the eye, the skin, the arm, or whatever the affected part may be. The normal self thereupon regains possession, sees, feels, and is able to move again. In this way M. Jules Janet easily cured the subject Witt... of all sorts of afflictions which, until he had discovered the secret of her deeper trance, it had been difficult to subdue. "*Cessez cette mauvaise plaisanterie* [cease this poor joke]," he said to the secondary self, and the latter obeyed. The way in which the various personages share the stock of possible sensations between them seems to be amusingly illustrated in this young woman. When awake, her skin is insensible everywhere except on a zone about the arm where she habitually wears a gold bracelet. This zone has feeling; but in the deeper trance, when all the rest of her body feels, this particular zone becomes absolutely anæsthetic.

Sometimes the mutual ignorance of the selves leads to incidents which are strange enough. The acts and movements performed by the sub-conscious self are withdrawn from the conscious one, and the subject will do all sorts of incongruous, things, of which he remains quite unaware.

> I order Lucie [by the method of *distraction*] to make a *pied de nez* {thumbing one's nose}, and her hands go forthwith to the end of her nose. Asked what she is doing, she replies that she is doing nothing, and continues for a long time talking, with no apparent suspicion that her fingers are moving in front of her nose. I make her walk about the room, she continues to speak, and believes herself sitting down.

M. Janet observed similar acts in a man in alcoholic delirium. While the doctor was questioning him, M. Janet made him, by whispered suggestion, walk, sit, kneel, and even lie down on his face on the floor, he all the while believing himself to be standing beside his bed. Such *bizarreries* sound incredible until one has seen their like. Long ago, without understanding it, I myself saw a small example of the way in which a person's knowledge may be shared by the two selves. A young woman, who had been writing automatically, was sitting with a pencil in her hand, trying to recall, at my request, the name of a gentleman whom she had once seen. She could only recollect the first syllable. *Her hand*, meanwhile, without her knowledge, wrote down the last two syllables. In a perfectly healthy young man who can write with the planchette, I lately found the hand to be entirely anesthetic during the writing act. I could prick it severely without the subject knowing the fact. The planchette, however, accused me in strong terms of hurting the hand. Pricks on the *other* (non-writing) hand, meanwhile, which awakened strong protest from the young man's vocal organs, were denied to exist by the self which made the planchette go.

We get exactly similar results in post-hypnotic suggestion. It is a familiar fact that certain subjects, when told during a trance to perform an act or to experience an hallucination after waking, will, when the time comes, obey the command. How is the command registered? How is its performance so accurately timed? These problems were long a mystery, for the primary personality remembers nothing of the trance or the suggestion, and will often trump up an improvised pretext for yielding to the unaccountable impulse which comes over him so suddenly, and which he cannot resist. Edmund Gurney was the first to discover, by means of automatic writing, that the secondary self was awake, keeping its attention constantly fixed on the command and watching for the signal of its execution. Certain trance-subjects, who were also automatic writers, when roused from trance and put to the planchette—not knowing then what they wrote, and having their upper attention fully engrossed by reading aloud, talking, or solving problems in mental arithmetic—would inscribe the orders they had received, together with notes relative to the time elapsed and the time yet to run before the execution. It is therefore to no "automatism," in the mechanical sense, that such acts are due: a self presides over them, a split-off, limited, and buried, but yet a fully conscious self. More than this, the buried self often comes to the surface and drives out the other self while the acts are performing. In other words, the subject lapses into trance again when the moment arrives for execution, and has no subsequent recollection of the act which he has done. Gurney and Beaunis established this fact, which has since been verified on a large scale; and Gurney also showed that the patient became *suggestible* again during the brief time of the performance. M. Janet's observations, in their turn, well illustrate the phenomenon.

> I tell Lucie to keep her arms raised after she shall have awakened. Hardly is she in the normal state when up go her arms above her head, but she pays no attention to them. She goes, comes, converses, holding her arms high in the air. If asked what her arms are doing, she is surprised at such a question and says, very sincerely: 'My hands are doing nothing they are just like yours.' I command her to weep, and when awake she really sobs, but continues in the midst of her tears to talk of very gay matters. The sobbing over, there remains no trace of this grief, which seemed to have been quite sub-conscious.

The primary self often has to invent an hallucination by which to mask and hide from its own view the deeds which the other self is enacting. Léonie 3 writes real letters, while Léonie 1 believes that she is knitting; or Lucie 3 really comes to the doctor's office, while Lucie 1 believes herself to be at home. This is a sort of delirium. The alphabet, or the series of numbers, when handed over to the attention of the secondary personage, may, for the time being, be lost to the normal self. While the hand writes the alphabet, obediently to command, the "subject," to her great stupefaction, finds herself unable to recall it, etc. Few things are more curious than these relations of mutual exclusion, of which all gradations exist, between the several partial consciousnesses.

How far this splitting up of the mind into separate consciousnesses may obtain in each one of us is a problem. M. Janet holds that it is only possible where there is abnormal weakness, and consequently a defect of unifying or coordinating power. An hysteric woman abandons part of her consciousness because she is too weak nervously to hold it all together. The abandoned part, meanwhile, may solidify into a secondary or sub-conscious self. In a perfectly sound subject, on the other hand, what is dropped out of mind at one moment keeps coming back at the next. The whole fund of experiences and knowledges remains integrated, and no split-off portions of it can get organized stably enough to form subordinate selves. The stability, monotony, and stupidity of these latter is often very striking. The post-hypnotic self-consciousness seems to think of nothing but the order which it last received; the cataleptic sub-consciousness, of nothing but the last position imprinted on the limb. M. Janet could cause definitely circumscribed reddening and tumefaction of the skin, on two of his subjects, by suggesting to them in hypnotism the hallucination of a mustard-poultice of any special shape. *"J'ai tout le temps pensé à votre sinapisme* [I think about your mustard-poultice all the time]," says the subject, when put back into trance after the suggestion has taken effect. A man, N——, whom M. Janet operated on at long intervals, was between whiles tampered with by another operator, and when put to sleep again by M. Janet, said he was "too far away to receive orders, being in Algiers." The other operator, having suggested that hallucination, had forgotten to remove it before waking the subject from his trance, and the poor, passive, trance-personality had stuck for weeks in the stagnant dream. Léonie's sub-conscious performances having been illustrated to a caller by a *pied de nez*, executed with her left hand in the course of conversation, when, a year later, she meets him again up goes the same hand to her nose again, without Léonie 1 suspecting the fact.

And this leads me to what, after all, is the really important part of these investigations—I mean their possible application to the relief of human misery. Let one think and say what one will about the crudity and intellectual barbarism of much of the philosophizing of our contemporary nerve-doctors; let one dislike as much as one may please the thoroughly materialistic attitude of mind which many of them show; still, their work, as a whole, is sanctified by its positive, practical fertility. Theorems about the unity of the thinking principle will always be, as they always have been, *barren*; but observations of fact lead to new issues *in infinitum*. And when one reflects that nothing less than the cure of insanity—that direst of human afflictions—lies possibly at the end of such inquiries as those which M. Janet and his *confrères* are beginning, one feels as if the disdain which some spiritualistic psychologists exhibit for such researches were very poorly placed. The way to redeem people from barbarism is not to stand aloof and sneer at their awkward attempts, but to show them how to do the same things better. Ordinary hypnotic suggestion is proving itself immensely fertile in the therapeutic field; and the subtler knowledge of sub-conscious states which we are now gaining will certainly increase our powers in this direction many fold. Who knows how many pathological states (not simply nervous and functional ones, but organic ones too) may be due to the existence of some perverse buried fragment of consciousness obstinately nourishing its narrow memory or delusion, and thereby inhibiting the normal flow of life? A concrete case will best exhibit what I mean. On the whole, it is more deeply suggestive to me than anything in Janet's book.

The story is that of a young girl of nineteen named Marie, who came to the hospital in an almost desperate condition, with monthly convulsive crises, chill, fever, delirium, attacks of terror, etc., lasting for days, together with various shifting anesthesias and contractures all the time, and a fixed blindness of the left eye. At first M. Janet, divining no particular psychological factor in the case, took little interest in the patient, who remained in the hospital for seven months, and had all the usual courses of treatment applied, including water-cure and ordinary hypnotic suggestions, without the slightest good effect.

She then fell into a sort of despair, of which the result was to make M. Janet try to throw her into a deeper trance, so as to get, if possible, some knowledge of her remoter psychologic antecedents, and of the original causes of the disease, of which, in the waking state and in ordinary hypnotism, she could give no definite account. He succeeded even beyond his expectations; for both her early memories and the internal memory of her crises returned in the deep somnambulism, and she explained three things: Her periodical chill, fever, and delirium were due to a foolish immersion of herself in cold water at the age of thirteen. The chill, fever, etc., were consequences which then ensued; and now, years later, the experience then stamped in upon the brain for the first time was *repeating itself* at regular intervals in the form of an hallucination undergone by the sub-conscious self, and of which the primary personality only experienced the outer results. The attacks of terror were accounted for by another shocking experience. At the age of sixteen she had seen an old woman killed by falling from a height; and the sub-conscious self, for reasons best known to itself, saw fit to believe itself present at this experience also whenever the other crises came on. The hysterical blindness of her left eye had the same sort of origin, dating back to her sixth year, when she had been forced, in spite of her cries, to sleep in the same bed with another child, the left half of whose face bore a disgusting eruption. The result was an eruption on the same parts of her own face, which came back for several years before it disappeared entirely, and left behind it an anesthesia of the skin and the blindness of the eye.

So much for the origin of the poor girl's various afflictions. Now for the cure! The thing needed was, of course, to get the sub-conscious personality to leave off having these senseless hallucinations. But they had become so stereotyped and habitual that this proved no easy task to achieve. Simple commands were fruitless; but M. Janet at last hit upon an artifice, which shows how many resources the successful mind-doctor must possess. He carried the poor Marie back in imagination to the earlier dates. It proved as easy with her as with many others when entranced, to produce the hallucination that she was again a child, all that was needed being an impressive affirmation to that effect. Accordingly M. Janet, replacing her in this wise at the age of six, made her go through the bed-scene again, but gave it a different *dénouement*. He made her believe that the horrible child had no eruption and was charming, so that she was finally convinced, and caressed without fear this new object of her imagination. He made her re-enact the scene of the cold immersion, but gave it also an entirely different result. He made her live again through the old woman's accident, but substituted a comical issue for the old tragical one which had made so deep an impression. The sub-conscious Marie, passive and docile as usual, adopted these new versions of the old tales; and was apparently either living in monotonous contemplation of them or had become extinct altogether when M. Janet wrote his book. For all morbid symptoms ceased as if by magic. "It is five months," our author says, "since these experiments were performed. Marie shows no longer the slightest mark of hysteria. She is well; and, in particular, has grown quite stout. Her physical aspect has absolutely changed." Finally, she is no longer hypnotizable, as often happens in these cases when the health returns.

The mind-curers and Christian scientists, of whom we have lately heard so much, unquestionably get, by widely different methods, results, in certain cases, no less remarkable than this. The ordinary medical man, if he believes the facts at all, dismisses them from his attention with the cut-and-dried remark that they are "only effects of the imagination." It is the great merit of these French investigators, and of Messrs. Myers, Gurney, and the "psychical researchers," that they are for the first time trying to read some sort of a definite meaning into this vaguest of phrases. Little by little the meaning will grow more precise. It seems to me a very great step to have ascertained that the secondary self, or selves, coexist with the primary one, the trance-personalities with the normal one, during the waking state. But just what these secondary selves may be, and what are their remoter relations and conditions of existence, are questions to which the answer is anything but clear. My own decided impression is that M. Janet's generalizations are based on too limited a number of cases to cover the whole ground. He would have it that the secondary self is always a symptom of hysteria, and that the essential fact about hysteria is the lack of synthetizing power and consequent disintegration of the field of consciousness into mutually exclusive parts. The secondary and the primary consciousnesses added together can, on M. Janet's theory, never exceed the normally total consciousness of the individual. This theory certainly expresses pretty well the facts which have fallen under its author's own observation, though even here, if this were a critical article, I might have something to say. But there are trances which obey another type. I know a non-hysterical woman who, in her trances, knows facts which altogether transcend her *possible* normal consciousness, facts about the lives of people whom she never saw or heard of before. I am well aware of all the liabilities to which this statement exposes me, and I make it deliberately, having practically no doubt whatever of its truth. My *own* impression is that the trance-condition is an immensely complex and fluctuating thing, into the understanding of which we have hardly begun to penetrate, and concerning which any very sweeping generalization is sure to be premature. *A comparative study of trances and sub-conscious states* is meanwhile of the most urgent importance for the comprehension of our nature. It often happens that scattered facts of a certain kind float around for a long time, but that nothing scientific or solid comes of them until some man writes just enough of a book to give them a possible body and meaning. Then they shoot together, as it were, from all directions, and that book becomes the center of crystallization of a rapid accumulation of new knowledge. Such a book I am sure that M. Janet's ought to be; and I confidently prophesy that anyone who may be induced by this article to follow the path of study in which it is so brilliant a pioneer will reap a rich reward.

2

WHAT PSYCHICAL RESEARCH HAS ACCOMPLISHED

In this laudatory essay about the Society for Psychical Research, William James reviews the first ten years of the Society's history and activities, providing his own assessments of them along the way. It first appeared in an 1892 issue of the well-respected journal, *The Forum*, which focused on science, politics, and society.

Five years later, in 1897, James published a revised version of the article under the same title, much edited and with content added from "The Hidden Self" (Chapter 1) and "Address of the President Before the Society for Psychical Research" (Chapter 3).[1] The present version has rarely been reprinted, and the three pieces together give a more thorough understanding of James's views on psychical research than the later edited piece. Indeed, read in sequence they seem almost like James was methodically laying out the case for the reality of psychic phenomena over a period of years.

If to have one's name knocked about in conversation and in newspapers be fame, the Society for Psychical Research is famous. Yet it is probable

---

[1] For the abridged and reworked version of "What Psychical Research Has Accomplished," see William James (1896) *The Will to Believe and Other Essays in Popular Philosophy*. London: Longman's Green.

that any real acquaintance with its history, its aims, and its work hardly exists outside the narrow circle of its membership. Believing, as I do, that the Society fulfils a function which, though limited, is decidedly important in the organization of science, I am glad to give a brief account of it to the uninstructed reader.

According to the newspaper and drawing-room myth, soft-headedness and idiotic credulity are the bond of sympathy in the Society, and general wonder-sickness is its dynamic principle. A glance at the membership fails, however, to corroborate this view. The president is Prof. Henry Sidgwick, known by his other deeds as the most incorrigibly and exasperatingly critical and sceptical mind in England. The hard-headed Arthur Balfour is one vice-president, and the hard-headed Prof. S. P. Langley, secretary of the Smithsonian Institution, is another. Such men as Professor Lodge, the eminent English physicist, and Professor Richet, the eminent French physiologist, are amongst the most active contributors to the Society's *Proceedings*; and through the catalogue of membership are sprinkled names honored throughout the world for their scientific capacity. In fact, were I asked to point to a scientific journal where hard-headedness and never-sleeping suspicion of sources of error might be seen in their full bloom, I think I should have to fall back on the *Proceedings of the Society for Psychical Research*. The common run of papers, say on physiological subjects, which one finds in other professional organs, are apt to show a far lower level of critical consciousness. Indeed, the rigorous canons of evidence applied a few years ago to testimony in the case of certain "mediums" led to the secession from the Society of a number of spiritualists. Messrs. Stainton Moses and Alfred Russel Wallace, amongst others, thought that no experiences based on mere eyesight could ever have a chance to be admitted as true, if such an impossibly exacting standard of proof were insisted on in every case.

The Society for Psychical Research was founded in February, 1882, by a number of gentlemen, foremost amongst whom seem to have been Professors Henry Sidgwick, W. F. Barrett, and Balfour Stewart, and Messrs. R. H. Hutton, Hensleigh Wedgwood, Edmund Gurney, and F. W. H. Myers. Their purpose was twofold: first, to carry on systematic experimentation with hypnotic subjects, mediums, clairvoyants, and others; and, secondly, to collect evidence concerning apparitions, haunted houses, and similar phenomena which are incidentally reported, but which, from their fugitive character, admit of no deliberate control. Professor Sidgwick, in his introductory address, insisted that the divided state of public opinion on all these matters was a scandal to science, absolute disdain on à priori grounds characterizing what may be called professional opinion, whilst completely uncritical and indiscriminate credulity was too often found amongst those who pretended to have a first-hand acquaintance with the facts.

As a sort of weather bureau for accumulating reports of such meteoric phenomena as apparitions, the S. P. R. (as I shall continue briefly to call it) has done an immense amount of work. As an experimenting body, it cannot be said to have completely fulfilled the hopes of its founders. The reasons for this lie in two circumstances: first, the clairvoyant and other subjects who will allow themselves to be experimented upon are few and far between; and, secondly, work with them takes an immense amount of time, and in the case of the Society has had to be carried on at odd intervals by members engaged in other pursuits. The Society has not yet been rich enough to control the undivided services of skilled experimenters in this difficult field. The loss of the lamented Edmund Gurney, who more than anyone else had leisure to devote, has been so far irreparable. But were there no experimental work at all, and were the Society nothing but a weather bureau for catching sporadic apparitions, etc., in their freshness, I am disposed to think its function indispensable in the scientific organism. If any one of my readers, spurred by the thought that so much smoke must needs betoken fire, has ever looked into the existing literature of the supernatural for proof, he will know what I mean. This literature is enormous, but it is practically quite worthless for evidential purposes. Facts enough are there, indeed; but the records of them are so fallible and uncritical that the most they do is to confirm the presumption that it may be well to keep a window open in one's mind upon that quarter.

In the Society's *Proceedings*, on the contrary, a different law prevails. Quality, and not mere quantity, is what has been mainly kept in mind. The most that could be done with every reported case has been done. The witnesses, where possible, have been cross examined personally, the collateral facts have been looked up, and the narrative appears with its precise coefficient of evidential worth stamped on it, so that all may know just what its weight as proof may be. Outside of these *Proceedings*, I know of no systematic attempt to weigh the evidence for the supernatural. This makes the value of the seven volumes already published unique, and I firmly believe that as the years go on and the ground covered grows still wider, the Society's *Proceedings* will more and more tend to supersede all other sources of empirical information concerning phenomena traditionally deemed occult. If the Society could continue to exist long enough for the public to become familiar with its presence, so that any case of apparition or of a house or person infested with unaccountable noises or disturbances of material objects would, as a matter of course, be reported to its officers, who thereupon would take down the evidence in as thorough a way as possible, we should end ere long by having a mass of facts concrete enough to found a decent theory upon.

Those who are now sustaining the Society should accustom themselves to the idea that its first duty is simply to exist from year to year and perform this recording function well, though no conclusive results of any sort emerge in the first generation. All our learned societies have begun in some such modest way. Three years after the English Society was founded, Professor Barrett came to this country and stirred up some scientific men in Boston, so that the American Society for Psychical Research was founded as a separate organization. After five years this Society perished. Providence had raised up no one in its midst who had both leisure and aptitude for doing work of the sort required. But though the organization was abandoned, its associates for the most part joined the English Society, which thereupon constituted an "American Branch," with Professor Langley and the present writer as its honorary vice-presidents and Mr. Richard Hodgson as its salaried secretary and executive agent. The "American Branch" has suffered from the same defect as the American Society. The secretary is the only individual connected with it who is able to make any solid contribution to its work. It requires, moreover, a large increase of membership to become self-supporting.

One cannot by mere outward organization make much progress in matters scientific. Societies can back men of genius, but can never take their place. The contrast between the parent Society and the "American Branch" illustrates this. In England, a little group of men with enthusiasm and genius for the work supplied the nucleus; in this country, Mr. Hodgson had to be imported from Europe before any tangible progress was made. What perhaps more than anything else has held the Society together in England is Professor Sidgwick's extraordinary gift of inspiring confidence in diverse sorts of people. Such tenacity of interest in the result and such absolute impartiality in discussing the evidence are not once in a century found in an individual. His obstinate belief that there is something yet to be brought to light communicates patience to the discouraged; his constitutional inability to draw any precipitate conclusion reassures those who are afraid of being dupes. Mrs. Sidgwick – a sister, by the way, of the great Arthur Balfour – is a worthy ally of her husband in this matter, showing a similarly extraordinary power of holding her judgment in suspense, and a keenness of observation and capacity for experimenting with human subjects which are rare in either sex.

The *worker* of the Society, as originally constituted, was Edmund Gurney. Gurney was a man of the rarest sympathies and gifts. Although, like Carlyle, he used to groan under the burden of his labors, he yet exhibited a colossal power of dispatching business and getting through drudgery of the most repulsive kind. His two thick volumes on the *Phantasms of the Living*, collected and published in three years, are a proof of this. Besides this, he had exquisite artistic instincts, and his massive volume on *The Power of Sound* is certainly the most important work on æsthetics in the English language. He had also the tenderest heart and a mind of rare metaphysical power, as his volume of essays, *Tertium Quid*, will prove to any reader. Mr. F. W. H. Myers, already well known as one of the most brilliant of English essayists, is the *ingenium præfervidum* of the S. P. R. Of the value of Mr. Myers' theoretic writings I will say a word later. Mr. Hodgson, the American secretary, is distinguished by a balance of mind almost as rare in its way as Sidgwick's. He is persuaded of the reality of many of the phenomena called spiritualistic, but he also has uncommon keenness in detecting error; and it is impossible to say in advance whether it will give him more satisfaction to confirm or to smash a given "case" offered to his examination. Other names in the *Proceedings* are those of Mr. Malcolm Guthrie, Mr. Frank Podmore, Prof. Oliver Lodge, Prof. Ch. Richet, and M. Léon Marillier.

It is now time to cast a brief look upon the actual contents of these *Proceedings*[2]. The first two years were largely taken up with experiments in thought-transference. The earliest lot of these were made with the

---

[2] The Society, in addition to the *Proceedings*, prints privately a monthly journal, which is issued to members only. This contains what may be called raw materials, imperfectly corroborated interviews and provisional discussions only; whereas the *Proceedings*, which appear thrice a year in parts numbering from 150 to 300 pages, contain worked-up reports of facts and such theoretical contributions as may receive the *imprimatur* of a special committee. The best way in this country to get the *Proceedings* regularly is to join the Branch. They may also be bought singly from the secretary, R. Hodgson, 5 Boylston Place, Boston, Mass., and from Damrell & Upham, booksellers, Washington and School streets, Boston.

daughters of a clergyman named Creery, and convinced Messrs. Balfour Stewart, Barrett, Myers, and Gurney that the girls had an inexplicable power of guessing names and objects thought of by other persons. Two years later, Mrs. Sidgwick and Mr. Gurney, recommencing experiments with the same girls, detected them signaling to each other. This makes it impossible to accept the record of their previous performances. It is true that for the most part the conditions had then excluded signaling, and it is also possible that the cheating may have grafted itself on what was originally a genuine phenomenon. Yet Gurney was wise in abandoning the entire series to the skepticism of the reader. Three other thought transference subjects were experimented upon at great length during the first two years: one was Mr. G. A. Smith; the other two were young ladies in Liverpool in the employment of Mr. Malcolm Guthrie.

It is the opinion of all who took part in these experiments that sources of conscious and unconscious deception were sufficiently excluded, and that the large percentage of correct reproductions by the subjects of words, diagrams, and sensations occupying other people's consciousness were entirely inexplicable as results of chance. The present writer confesses that the reading of the records leaves on him a similar impression. But the odd thing about this sort of "thought-transference" is that since the first three years of the Society's existence no new subjects have turned up with whom extensive and systematic experiments could be carried on. All the later reports are of brief series and semi-sporadic results, leaving no ground for certainty. Meanwhile the witnesses of Mr. Smith's, Miss Ralph's, and Miss Edwards' performances were all so satisfied of the genuineness of the phenomenon that "telepathy" has figured freely in the papers of the *Proceedings* and in Gurney's book on *Phantasms* as a *vera causa* on which additional hypotheses might be built. No mere reader can be blamed, however, if he refuse to espouse so revolutionary a belief until a larger bulk of testimony be supplied.

Volume I contains another experimental paper, that on the divining-rod, by Mr. Edward R. Pease, with inconclusive results. The divining-rod has never again shown its face in the *Proceedings*. Gurney's papers on hypnotism must be mentioned next. Some of them are less concerned with establishing new facts than with analyzing old ones, the papers on memory during hypnotism, for example. Omitting these, we find that in the line of pure observation Gurney claims to have ascertained in more than one subject the following phenomenon, of which the theoretic explanation is doubtful: The subject's hands are thrust through a blanket, which screens the operator from his eyes, and his mind is absorbed in conversation with a third person. The operator meanwhile points with his finger to one of the fingers of the subject, which finger alone responds to this silent selection by becoming stiff or anæsthetic, as the case may be. The interpretation is difficult, but the phenomenon, which I have myself witnessed, seems authentic.

Another observation made by Gurney seems to prove the possibility of the subject's mind being directly influenced by the operator's. The hypnotized subject responds or fails to respond to questions asked by a third party according to the operator's silent permission or refusal. Of course, in these experiments all obvious sources of deception were considered. But Gurney's most important contribution by far to our knowledge of hypnotism was his series of experiments on the automatic writing of subjects who had received post-hypnotic suggestions. For example, a subject during trance is told that he will poke the fire in six minutes after waking. On being waked he has no memory of the order, but while he is engaged in conversation his hand is placed on a *planchette*, which immediately writes the sentence, "P., you will poke the fire in six minutes." Experiments like this, which were repeated in great variety, prove that below the upper consciousness the hypnotic consciousness persists, engrossed with the suggestion and able to express itself through the involuntarily moving hand.

Gurney shares, therefore, with Janet and Binet, whose observations were made with widely differing subjects and methods, the credit of demonstrating the simultaneous existence of two different strata of consciousness, ignorant of each other, in the same person. The "extra-consciousness," as one may call it, can be kept on tap, as it were, by the method of automatic writing. This discovery marks a new era in experimental psychology; it is impossible to overrate its importance. But Gurney's greatest piece of work is his laborious *Phantasms of the Living*. As an example of the drudgery stowed away in the volumes, it may suffice to say that in looking up the proofs for the alleged physical phenomena of witchcraft, Gurney reports a careful search through two hundred and sixty books on the subject, with the result of finding no first-hand evidence recorded in the trials except the confessions of the victims themselves, and these, of course, are presumptively based on hallucinations. This statement, made in an unobtrusive note, is only one instance of the care displayed throughout the volumes. In the course of these, Gurney discusses about seven hundred cases of apparitions which he collected. A large number of these were "veridical," in the sense of coinciding with some calamity happening to the person who appeared.

Gurney's explanation is that the mind of the person undergoing the calamity was at that moment able to impress the mind of the percipient with a hallucination.

Apparitions, on this "telepathic" theory, may be called "objective" facts, although they are not "material" facts. In order to test the likelihood of such veridical hallucinations being due to mere chance, Gurney instituted the "census of hallucinations," which has been continued with the result of obtaining answers from some twenty-five thousand people, asked at random in different countries whether, when in good health and awake, they had ever heard a voice, seen a form, or felt a touch which no material presence could account for. The result seems to be, roughly speaking, that about one adult in ten has had such an experience at least once in his life, and of the experiences themselves 14 percent coincide with some real distant event. In other words, one person out of every one hundred and forty in the community has had a veridical hallucination of some sort or other, vague or precise. The question is, Is this degree of frequency too great to be deemed fortuitous, and must we suppose an occult connection between the two events? My own position is still one of doubt, although I tend to accept the occult connection. In but few cases is the evidence as complete as one could wish, and the data themselves are all too crude for a mathematical computation of probability. The great use of the census is to have been the means of collecting an enormous amount of material for study. The admirable report upon it which Mrs. Sidgwick will make to the International Congress of Experimental Psychology next August will continue Gurney's labors, and put the entire subject of hallucinations on a new empirical basis.

The next experimental topic worth mentioning in the *Proceedings* is the discussion of the physical phenomenon of mediumship (slate-writing, furniture-moving, and so forth) by Mrs. Sidgwick, Mr. Hodgson, and "Mr. Davey." This, so far as it goes, is destructive of the claims of all the mediums examined. In the way of "control," "Mr. Davey" himself produced fraudulent slate-writing of the highest order, while Mr. Hodgson, a "sitter" in his confidence, reviewed the written reports of the series of his other sitters—all intelligent per sons—and shows that in every case they failed to see the essential features of what was done before their eyes. This Davey-Hodgson contribution is probably the most damaging document concerning eye-witnesses' evidence which has ever been produced. Another substantial bit of work based on personal observation is Mr. Hodgson's report of Madame Blavatsky's claims to physical mediumship. This is adverse to the lady's pretensions; and although some of Madame Blavatsky's friends make light of it, it is a stroke from which her reputation will hardly recover. Although the S. P. R. has thus found that the evidence for matter moving without contact is as yet insufficient, its observations on an American medium, Mrs. Piper, tend to substantiate the claim that hyper-normal intelligence may be displayed in the trance state. A tediously long report of sittings with Mrs. Piper in England, followed by a still longer ditto in America, gives proof (entirely conclusive to the present writer's mind) that this lady has shown in her trances a knowledge of the personal affairs of living and dead people which it is impossible to suppose that she can have gained in any "natural" way. A satisfactory explanation of the phenomenon is yet to seek. It offers itself as spirit-control; but it is as hard to accept this theory without protest as it is to be satisfied with such explanations as clairvoyance or reading the sitter's mind.

One of the most important experimental contributions to the *Proceedings* is the article of Miss X— on "Crystal Vision." Many persons who look fixedly into a crystal or other vaguely luminous surface fall into a kind of daze and see visions. Miss X— has this susceptibility in a remarkable degree, and is, moreover, an unusually intelligent critic. She reports many visions which can only be described as apparently clairvoyant, and others which beautifully fill a vacant niche in our knowledge of subconscious mental operations. For example, looking into the crystal before breakfast one morning she reads in printed characters of the death of a lady of her acquaintance, the date and other circumstances all duly appearing in type. Startled by this, she looks at *The Times* of the previous day for verification, and there amongst the deaths are the identical words which she has seen. On the same page of *The Times* are other items which she remembers reading the day before; and the only explanation seems to be that her eyes then inattentively observed, so to speak, the death item, which forthwith fell into a special corner of her memory and came out as a visual hallucination when the peculiar modification of consciousness induced by the crystal-gazing set in.

Passing from papers based on observation to papers based on narrative, we have a number of ghost stories, etc., sifted by Mrs. Sidgwick and discussed by Messrs. Myers and Podmore. They form the best ghost literature I know of from the point of view of emotional interest. As to the conclusions drawn, Mrs. Sidgwick is rigorously non-committal, while Mr. Myers and Mr. Podmore show themselves respectively hospitable and inhospitable to the notion that such stories have a basis of objectivity dependent on the continued existence of the dead.

I must close my gossip about the *Proceedings* by naming what, after all, seems to me the most important part of its contents. This is the long series of articles by Mr. Myers on what he now calls the "subliminal self," or what I have designated above as the "extra-consciousness." The result of Myers' learned and ingenious studies in hypnotism, hallucinations, automatic writing, mediumship, and the whole series of allied phenomena is a conviction which he expresses in the following terms:

> Each of us is in reality an abiding psychical entity far more extensive than he knows—an individuality which can never express itself completely through any corporeal manifestation. The self manifests itself through the organism, but there is always some part of the self unmanifested, and always, as it seems, some power of organic expression in abeyance or reserve.

The ordinary consciousness Mr. Myers likens to the visible part of the solar spectrum; the total consciousness is like that spectrum prolonged by the inclusion of the ultra-red and ultra-violet rays. In the psychic spectrum the "ultra" parts may embrace a far wider range, both of physiological and of psychical activity, than is open to our ordinary consciousness and memory. At the lower end, beyond the red, as it were, we have the *physiological* extension, mind-cures, "stigmatization" of ecstatics, etc.; in the upper or ultra-violet region, we have the hyper-normal cognitions of the medium-trance. Whatever the judgment of the future may be on Mr. Myers' speculations, the credit will always remain to them of being the first attempt in our language, and the first thoroughly inductive attempt in any language, to consider the phenomena of hallucination, hypnotism, automatism, double personality, and mediumship as connected parts of one whole subject. No one seems to me to have grasped the problem in a way both so broad and so sober as he has done.

One's reaction on hearsay testimony is always determined by one's own experience. Most men who have once convinced themselves, by what seems to them a careful examination, that any one species of the supernatural exists, begin to relax their vigilance as to evidence, and throw the doors of their minds more or less wide open to the supernatural along its whole extent. To a mind that has thus made its *salto mortale*, the minute work over insignificant cases and quiddling discussion of "evidential values," of which the Society's reports are full, seems insufferably tedious. And it is so; few species of literature are more truly dull than reports of phantasms. Cases which one collects one's self from the witnesses may acquire a personal interest; but cases merely found printed as having occurred to strangers are hard to read or to remember without some definite purpose in one's mind, such as trying to classify them, or seeing how they may affect a theory or fill gaps in a growing series. Taken simply by themselves, as separate facts to stare at, they appear so devoid of meaning and sweep that even were they certainly true, one would be tempted to leave them out of one's universe for being so idiotic. Every other sort of fact has some context and continuity with the rest of nature. These alone are contextless and discontinuous.

Hence I think that the sort of loathing—no milder word will do—which the very words "psychical research" and "psychical researcher" awaken in so many honest scientific breasts is not only natural, but in a sense praiseworthy. A man who is unable himself to conceive of any *orbit* for these mental meteors can only suppose that Messrs. Gurney, Myers & Co.'s mood in dealing with them must be that of silly marveling at so many detached prodigies. And *such* prodigies! Whereas the only thing that really interests these "researchers" is the glimpse that they gain of the orbit itself. Thus between the spiritualists and theosophists, who have so much orbit that they are sickened by the methods, and the scientists, who have so little that they are sickened by the facts, of the S. P. R., the latter stands in a rather forsaken position. And yet it is a position of peculiar merit, as I think that a little reflection will show.

Orthodoxy is almost as much a matter of authority in science as it is in the Church. We believe in all sorts of laws of nature which we cannot ourselves understand, merely because men whom we admire and trust vouch for them. If Messrs. Helmholtz, Huxley, Pasteur, and Edison were simultaneously to announce themselves as converts to clairvoyance, thought-transference, and ghosts, who can doubt that there would be a prompt popular stampede in that direction? We should have as great a slush of "telepathy" in the scientific press as we now have of "suggestion" in the medical press. We should hasten to invoke mystical explanations without winking, and fear to be identified with a by-gone *régime* if we held back. In society we should eagerly let it be known that we had always thought there was a basis of truth in haunted houses, and had, as far back as we could remember, had faith in demoniacal possession.

Now, it is certain that if the cat ever does jump this way, the cautious methods of the S. P. R. will give it a position of extraordinary influence. As, one after another, the fashion-setting converts dropped in and the popular credulity began, its efforts at exactitude about evidence and its timidity in speculating would seem supremely virtuous. Sober-headed scientists would look to its temper as a bulwark; whilst its poor little detached facts, no longer so idiotic and neglectable, would prove the least of possible entering wedges for theosophists and others who had ready-made supernaturalistic philosophies to propagate. In short, the S. P. R. would be a surprisingly useful mediator between the old order and the new.

All this on the supposition that the Helmholtzes and Huxleys did become converted. Now, the present writer (not wholly insensible to the ill consequences of putting himself on record as a false prophet) must candidly express his own suspicion that sooner or later the cat must jump this way. The special means of his conversion have been the trances of the medium whose case in the *Proceedings* was alluded to above. Knowing these trances at first hand, he cannot escape the conclusion that in them the medium's knowledge of facts increases enormously, and in a manner impossible of explanation by any principles of which our existing science takes account. Facts are facts, and the larger includes the less; so these trances doubtless make me the more lenient to the other facts recorded in the *Proceedings*. I find myself also suspecting that the thought-transference experiments, the veridical hallucinations, the crystal-vision, yea, even the ghosts, are sorts of thing which with the years will tend to establish themselves. All of us live more or less on some inclined plane of credulity. The plane tips one way in one man, another way in another; and may he whose plane tips in *no* way be the first to cast a stone! But whether the other things establish themselves more and more or grow less and less probable, the trances I speak of have broken down for my own mind the limits of the admitted order of nature. Science, so far as science denies such exceptional facts, lies prostrate in the dust for me; and the most urgent intellectual need which I feel at present is that science be built up again in a form in which such facts shall have a positive place. Science, like life, feeds on its own decay. New facts burst old rules; then newly divined conceptions bind old and new together into a reconciling law.

And here finally is the real instructiveness of Messrs. Myers and Gurney's work. They are trying with the utmost conscientiousness to find a reconciling conception which shall subject the old "laws of nature" to the smallest possible strain. Mr. Myers uses that method of gradual approach which has performed such wonders in Darwin's hands. When Darwin met a fact which seemed a poser to his theory, his regular custom, as I have heard an ingenious friend say, was to *fill in* all round it with smaller facts, and so mitigate the jolt, as a wagoner might heap dirt round a big rock in the road, and thus get his team over without upsetting. So Mr. Myers, starting from the most ordinary facts of inattentive consciousness, follows this clue through a long series which terminates in ghosts, and seeks to show that these are but extreme manifestations of a common truth, the truth that our normal conscious life is but the visible segment of a spectrum indefinitely long, of which the invisible segments are capable, under rarely realized conditions, of acting and being acted upon by the invisible segments of other conscious lives. This may not be ultimately true (for the theosophists, with their astral bodies and the like, may, for aught I know, prove to be on the correcter trail), but no one can deny that it is *scientific*.

Science always takes a known kind of phenomenon and tries to extend its range. Sensorial hallucination is a known phenomenon; and it is also a known phenomenon that impressions received by the "subliminal"[3] strata of consciousness may be hallucinatory in their intensity—witness the phenomena of dreams and the hypnotic trance. Mr. Myers accordingly seeks to interpret mediumistic experiences and ghostly apparitions as so many effects of the impact upon the subliminal consciousness of causes "behind the veil." The *effects*, psychologically speaking, are hallucinations; yet so far as they are "veridical" they must be held probably to have an "objective" cause. What that objective cause may be Mr. Myers does not decide; yet from the context of many of the hallucinations it would seem to be an intelligence other than that of the medium's or seer's ordinary self, and the interesting question is, Is it what I have called the extra-conscious intelligence of persons still living, or is it the intelligence of persons who have themselves passed behind the veil? Only the most scrupulous examination of the "veridical" effects themselves can decide. I do not myself see how any candid mind can doubt that Mr. Myers' scrupulous testing of the minutest cases is in the line of the best scientific tradition. I do not see, whatever prove the fate of his hypothesis, how his "working of it for all it is worth" can fail to mark a distinct step onward in our knowledge of the truth.

---

[3] Subliminal, from *sub* and *limen*: "beneath the threshold."

I have myself, during the past two years as American agent for the census, collected some five hundred cases of "hallucination" in healthy people. The result is to make me feel that we all have potentially a "subliminal" self, which may make at any time irruption into our ordinary lives. In its lowest phases it is only the depository of our forgotten memories; in its highest, we don't know what it is at all. Take, for instance, a series of cases. During sleep many persons have something in them which measures the flight of time better than the waking self does. It wakes them at a preappointed hour; it acquaints them with the moment when they first awake. It may produce a hallucination, as in a lady who informs me that at the instant of waking she has a vision of her watch-face with the hands pointing (as she has often verified) to the exact time. Whatever it is, it is subconscious.

A subconscious something may also preserve experiences to which we do not openly attend. A lady taking her lunch in town finds herself without her purse. Instantly a sense comes over her of rising from the breakfast-table and hearing her purse drop on the floor. On reaching home she finds nothing under the table, but summons the servant to say where she has put the purse. The servant produces it, saying: "How did you know where it was? You rose and left the room as if you didn't know you'd dropped it." The same subconscious something may recollect what we have forgotten. A lady used to taking salicylate of soda for muscular rheumatism awakens one early winter morning with an aching neck. In the twilight she takes what she supposes to be her customary powder from a drawer, dissolves it in a glass of water, and is about to drink it down, when she feels a sharp slap on her shoulder and hears a voice in her ear saying, "Taste it!" On examination, she finds she has got a morphine powder by mistake. The natural interpretation is that a sleeping memory of the morphine powders awoke in this quasi-explosive way. A like explanation offers itself as most plausible for the following case: A lady, with little time to catch the train, and the expressman about to call, is excitedly looking for the lost key of a packed trunk. Hurrying upstairs with a bunch of keys, proved useless, in her hand, she hears an "objective" voice distinctly say, "Try the key of the cake-box." Being tried, it fits. This may well have been the effect of some long-eclipsed experience.

Now, the *effect* is doubtless due to the same hallucinatory mechanism, but the *source* is less easily assigned as we ascend the scale of cases. A lady, for instance, goes after breakfast to see about one of her servants who has become ill overnight. She is startled at distinctly reading over the bedroom door in gilt letters the word "smallpox." The doctor is sent for, and ere long pronounces small-pox to be the disease, although the lady says, "The thought of the girl's having small-pox never entered my mind till I saw the apparent inscription." Then come other cases of warning; e.g., that of a youth sitting in a wagon under a shed, who suddenly hears his dead mother's voice say, "Stephen, get away from here quick," and jumps out just in time to see the shed roof fall.

After this come the by no means infrequent experiences, usually visual, but sometimes both visual and auditory, of people appearing to distant friends at or near the hour of death. Then we have the trance-visions and utterances, which (as in the case of a circle of private persons with whom I have recently become acquainted) may appear astonishingly profuse and continuous and maintain a superior level intellectually. For all these higher phenomena, it seems to me that whilst the proximate mechanism is that of "hallucination," it is straining an hypothesis unduly to name any ordinary subconscious operation, such as expectation, recollection, or inference from inattentive perception, as the ultimate cause that starts it up. It is far better tactics to brand the narratives themselves as unworthy of trust. The trustworthiness of most of them is to my own mind far from proved. And yet, in the light of the medium-trance, which is proved, it seems as if they might well all be members of a "natural kind" of fact of which we do not yet know the full extent. Thousands of "sensitive" organizations in the United States today live as steadily in the light of these experiences and are as indifferent to modern "science" as if they lived in Bohemia in the twelfth century. They are indifferent to science, because science is so callously indifferent to their experiences. The essential "point" I wish to make to my readers is that by taking the experiences of these persons as they come and applying the ordinary methods of science to their discussion, the *Proceedings* of the S. P. R., whatever be their theoretic outcome, form a department of empirical natural history worthy of all encouragement and respect.

A final word about the practical outcome of inquiries into the extra consciousness may not be out of place. I remember saying, at a public meeting in Boston three years since, that a good psychical researcher let loose in an insane-asylum would be likely to discover facts in the patients which the doctors had overlooked. M. Pierre Janet, on the whole the most brilliant French inquirer into the extra – consciousness, gave a pretty verification of this prediction last year by the "Études sur un Cas d'Aboulie et d'Idées Fixes," ["Studies on a Case of Apathy and Obsession"] which he published in the *Revue Philosophique*. He is only a professor of philosophy, but he pursues his studies in the Paris hospitals, and in the Salpêtrière he had a patient named Marcella, aged nineteen, handed over to him.

Marcella was a melancholic girl whose character had gradually become so changed for the worse as to be unrecognizable, and whose life was a picture of invincible apathy and inertia, varied by occasional spells of violence—a sort of case that in our asylums is generally "let alone" as much as possible, in the hope that time may of itself effect a cure. M. Janet patiently and lovingly studied all her symptoms, and describes them at great length. The essential facts for my present purpose are these: He soon observed that she had periods of absent-mindedness, which he calls her "clouds." During these "clouds" she responded to no questions, and after them had no memory of what had taken place in them. But by piecing together various partial clues which he elicited, he discovered that although so outwardly impassive, she was a prey throughout these "clouds" to monotonous hallucinations of a terrifying sort. When I say that what she told when hypnotized was one of his clues, and that her automatic writing was another, the reader will see why I speak of M. Janet's methods as those of a psychical researcher.

The next thing which he made out was that her inertia and melancholy were in great part after-effects of these hallucinations. M. Janet tried all usual methods, including ordinary hypnotic commands, with only transient success. Only when he entered into her hallucinations, confining them in part, but mixing other elements with them and giving them new terminations, did marked benefit result. But here a fresh difficulty came up. After each successive delusion that was exorcised, the patient became better than ever before; but each one was replaced after some days by another more obstinate and bad. At last there came a delusion, based on hallucinations of hearing, which made her refuse her food. It persisted so long that, at the end of his resources one day, M. Janet put a pencil into her hand to see if she might not automatically prescribe for herself. *"Il faut la forcer, et ce sera fini,"* ["You must force it, and it will be over"] the hand "unconsciously" wrote. But when force was applied, Marcella fell into an alarming hystero-epileptic attack which lasted two hours and made the experimenter momentarily regret his rashness.

From this attack she unexpectedly emerged quite well, and remained so for twelve days. Then she relapsed into the same delusion coupled with the additional refusal to speak; and this condition, terminating by a similar convulsive crisis, never returned again. Before long, however, a frenzied attack of suicidal mania set in, lasted fifteen days, and then spontaneously disappeared, leaving the girl practically cured and oblivious of all that had happened in the previous weeks. Her condition, for several months at least, was normal. But the remarkable aspect of the case is one of which M. Janet saw the significance only late in the series of his operations. The hallucinations were largely based on painful experiences in the girl's life, which came up, as if present again, in her "clouds." Her morbid waking state was a sort of resultant effect of the accumulation of these influences; and each later hallucination that was peeled off, so to speak, by M. Janet gave an older one a chance to become more acute, until the whole regressive series was run through. Her mind was thus gradually freed of a deposit of obsessions that had accumulated during five years. The refusal to eat and the suicidal frenzy were repetitions of crises that she had gone through at the beginning of her malady, and once having thrown them off she got entirely well. Might not such a case well lead our younger medical men to explore their patients' "subliminal selves" a little more than they yet do?

3

ADDRESS OF THE PRESIDENT BEFORE THE SOCIETY FOR PSYCHICAL RESEARCH

After some persuasion by Fredric Myers, William James became President of the Society for Psychical Research for two years, 1895-1896.[1] The following is the speech he wrote for the SPR upon retiring from the position, which was published in the *Proceedings of the Society for Psychical Research*. The piece was reprinted the same year in the "mainstream" journal *Science*, a publication of the American Association for the Advancement of Science, showing James's dedication to promoting psychical research as legitimate scientific inquiry.

In addition to pointing out the successes and limitations of SPR investigations up that time, James also presents a logical argument against the skeptical dismissal of evidence for psi – effectively an indictment of the closed-minded attitudes that continue to reverberate with some of today's professional skeptics.

* * *

---

[1] For the 1893 exchange of letters between James and Myers regarding the SPR presidency, see Ralph Barton Perry (1935) *The Thought and Character of William James*, Vol. II. Boston: Little Brown, 156-58.

The Presidency of the Society for Psychical Research resembles a mousetrap. Broad is the path and wide is the way that leadeth thereinto. Flattering bait is spread before the entrance: the distinguished names of one's predecessors in the office; the absence of any active duties; England and America symbolically made one in that higher republic where no disputed frontiers or foreign offices exist; –and all the rest of it. But when the moment comes to retrace one's steps and go back to private life, like Cincinnatus to his plow, then comes the sorrow, then the penalty for greatness. The careless presidential mouse finds the wires all pointing now against him, and to get out there is no chance, unless he leave some portion of his fur. So in resigning my office to my worthier successor, I send this address to be read across the ocean as my ransom, not unaware, as I write it, that the few things I can say may well fall short of the dignity of the occasion and the needs of the cause for which our Society exists.

Were psychical research as well organized as the other sciences are, the plan of a presidential address would be mapped out in advance. It could be nothing but a report of progress, an account of such new observations and new conceptions as the interim might have brought forth. But our active workers are so few compared with those engaged in more familiar departments of natural learning, and the phenomena we study so fortuitous and occasional, that two years must, as a rule, prove too short an interval for regular accounts of stock to be taken. Looking back, however, on our whole dozen years or more of existence, one can appreciate what solid progress we have made. Disappointing as our career has doubtless been to those of our early members who expected definite corroboration or the final *coup de grâce* to be given in a few short months to such baffling questions as that of physical mediumship, to soberer and less enthusiastic minds the long array of our volumes of *Proceedings* must suggest a feeling of anything but discouragement. For here, for the first time in the history of these perplexing subjects, we find a large collection of records to each of which the editors and reporters have striven to attach its own precise coefficient of evidential value, great or small, by getting at every item of firsthand evidence that could be attained, and by systematically pointing out the gaps. Only those who have tried to reach conclusions of their own by consulting the previous literature of the occult, as vague and useless, for the most part, as it is voluminous, can fully appreciate the immense importance of the new method which we have introduced. Little by little, through consistently following this plan, our *Proceedings* are extorting respect from the most unwilling lookers-on, and I should like emphatically to express my hope that the impartiality and completeness of record which has been their distinguishing character in the past, will be held to even more rigorously in the future. It is not as a vehicle of conclusions of our own, but as a collection of documents that may hereafter be resorted to for testing the conclusions and hypotheses of *anybody*, that they will be permanently important. Candor must be their very essence, and all the hesitations and contradictions that the phenomena involve must appear unmitigatedly in their pages. Collections of this sort are usually best appreciated by the rising generation. The young anthropologists and psychologists who will soon have full occupancy of the stage will feel, as we have felt, how great a scientific scandal it has been to leave a great mass of human experience to take its chances between vague tradition and credulity on the one hand and dogmatic denial at long range on the other, with no body of persons extant who are willing and competent to study the matter with both patience and rigor. There have been isolated experts, it is true, before now. But our Society has for the first time made their abilities mutually helpful.

If I were asked to give some sort of dramatic unity to our history, I should say first that we started with high hopes that the hypnotic field would yield an important harvest, and that these hopes have subsided with the general subsidence of what may be called the hypnotic wave. Secondly, I should say that experimental thought-transference has yielded a less abundant return than that which in the first year or two seemed not unlikely to come in. Professor Richet's supposition that if the unexplained thing called thought-transference be ever real, its causes must, to some degree, work in everybody at all times (so that in any long series of card-guessing, for example, there ought always to be some excess of right answers above the chance number), is, I am inclined to think, not very well substantiated. Thought-transference may involve a critical point, as the physicists call it, which is passed only when certain psychic conditions are realized, and otherwise not reached at all – just as a big conflagration will break out at a certain temperature, below which no conflagration whatever, whether big or little, can occur. We have published records of experiments on at least thirty subjects, roughly speaking, and many of these were strikingly successful. But their types are heterogeneous; in some cases the conditions were not faultless; in others the observations were not prolonged; and generally speaking, we must all share in a regret that the evidence, since it has reached the point it has reached, should not grow more voluminous still. For whilst it cannot be ignored by the candid mind, it yet, as now stands, may fail to convince coercively the skeptic. Any day, of course, may bring in fresh experiments in successful picture-guessing. But meanwhile, and lacking that, we can only point out that our present data are strengthened in the flank, so to speak, by all observations that tend to corroborate the possibility of other kindred phenomena, such as telepathic impression, clairvoyance, or what is called "test mediumship." The wider genus will naturally cover the narrower species with its credit.

Now, as regards the work of the Society in these latter regards, we can point to a solid progress. First of all we have that masterpiece of intelligent and thorough scientific work – I use my words advisedly – the Sidgwick *Report on the Census of Hallucinations*. Against the conclusion of this report, that death apparitions are 440 times more numerous than they should be according to chance, the only rational answer that I can see is that the data are still too few, that the net was not cast wide enough, and that we need, to get fair averages, far more than 17,000 answers to the Census-question. This may, of course, be true, though it seems exceedingly unlikely, and in our own 17,000 answers veridical cases may have heaped themselves unduly. So neither by this report then taken alone, is it absolutely necessary that the skeptic be definitively convinced. But then we have, to strengthen *its* flank in turn, the carefully studied cases of "Miss X" and Mrs. Piper, two persons of the constitution now coming to be nicknamed "psychic" (a bad term, but a handy one), each person of a different psychic type, and each presenting phenomena so chronic and abundant that, to explain away the supernormal knowledge displayed, the disbeliever will certainly rather call the subjects deceivers, and their believers dupes, than resort to the theory of chance coincidence. The same remark holds true of the extraordinary case of Stainton Moses, concerning which Mr. Myers has recently given us such interesting documents. In all these cases (as Mr. Lang has well said of the latter one) we are, it seems to me, fairly forced to choose between a physical and a moral miracle. The physical miracle is that knowledge may come to a person otherwise than by the usual use of eyes and ears. The moral miracle is a kind of deceit so perverse and successful as to find no parallel in usual experience. But the limits of possible perversity and success in deceit are hard to draw – so here again the skeptic may fall back on his general *non possamus* ["we cannot," i.e., stating that something is impossible], and without pretending to explain the facts in detail, say the presumption from the ordinary course of Nature still holds good against their supernormal interpretation. But the oftener one is forced to reject an alleged sort of fact by the method of falling back on the mere presumption that it can't be true because, so far as we know, Nature runs altogether the other way, the weaker does the presumption itself get to be; and one might in course of time use up one's presumptive privileges in this way, even though one started (as our anti-telepathists do) with as good a case as the great induction of psychology that all our knowledge comes by the use of our eyes and ears and other senses. And we must remember also that this undermining of the strength of a presumption by reiterated report of facts to the contrary does not logically require that the facts in question should all be well proved. A lot of rumors in the air against a businessman's credit, though they might all be vague, and no one of them amount to proof that he is unsound, would certainly weaken the *presumption* of his soundness. And all the more would they have this effect if they formed what our lamented Gurney called a faggot and not a chain, that is, if they were independent of each other, and came from different quarters. Now our evidence for telepathy, weak and strong, taken just as it comes, forms a faggot and not a chain. No one item cites the content of another item as part of its own proof. But, taken together, the items have a certain general consistency: there is a method in their madness, so to speak. So each of them adds presumptive value to the lot; and cumulatively, as no candid mind can fail to see, they subtract presumptive force from the orthodox belief that there can be nothing in anyone's intellect that has not come in through ordinary experiences of sense.

But it is a miserable thing for a question of truth to be confined to mere presumption and counter-presumption, with no decisive thunderbolt of fact to clear the baffling darkness. And sooth to say, in talking so much of the merely presumption-weakening value of our records, I have been willfully taking the point of view of the so-called "rigorous scientific" disbeliever, and making an *ad hominem* plea. My own point of view is different. For me the thunderbolt has fallen, and the orthodox belief has not merely had its presumption weakened, but the truth itself of the belief is decisively overthrown. If you will let me use the language of the professional logic-shop, a universal proposition can be made untrue by a particular instance. If you wish to upset the law that all crows are black, you mustn't seek to show that all crows are black; it is enough if you prove one single crow to be white. My own white crow is Mrs. Piper. In the trances of this medium, I cannot resist the conviction that knowledge appears which she has never gained by the ordinary waking use of her eyes and ears and wits. What the source of this knowledge maybe I know not, and have not the glimmer of explanatory suggestion to make; but from admitting the fact of such knowledge, I can see no escape. So when I turn to the rest of our evidence, ghosts and all, I cannot carry with me the irreversibly negative bias of the rigorously scientific mind, with its presumption as to what the true order of nature ought to be. I feel as if, though the evidence be flimsy in sports, it may nevertheless collectively carry heavy weight. The rigorously scientific mind may, in truth, easily overreach itself. Science means, first of all, a certain dispassionate method. To suppose that it means a certain set of results that one should pin one's faith upon and hug forever, is sadly to mistake its genius, and degrades the scientific body to the status of a sect.

But I am devoting too many words to scientific logic, and too few to my review of our career. In the question of physical mediumship, we have left matters as baffling as we found them, neither more nor less. For if, on the one hand, we have brought out new documents concerning the physical miracles of Stainton Moses, on the other hand we have, by the Hodgson-Davey experiments, and the Paladino episode, very largely increased the probability that testimony based on certain sorts of observation may be quite valueless as proof. Eusapia Paladino has been to us both a warning and an encouragement. An encouragement to pursue unwaveringly the rigorous method in such matters from which our *Proceedings* have never departed, and a warning against drawing any prompt inference whatever from things that happen in the dark. The conclusions to which some of us had been hastily led on "the island," melted away when, in Cambridge, the opportunity for longer and more cunning observation was afforded. Someday, it is to be hoped, our *Proceedings* may be enabled to publish a complete study of this woman's life. Whatever were the upshot of such a study, few documents could be more instructive in all ways for psychical research.

It is pleasant to turn from phenomena of the dark-sitting and rat-hole type (with their tragic-comic suggestion that the whole order of nature might possibly be overturned in one's own head, by the way in which one imagined oneself, on a certain occasion, to be holding a tricky peasant woman's feet) to the "calm air of delightful studies." And on the credit side of our Society's account a heavy entry must next be made in favor of that immense and patient collecting of miscellaneous first-hand documents that alone has enabled Mr. Myers to develop his ideas about automatism and the subliminal self. In Mr. Myers' papers on these subjects we see, for the first time in the history of men's dealings with occult matters, the whole range of them brought together, illustrated copiously with unpublished contemporary data, and treated in a thoroughly scientific way. All constructions in this field must be provisional, and it is as something provisional that Mr. Myers offers us his attempt to put order into the tangle. But, thanks to his genius, we begin to see for the first time what a vast interlocked and graded system these phenomena, from the rudest motor automatisms to the most startling sensory apparition, form. Mr. Myers' methodical treatment of them by classes and series is the first great step towards overcoming distaste of orthodox science to look at them at all.

But our *Proceedings* contain still other veins of ore for future working. Ghosts, for example, and disturbances in haunted houses. These, whatever else may be said of them at present, are not without bearing on the common scientific presumption of which I have already perhaps said too much. Of course, one is impressed by such narratives after the mode in which one's impressibility is fashioned. I am not ashamed to confess that in my own case, although my *judgment* remains deliberately suspended, my *feeling* towards the way in which the phenomena of physical mediumship should be approached has received from ghost and disturbance stories a distinctly charitable lurch. Science may keep saying: "such things are simply impossible;" yet, so long as the stories multiply in different lands, and so few are positively explained away, it is bad method to ignore them. They should at least accrete for future use. As I glance back at my reading of the past few years (reading accidental so far as these stories go, since I have never followed up the subject) ten cases immediately rise to mind. The Phelps case at Andover, recorded by one of the family, in *McClure's Magazine* for this month; a case in China, in Nevius's *Demon Possession*, published last year; the case in John Wesley's life; the "*Amherst Mystery*" in Nova Scotia (New York, 1888); the case in Mr. Willis's house at Fitchburg, recorded in *The Atlantic Monthly* for August, 1868 (XXII, 129); the Telfair-Mackie case, in Sharpe's *History of Witchcraft in Scotland*; the Morse case, in Upham's *Salem Witchcraft*; the case recounted in the introduction of W. v. Humboldt's *Briefe an eine Freundin*; a case in the *Annales des Sciences Psychiques* for last year (p. 86); the case of the carpenter's shop at Swanland, near Hull, in our *Proceedings*, Vol. VII, Part XX, p. 383-394. In all of these, if memory doesn't deceive me, material objects are said to have been witnessed by many persons moving through the air in broad daylight. Often the objects were multitudinous – in some cases they were stones showered through windows and down-chimney. More than once it was noted that they fell gently and touched the ground without shock. Apart from the exceptionality of the reputed occurrences, their mutual resemblances suggest a natural type, and I confess that until these records, or others like them, are positively explained away, I cannot feel (in spite of such vast amounts of detected fraud) as if the case against physical mediumship itself as a freak of nature were definitively closed. But I admit that one man's psychological reaction cannot here be like unto another's; and one great duty of our Society will be to pounce upon any future case of this "disturbance" type, catch it while red-handed and nail it fast, whatever its quality be.

We must accustom ourselves more and more to playing with the role of meteorological bureau, be satisfied for many a year to go without definitive conclusions, confident that if we only keep alive and heap up data, the natural types of them (if there are any) will surely crystallize out; whilst old material that is baffling will get settled as we proceed, through its analogy with new material that will come with the baffling character removed.

But I must not weary your patience with the length of my discourse. One general reflection, however, I cannot help asking you to let me indulge in before I close. It is relative to the influence of psychical research upon our attitude towards human history. Although, as I said before, Science taken in its essence should stand only for a method, and not for any special beliefs, yet, as habitually taken by its votaries, Science has come to be identified with certain fixed general belief, the belief that the deeper order of Nature is mechanical exclusively, and that non-mechanical categories are irrational ways of conceiving and explaining even such a thing as human life. Now this mechanical rationalism, as one may call it, makes, if it becomes one's only way of thinking, a violent breach with the ways of thinking that have, until our own time, played the greatest part in human history. Religious thinking, ethical thinking, poetical thinking, teleological, emotional, sentimental thinking, what one might call the personal view of life to distinguish it from the impersonal and mechanical view, and the romantic view of life to distinguish it from the rationalistic view, have been, and even still are, outside of well-drilled scientific circles, the dominant forms of thought. But for mechanical rationalism, personality is an insubstantial illusion; the chronic belief of mankind, that events may happen for the sake of their personal significance, is an abomination; and the notions of our grandfathers about oracles and omens, divinations and apparitions, miraculous changes of heart and wonders worked by inspired persons, answers to prayer and providential leadings, are a fabric absolutely baseless, a mass of sheer *un*truth. Now, of course, we must all admit that the excesses to which the romantic and personal view of Nature may lead, if wholly unchecked by impersonal rationalism, are direful. Central Africa Mumbo-jumboism is one of the unchecked romanticism's fruits. One ought accordingly to sympathize with that abhorrence of romanticism as a sufficient world-theory; one ought to understand that lively intolerance of the least grain of romanticism in the views of life of other people, which are such characteristic marks of those who follow the scientific professions today. Our debt to Science is literally boundless, and our gratitude for what is positive in her teachings must be correspondingly immense.

But our own *Proceedings* and *Journals* have, it seems to me, conclusively proved one thing to the candid reader, and that is that the verdict of pure insanity, of gratuitous preference for error, of superstition without an excuse, which the scientists of our day are led by their intellectual training to pronounce upon the entire thought of the past, is a most shallow verdict. The personal and romantic view of life has other roots beside wanton exuberance of imagination and perversity of heart. It is perennially fed by *facts of experience*, whatever the ulterior interpretation of those facts may prove to be, and at no time in human history would it have been less easy than now – at most times it would have been much more easy – for advocates with a little industry to collect in its favor an array of contemporary documents as good as those which our publications present. These documents all relate to real experiences of persons. These experiences have three characters in common: They are capricious, discontinuous, and not easily controlled; they require peculiar persons for their production; their significance seems to be wholly for personal life. Those who preferentially attend to them, and still more those who are individually subject to them, not only easily *may* find but are logically bound to find in them valid arguments for their romantic and personal conception of the world's course. Through my slight participation in the investigations of the Society for Psychical Research, I have become acquainted with numbers of persons of this sort, for whom the very word Science has become a name of reproach, for reasons that I now both understand and respect. It is the intolerance of Science for such phenomena as we are studying, her peremptory denial either of their existence, or of their significance except as proofs of man's absolute innate folly, that has set Science so apart from the common sympathies of the race. I confess that it is on this, its humanizing mission, that our Society's best claim to the gratitude of our generation seems to me to depend. We have restored continuity to history. We have shown some reasonable basis for the most superstitious aberrations of the foretime. We have bridged the chasm, healed the hideous rift that Science, taken in a certain narrow way, has shot into the human world.

I will even go one step further. When from our present advanced standpoint we look back upon the past stages of human thought, whether it be scientific thought or theological thought, we are amazed that a Universe which appears to us of so vast and mysterious a complication should ever have seemed to anyone so little and plain a thing. Whether it be Descartes' world or Newton's; whether it be that of the materialists of the last century or that of the Bridgewater treatises of our own; it always looks the same to us – incredibly perspectiveless and short. Even Lyell's, Faraday's, Mill's, and Darwin's consciousness of their respective subjects are already beginning to put on an infantile and innocent look. Is it then likely that the Science of our own day will escape the common doom, that the minds of its votaries will never look old-fashioned to the grandchildren of the latter? It would be folly to suppose so. Yet, if we are to judge by the analogy of the past, when our Science once becomes old-fashioned, it will be more for its omissions of fact, for its ignorance of whole ranges and orders of complexity in the phenomena to be explained, than for any fatal lack in its spirit and principles. The spirit and principles of Science are mere affairs of method; there is nothing in them that need hinder Science from dealing successfully with a world in which personal forces are the starting point of the new effects. The only form of thing that we directly encounter, the only experience that we concretely have, is our own personal life. The only complete category of our thinking, our professors of philosophy tell us, is the category of personality, every other category being one of the abstract elements of that. And this systematic denial on Science's part of personality as a condition of events, this rigorous belief that in its own essential and innermost nature our world is a strictly impersonal world, may conceivably, as the whirligig of time goes round, prove to be the very defect that our descendants will be most surprised at in our own boasted Science, the omission that, to their eyes, will most tend to make *it* look perspectiveless and short.

But these things lie upon the knees of the gods. I must leave them there, and close now this discourse, which I regret that *I* could not make more short. If it has made you feel that (however it turn out with modern Science) our own Society, at any rate, is not "perspectiveless," it will have amply served its purpose; and the next President's address may have more definite conquests to record.

4

PSYCHICAL RESEARCH

In response to James's "Address," (Chapter 3) James McKeen Cattell wrote a critical letter in the *Psychological Review*.[1] Like James, Cattell was an important American psychologist, though in contrast he was a confirmed skeptic about psychical phenomena. He believed that James was wasting his time on the subject, and that the SPR was damaging to the progress and reputation of proper psychology. Cattell was particularly critical of James's argument regarding the sheer number of cases of such phenomena, and used his "white crow" analogy against him:

When we have an enormous number of cases, and cannot find among them all a single one that is quite conclusive, the very number of cases may be interpreted as an index of the weakness of the evidence. The discovery of a great many gray crows would not prove that any crows are white, rather the more crows we examine and find to be black or gray, the less expectation have we of finding one that is white.

Though Cattell held James himself in high esteem, he added:

---

[1] James McKeen Cattell (1909) "Psychical Research." *Psychological Review*, Volume 3 No. 1, 582-83.

The ablest of men have followed alchemy and astrology, have worshiped strange gods, have consulted witches and burned them. Geese have before now been mistaken for swans, and often to the honor of those who made the mistake. One white crow is enough, but its skin should be deposited in a museum.

The following is James's response to Cattell, published in the same journal in 1896.

"Psychical Research" has so many enemies, fair and foul, to elude before she gets her scientific position recognized, and is moreover so easily vulnerable in her present stage of development, that I may be excused, as one of her foster-fathers, for uttering a word that may turn the edge of Prof. Cattell's amiable *persiflage* in the last number of this *Review*. He seems not quite to have caught the argument of my presidential address. The inquiry, I said in substance, still remains baffling over a large part of its surface, for the evidence in innumerable cases can neither be made more perfect, *nor*, on the other hand, be positively explained away. It *may* be mal-observation, illusion, fraud or accidental coincidence; it *may* be good and true report. One can only go by its probabilities and improbabilities; and the scientist, who goes by the *presumption* that the usual laws of nature are superabundantly proved, feels the improbability of "occult" phenomena to be so infinitely great that he is practically certain that the evidence in their favor must be bad, even though he can't show in the particular case where the badness comes in. The issue between Prof. Cattell and myself is as to the general logic of presumption here. I urged that the force of the scientist's presumption, *quâ* presumption, might someday be worn out by the accumulation of "psychic" cases, long before his doctrine of nature was radically overthrown, as it would be were a single case conclusively proved. Prof. Cattell says: "When we have an enormous number of cases, and cannot find among them a single one that is quite conclusive, the very number of cases may be interpreted as an index of the weakness of the evidence;" apparently holding the scientist's presumption to be actually strengthened by the quantity and quality, taken together, of the psychical research reports. It would indeed be strengthened if, *pari passu* with the accumulation of reports, there went for each concrete type of case a parallel accumulation of demonstrations of its erroneousness. And as this is just what happened in the "physical mediumship" type, the work of the S. P. R. in that field has been mainly destructive. But it has happened practically nowhere else. In the veridical apparitions, in the chief thought-transference experiments, fallacy has been assumed, but not clearly demonstrated. The presumption has remained presumption merely, the scientist saying, "I can't believe you're right," whilst at the same time he has been unable to show how or where we were wrong, or even except in one or two cases to point out what the error most probably may have been. In such a state of things people trust their instincts merely, while waiting for a final proof. Many naturalists, for instance, consider the evidence for the sea-serpent practically sufficient. In others it provokes a smile. Meanwhile a single sea-serpent dragged up on the beach would settle the matter forever. I spoke of my own final proof or psychical sea-serpent-corpse, under the name of a "white crow." Professor Cattell says: Can the exhibition of any number of gray crows prove that any crows are white? But our reports are not of gray crows; at the very worst they are of white crows without the skins brought home, of sea serpents without the corpse to show; and where there are such obvious reasons why it must be easier to see a wild beast than to capture him, who can seriously maintain that continued reports of merely seeing him tend positively to decrease the probability that he exists? In the case of telepathy, ghosts, death-apparitions, etc., the reasons why the evidence is always likely to be imperfect rather than perfect are equally obvious, and the logic is the same as in the wild beast case. Continued reports, far from strengthening the presumption that such things cannot exist, can only detract from its force.

Both here and in my address I have played into the hands of the scientist, and granted him every conceivable concession about the facts for the sake of making my point as to the logic of presumption all the more clear. But there is such a thing as being too fair-minded, so that one wades in a very bog of over-reasonableness. For, in point of fact, the concrete evidence for most of the "psychic" phenomena under discussion is good enough to hang a man twenty times over. The scientist's objections, on the other hand, are either shallow on their face (as where apparitions at the time of death are disposed of as mere "folklore," or swept away as a mass of fiction due to illusion of memory), or else they are proved to be shallow by further investigation, as where they are ascribed to chance-coincidence. May I add a word to illustrate this?

On page 69 of Vol. II. of this *Review*, I summarized the elaborate Sidgwick's report on the *Census of Hallucinations*. That paper concluded that the stories of apparitions occurring on the day of the death of the person appearing were 440 times too numerous for the phenomenon to be fairly ascribed to chance. I said that the chief objection practically to this conclusion was that the census, covering only 17,000 cases, was still too small. Last spring I wrote a letter to Professor Sidgwick, giving, for quotation at the Munich Congress, the results of my American census of 7,123 cases. They prolong and corroborate his own. The 'yes' cases were 1,051 in number, or 14.75% of the whole. I cite part of my letter:

> Of these yeses 429 were without particulars, and in 36 the percipient had not signed the account. Only 586 subjects thus remained for statistical treatment.
>
> Of these, eliminating all who had the experience before they were 10 years old; and all who gave vaguely plural experiences, there remain 62 subjects with *71 cases of visual hallucination of some recognized living person. Of these, 42 are reported to have occurred on the day of the death of the person seen.*
>
> These numbers are so small that I have not ventured to reduce by any elimination of "suspicious" cases, as you did, but as a correction for oblivion have multiplied the whole lot by your figure 6 1/2.
>
> 71 x 6 1/2 = 462 (in round number).
>
> *Let this 462 represent the probable whole number* of visual hallucinations of living persons really seen by the percipients since their tenth birthday. The 12 veridicals are in round numbers 1/39 of 462. Therefore 1/39 is the probability induced from facts, and due to the unknown cause of apparitions, that if a man "appear" at all it will be on his death-day.
>
> On the other hand (the U. S. death rate being practically the same as that of England) the *pure chance* that if any one appear on a certain day it will be one who is dying on that day is only 1/19000. But 1/39 = 1/19000 x 487; so that *apparitions on the day of death are, according to our statistics, 487 times more numerous than pure chance ought to make them.*
>
> 'The details will be sent later, but I append now a few remarks. Of the 71 cases, all but the 12 that were death-apparitions are treated as insignificant in the statistical result. But this, though inevitable, is unfair to an occultist theory of their origin, since 16 of them, though not veridical of death, were coincidental in other ways. e.g., 6 were collective, 2 were reciprocal, 1 was voluntarily produced by the distant

agent, 2 were premonitory and 3 were veridical, but not of death. But let this pass. There remains another unfairness to occultism in our systematic rejection of all vaguely plural cases. I rejected 19 percipients in all for this reason, but 7 of these percipients gave us coincidental cases, 2 of them being apparitions at time of death.

We can afford to be very generous. Suppose we throw in these 19 subjects as if each stood for one non-coincidental case. Suppose we multiply for oblivion by 10 instead of 6 1/2, making 900 cases in all. Suppose we take only 1/2 of our 12 veridicals. We shall still get 6/900 = 1/150 =126 times 1/19000, the chance probability.

The objections to be urged are:
1. *Smallness* of numbers. But the agreement of our figures with yours goes against this.
2. *The collectors packed their sheets with veridicals.* As a matter of fact, they say they knew the answer beforehand in 3, possibly in 4 cases. In 5 cases they state their ignorance. In 3 they say nothing. From the warning against packing with yeses and the very large number of veridicals that the collectors furnish separately, this objection is probably not very important.
3. *The veridical cases are not strong.* They are not. Only 5 have any corroboration, and in no case is it first-rate. Our best cases are not among these. But this is an argument at any rate in favor of the sincerity of the *Census*; and since coincidentals and non-coincidentals are treated homogeneously (at least all the deliberate treatment going against the statistical result, where they are treated otherwise than similarly), the ratio of the surface figures is perhaps a fair one.

But I never believed and do not now believe that these figures will ever conquer disbelief. They are only useful to rebut the assurance of the scientists that the death-warnings, if not lies, are chance coincidences. Better call them lies and have done with it.

I make this quotation, first because of the facts themselves, but mainly because I have above too easily granted the ambiguity of the evidence for such phenomena, and I wish to show, by a new example, how, when two interpretations are possible, it is not always the scientist's which has the greater numerical probability in its favor, or which is the more carefully or conscientiously weighed.

5

SENSE OF PRESENCE

As with *Principles of Psychology* and other prominent works for which James is famous, themes related to psychical research occur throughout *The Varieties of Religious Experience*. The long descriptions of and discussions about feelings of a divine presence, of mystical states, "mind-cures," and the transformative qualities of extraordinary experiences all cross over into parapsychological considerations.

However, the focus on the personally transformative quality of such experiences is where *Varieties* diverges from the themes of the present book, for James's primary concern was with the "fruits" of religious experiences rather than with their origins and true nature. One exception is the short excerpt below, concerning the hypothesis that the origins of beliefs in gods derived from a paranormal sense of presence (starting with ancient Greece as an example). In common with contemporaries such as Andrew Lang and Edward Burnett Tylor, this is an early example of what would later be called by David Hufford the "experiential source hypothesis."[1]

---

[1] See Edward Burnett Tylor (1871; rpt. 1920) *Primitive Culture*, vol. 2. London: Murray, 46-49; Andrew Lang (1900; 2nd ed.) *The Making of Religion*. London: Longmans Green, 105ff, 140ff; David Hufford (1982) *The Terror that Comes in the Night: An Experience-Centered Study of Supernatural Assault Traditions*. Philadelphia: University of Pennsylvania Press.

The Postscript to *Varieties of Religious Experience* will be found at the end of this book, though interested readers will undoubtedly find the full volume rewarding, and its status as a classic of psychology and religion is fully justified.

From Lecture III: The Reality of the Unseen

Examples of "Sense of Presence"

As regards the origin of the Greek gods, we need not at present seek an opinion. But the whole array of our instances leads to a conclusion something like this: It is as if there were in the human consciousness a *sense of reality, a feeling of objective presence, a perception* of what we may call *"something there,"* more deep and more general than any of the special and particular "senses" by which the current psychology supposes existent realities to be originally revealed. If this were so, we might suppose the senses to waken our attitudes and conduct as they so habitually do, by first exciting this sense of reality; but anything else, any idea, for example, that might similarly excite it, would have that same prerogative of appearing real which objects of sense normally possess. So far as religious conceptions were able to touch this reality-feeling, they would be believed in in spite of criticism, even though they might be so vague and remote as to be almost unimaginable, even though they might be such non-entities in point of *whatness*, as Kant makes the objects of his moral theology to be.

The most curious proofs of the existence of such an undifferentiated sense of reality as this are found in experiences of hallucination. It often happens that an hallucination is imperfectly developed: the person affected will feel a "presence" in the room, definitely localized, facing in one particular way, real in the most emphatic sense of the word, often coming suddenly, and as suddenly gone; and yet neither seen, heard, touched, nor cognized in any of the usual "sensible" ways. Let me give you an example of this, before I pass to the objects with whose presence religion is more peculiarly concerned.

An intimate friend of mine, one of the keenest intellects I know, has had several experiences of this sort. He writes as follows in response to my inquiries:

> I have several times within the past few years felt the so-called "consciousness of a presence." The experiences which I have in mind

are clearly distinguishable from another kind of experience which I have had very frequently, and which I fancy many persons would also call the "consciousness of a presence." But the difference for me between the two sets of experience is as great as the difference between feeling a slight warmth originating I know not where, and standing in the midst of a conflagration with all the ordinary senses alert.

It was about September, 1884, when I had the first experience. On the previous night I had had, after getting into bed at my rooms in College, a vivid tactile hallucination of being grasped by the arm, which made me get up and search the room for an intruder; but the sense of presence properly so called came on the next night. After I had got into bed and blown out the candle, I lay awake awhile thinking on the previous night's experience, when suddenly *felt* something come into the room and stay close to my bed. It remained only a minute or two. I did not recognize it by any ordinary sense, and yet there was a horribly unpleasant "sensation" connected with it. It stirred something more at the roots of my being than any ordinary perception. The feeling had something of the quality of a very large tearing vital pain spreading chiefly over the chest, but within the organism—and yet the feeling was not *pain* so much as *abhorrence*. At all events, something was present with me, and I knew its presence far more surely than I have ever known the presence of any fleshly living creature. I was conscious of its departure as of its coming: an almost instantaneously swift going through the door, and the "horrible sensation" disappeared.

On the third night when I retired my mind was absorbed in some lectures which I was preparing, and I was still absorbed in these when I became aware of the actual presence (though not of the *coming*) of the thing that was there the night before, and of the "horrible sensation." I then mentally concentrated all my effort to charge this "thing," if it was evil, to depart, if it was *not* evil, to tell me who or what it was, and if it could not explain itself, to go, and that I would compel it to go. It went as on the previous night, and my body quickly recovered its normal state.

On two other occasions in my life I have had precisely the same "horrible sensation." Once it lasted a full quarter of an hour. In all three instances the certainty that there in outward space there stood *something* was indescribably *stronger* than the ordinary certainty of companionship when we are in the close presence of ordinary living people. The something seemed close to me, and intensely more real than any ordinary perception. Although I felt it to be like unto myself, so to speak, or finite, small, and distressful, as it were, I didn't recognize it as any individual being or person.

Of course such an experience as this does not connect itself with the religious sphere. Yet it may upon occasion do so; and the same correspondent informs me that at more than one other conjuncture he had the sense of presence developed with equal intensity and abruptness; only then it was filled with a quality of joy.

> There was not a mere consciousness of something there, but fused in the central happiness of it, a startling awareness of some ineffable good. Not vague either, not like the emotional effect of some poem, or scene, or blossom, of music, but the sure knowledge of the close presence of a sort of mighty person, and after it went, the memory persisted as the one perception of reality. Everything else might be a dream, but not that.

My friend, as it oddly happens, does not interpret these latter experiences theistically, as signifying the presence of God. But it would clearly not have been unnatural to interpret them as a revelation of the deity's existence. When we reach the subject of mysticism, we shall have much more to say upon this head.

Lest the oddity of these phenomena should disconcert you, I will venture to read you a couple of similar narratives, much shorter, merely to show that we are dealing with a well-marked natural kind of fact. In the first case, which I take from the *Journal of the Society for Psychical Research*, the sense of presence developed in a few moments into a distinctly visualized hallucination—but I leave that part of the story out.

> I had read (the narrator says), some twenty minutes or so, was thoroughly absorbed in the book, my mind was perfectly quiet, and for the time being my friends were quite forgotten, when suddenly without a moment's warning my whole being seemed roused to the highest state of tension or aliveness, and I was aware, with an intenseness not easily imagined by those who had never experienced it, that another being or presence was not only in the room, but quite close to me. I put my book down, and although my excitement was great, I felt quite collected, and not conscious of any sense of fear. Without changing my position, and looking straight at the fire, I knew somehow that

my friend A. H. was standing at my left elbow, but so far behind me as to be hidden by the armchair in which I was leaning back. Moving my eyes round slightly without otherwise changing my position, the lower portion of one leg became visible, and I instantly recognized the gray-blue material of trousers he often wore, but the stuff appeared semi-transparent, reminding me of tobacco smoke in consistency[2] (and hereupon the visual hallucination came).

Another informant writes:

Quite early in the night I was awakened. ... I felt as if I had been aroused intentionally, and at first thought someone was breaking into the house. ... I then turned on my side to go to sleep again, and immediately felt a consciousness of a presence in the room, and singular to state, it was not the consciousness of a live person, but of a spiritual presence. This may provoke a smile, but I can only tell you the facts as they occurred to me. I do not know how to better describe my sensations than by simply stating that I felt a consciousness of a spiritual presence. ... I felt also at the same time a strong feeling of superstitious dread, as if something strange and fearful were about to happen.[3]

Professor Flournoy of Geneva gives me the following testimony of a friend of his, a lady, who has the gift of automatic or involuntary writing:

Whenever I practice automatic writing, what makes me feel that it is not due to a subconscious self is the feeling I always have of a foreign presence, external to my body. It is sometimes so definitely characterized that I could point to its exact position. This impression of presence is impossible to describe. It varies in intensity and clearness according to the personality from whom the writing professes to come. If it is someone whom I love, I feel it immediately, before any writing has come. My heart seems to recognize it.

In an earlier book of mine I have cited at full length a curious case of presence felt by a blind man. The presence was that of the figure of a gray-bearded man dressed in a pepper and salt suit, squeezing himself under the crack of the door and moving across the floor of

---

[2] *Journal of the SPR.*, February, 1895, p. 26.
[3] E. Gurney: *Phantasms of the Living*, I, 384.

the room towards a sofa. The blind subject of this quasi-hallucination is an exceptionally intelligent reporter. He is entirely without internal visual imagery and cannot represent light or colors to himself, and is positive that his other senses, hearing, etc., were not involved in this false perception. It seems to have been an abstract conception rather, with the feelings of reality and spatial outwardness directly attached to it—in other words, a fully objectified and exteriorized *idea*.

Such cases, taken along with others which would be too tedious for quotation, seem sufficiently to prove the existence in our mental machinery of a sense of present reality more diffused and general than that which our special senses yield. For the psychologists the tracing of the organic seat of such a feeling would form a pretty problem—nothing could be more natural than to connect it with the muscular sense, with the feeling that our muscles were innervating themselves for action. Whatsoever thus innervated our activity, or "made our flesh creep,"—our senses are what do so oftenest—might then appear real and present, even though it were but an abstract idea. But with such vague conjectures we have no concern at present, for our interest lies with the faculty rather than with its organic seat.

6

TWO REVIEWS:
COCK-LANE AND COMMON SENSE BY ANDREW LANG AND *DIE ENTDECKUNG DER SEELE DUREH DIE GEHEIMWISSENSCHAFTEN* BY CARL DU PREL

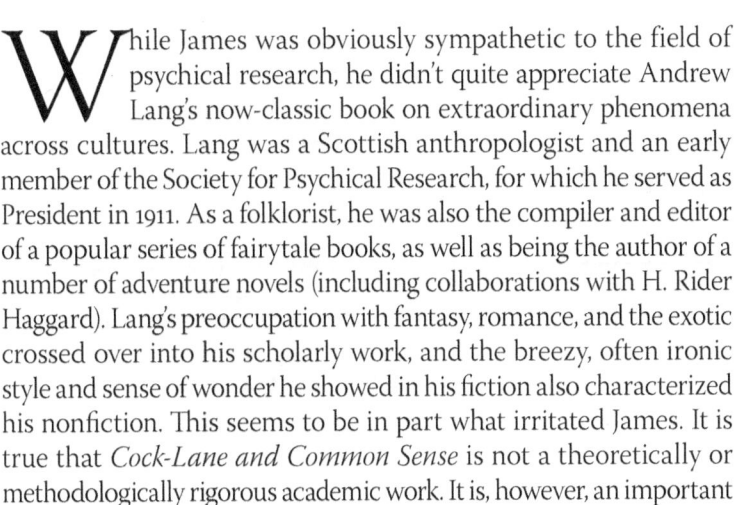

While James was obviously sympathetic to the field of psychical research, he didn't quite appreciate Andrew Lang's now-classic book on extraordinary phenomena across cultures. Lang was a Scottish anthropologist and an early member of the Society for Psychical Research, for which he served as President in 1911. As a folklorist, he was also the compiler and editor of a popular series of fairytale books, as well as being the author of a number of adventure novels (including collaborations with H. Rider Haggard). Lang's preoccupation with fantasy, romance, and the exotic crossed over into his scholarly work, and the breezy, often ironic style and sense of wonder he showed in his fiction also characterized his nonfiction. This seems to be in part what irritated James. It is true that *Cock-Lane and Common Sense* is not a theoretically or methodologically rigorous academic work. It is, however, an important book in the study of psychical research in anthropological contexts – what Lang called "psycho-folklore," and what later came to be known as paranthropology. Given that there was very little attention paid to the cross-cultural dimensions of such phenomena at the time, James's rather harsh review is somewhat surprising.

Carl du Prel was a German philosopher whose interests in mysticism and hypnotism aligned well with the interests of William James. Du Prel was also the founder of the German equivalent of the SPR, the Munich Psychological Society. Highly regarded by such luminaries as Sigmund Freud, Carl Jung, and Frederic Myers, du Prel's most well-known book – and the only one to be translated into English – is *Die Philosophie der Mystik (The Philosophy of Mysticism)*.[1] The book reviewed here by James can be translated as *The Discovery of the Soul Through the Occult Sciences*. Although James sees it as inferior to du Prel's other works, the contrast between his philosophical engagement with the book and his dismissiveness of Lang's book is stark. It is also interesting that while he criticized du Prel for an uncritical acceptance of accounts of psychical phenomena, he criticized Lang for being *too* skeptical and inconclusive.

Cock-Lane and Common Sense. Andrew Lang. London and New York, Longmans, 1894.
Die Entdeckung der Seele dureh die Geheimwissenschaften. Carl du Prel. Leipzig, Gunther, 1894.

Mr. Lang has the memory of a bookworm and the pen of a *fin-de-siècle* journalist. The result here is a very curious compound of erudition and flippancy, in which the author drags us up and down all the ages of history and to and from all the ends of the earth, in order to make us feel the improbability that clairvoyant trances, "levitations," knockings, scratchings, and other noises, stone-throwings, movements of furniture, ghostly apparitions and the like, which *semper et ubiqut* [always and everywhere] have been alleged forms of experience, should be due to nothing but an original folklore tradition perpetuated and copied by sporadically-recurring fraud. From these persistent and apparently natural types of phenomenon he distinguishes genuine folk-lore beliefs like that in brownies, fairies, and the witches' sabbath, which are much

---

[1] Carl Du Prel (1889) *The Philosophy of Mysticism* (2 vols.). London: Redway.

less omnipresent in human history. He makes very merry over the unexacting rules by which "Science" has hitherto held herself bound in giving explanation of these narratives, and finally he himself – declines to conclude! In all this his state of mind is the pattern and exemplar of what at all times has been that of the "man of the world." To be sure Mr. Lang, when his learning is considered, is a very rare man of the world. But he has the worldly lack of reverence even for "Science," as well as the worldly bias for fair play and relish for what he calls "sportsmanlike" treatment of a subject. He has the worldly suspicion that "where there is smoke there is fire," but also the worldly dislike to push a thing too far, the worldly reluctance to stand committed and responsible, and the worldly love of keeping some thrilling mystery perpetually open to play with. So his book baffles the reader as the subject has baffled the author; and the most one can say of it is that it is the typical expression of a state of mind that is now common enough. As a skirmisher in the cause of "psychical research" it will probably be effective; but it should have had an index, to make it useful to the more serious student of the sort of material which it contains.

If Mr. Lang feels baffled by his facts, not so does Baron du Prel. This writer has a *Schlagfertigkeit* [clever, quick-wittedness] at explanation quite equal to the great range of his learning, but the present work is a poor one by which to judge him on the theoretic side. The reasonings on which his theory of the "transcendental Subject" is grounded are more fully given in his other works. The present one rather takes the theory ready-made, and in a number of chapters gives illustrations of its way of working in such things as emotional and aesthetic expression, somnambulism, thought-transference, clairvoyance, premonition, automatic writing, and speech in foreign tongues. The book is in fact a collection of distinct essays with the transcendental Subject as their nucleus. Our conscious intelligence or Ego, according to Du Prel, is only a partial manifestation of our soul, dependent on the brain and the senses. It has its roots in an extension of the same soul, which in addition to possessing the non-sensuous powers of cognition manifested in trance-states, etc., is the architect of the body and guider of its organic processes, and consequently the original molder of the brain and senses themselves. This transcendental Subject is an individual entity, and so far Dr. Du Prel is not a Monist; though if we ascend to the substance of the world he admits that the various transcendental subjects may be englobed in the ultimate unity. In all this his hypothesis is more positive and elaborate than Mr. Myers's doctrine of the subliminal consciousness, and less elaborate than the "theosophic" theory of personality. In the ordinary dream-phenomenon of conversing with an external interlocutor whom on waking we recognize to be our own creation, he finds an analogue of the relations of the normal or sensuous consciousness to the transcendental Self. After the great awakening we may find our sense-life similarly reabsorbed into the wider transcendental unity. That the dreamlife plays a great part in the establishment of our author's ideas, those acquainted with his *Philosophy of Mysticism* will remember. In the present book he explains "premonitions" (as, for example, the giving-up of one's passage in a steamer on account of a sense of impending evil) as due to emotional vestiges in the waking consciousness of clairvoyant prophetic dreams whose sensible details have been forgotten. The slenderness of the clues which Baron du Prel is not afraid to follow is shown in the first essay, "On the psychic activity of the Artist," of which the thesis, briefly given, is that the power that produces works of genius is the same supersensuous Subject that makes the artist's own organism. The proof of this is that while talent copies nature, genius does not copy but produces works co-ordinate with nature, lending soul and life to the bodily things it represents, as in the personifications of nature in lyric poetry; and, as in the dramatic and pictorial expression of the emotions, giving body and object to the thoughts of the soul. The same soul that drew the gestures in Leonardo's Last Supper, etc., prompted those gestures in Leonardo's person, and organized Leonardo's nervous system for their execution.

The range of our author's anecdotes is very great, and his choice of them absolutely uncritical. He appears to hold for true anything which any one may ever have reported, the publications of the Psychical Research Society being almost the only source not drawn upon in his pages. Add to this his unchartered freedom of theorizing, and the result is of course completely "unsatisfactory," although the book remains "suggestive" enough. But in the present era of anarchy in these outlawed matters no one can be punished for any special sort of unsatisfactoriness in which he may prefer to indulge, so I say no more. Nevertheless between Mr. Lang's facility in leaving things unsettled, and Baron du Prel's facility in concluding them, it seems as if a better path might be found. Might not the earnest temper of science be combined somewhere with Du Prel's learning and the power of doubt of Lang? So far Mr. Myers's papers on the "Subliminal Self" seem to have kept nearest to this ideal; and both Lang's and Du Prel's books set off by contrast the superiority of his work.

PART II

TELEPATHY, AUTOMATISM, AND EXTENDED CONSCIOUSNESS

7

TELEPATHY

This article on telepathy was written by James for *Johnson's Universal Cyclopedia* from 1895. James had also been asked to write a contribution on Spiritualism, though he stated that it was "too much for me" and instead suggested Richard Hodgson.[1] "Telepathy" is an excellent overview of European research on the subject, and it is regrettable that James didn't write a similar summary of Spiritualism – or indeed a book-length introduction to psychical research.

Despite his characteristic caution on the subject, James was ultimately convinced that however rare, telepathy exists, writing that careful and well-controlled scientific experiments made it "unreasonable to doubt any longer the fact that occasionally a telepathic relation between one mind and another may exist." This contrasts interestingly with a current popular encyclopedia entry on telepathy, nearly a 130 years later – from the notoriously anti-psi Wikipedia: "There is no good evidence that telepathy exists, and the topic is generally considered by the scientific community to be pseudoscience."[2]

---

[1] See James's letter to J. Mark Baldwin, editor of the *Psychological Review*, 30 May, 1894. In William James (coll. 1986) *Essays in Psychical Research*. Frederick Burkhardt and Fredson Bowers (eds.) Cambridge, MA.: Harvard University Press, 468.

[2] "Telepathy." *Wikipedia* entry. https://en.wikipedia.org/wiki/Telepathy. Retrieved 16 September, 2023.

It is also interesting to note James's reference to Mrs. Piper in this article, viewing her abilities that so convinced him as telepathic rather than as mediumistic communication with souls of the dead.

Telep´athy [from Gr. *τήλε*, far + *παθος*, feeling]: thought-transference, or the phenomenon of the reception by the mind of an impression not traceable to any of the ordinarily recognized channels of sense, and assumed to be due to an influence from the mind of another person, near or remote. Thus the sphere of telepathy is not the same as that of *clairvoyance*, in which it is assumed that the mind of the subject may receive an impression of *impersonal facts*, or things at a distance. The subject who receives the impression is called the percipient, the one from whom the influence emanates is usually called the agent, in accounts of experiments on this phenomenon.

In the earlier works on animal magnetism there are many reports concerning subjects who are said to have developed the faculty of obeying the unspoken will of their magnetizer, going to sleep and waking, moving, acting, and speaking in accordance with his silent commands. More recently there have been public exhibitors of "mind-reading," and their performances have been imitated in private circles by the so-called willing-game. In most of these feats the agent is required to think intently of some act while he lays his hands on some part of the so-called mind-reader's person. The mind-reader, either promptly or hesitatingly, will then usually perform the act. It is safe to assume that wherever such personal contact between the pair is allowed, the percipient is guided by the encouragement or checking which the agent's hands more or less unconsciously exert upon his at first tentative movements; so that muscle-reading, and not mind-reading, is the proper name for this phenomenon. There are, it is true, reports of success in the willing game where no contact was allowed; but in the absence of authentic details, they cannot be taken as evidence that telepathy exists. For the same reason the earlier mesmeric reports have doubtful evidential value. The operators took too few precautions against "suggesting" to the subjects by other channels than speech what their will might be. It is only within recent years that we have learned to measure the acuteness with which an entranced person with his mind concentrated upon his hypnotizer will divine the intentions of the latter by indications which he gives quite unconsciously by voice or movement, or even by the mere order of sequence of what he does.

On these accounts, evidence in the strict sense for telepathy must be sought in a small number of experiments conducted by a few more careful observers since about 1880. These experiments, taken in the aggregate, appear to make it unreasonable to doubt any longer the fact that occasionally a telepathic relation between one mind and another may exist.

In a faultless experiment on thought-transference certain precautions must be observed. To avoid previous collusion between agent and percipient the agent should receive from a third party the idea to be transferred; and the latter should, when possible, select it by drawing lots or by some other appeal to chance. This is to exclude the possibility of himself and the percipient being led by number-habits, diagram-habits, or other parallel paths of inner association to a common result. The percipient should not be in the room when the idea is determined on; and when possible it should be chosen in silence, written down, and shown, if it need be shown beforehand, in written form. The percipient should, if possible, do his guessing in another room. In any case he should be blindfolded, and there should be no conversation with him during the performance, the signal that he must attend to his inner impressions being given by bell or other sound. Physical contact between agent and percipient must not occur, and if the percipient writes or draws his result the agent should not look on, since an unconscious commentary by changes in breathing, etc., might reveal to the percipient whether he was going right or wrong.

The *Proceedings of the Society for Psychical Research* contain some records of experiments made under approximately faultless conditions. In certain cases the ideas to be transferred were diagrams or drawings. A couple of examples will show the success reached when at its best. Fig. 1 is from a series with Mr. Blackburn, agent, G. A. Smith, percipient, in which out of thirty-three trials without contact, though with percipient and agent in one room, there were twenty-five reproductions as good as those here given of a figure prepared and kept outside of the room. Fig. 2 gives the first six trials of a series reported by Malcolm Guthrie, of Liverpool, he being agent and a

Fig. 1.

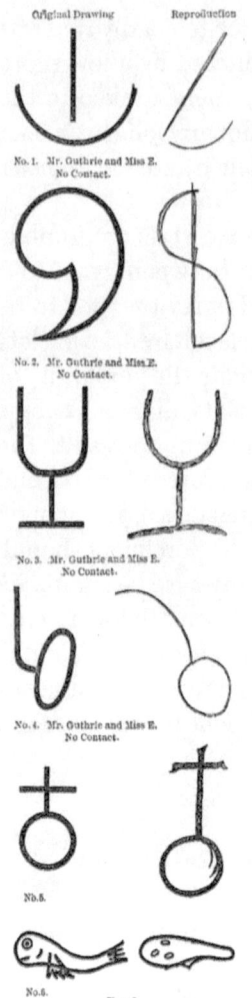

Miss E. percipient. The conditions seem almost faultless, if the account is accurate, though the figures are simpler than in the former series. In all, with various agents, Miss E. made 150 trials, the majority of which were successful entirely or in part. Sixteen specimens are printed in the report, all about as good as those in Fig. 2.

The same Miss E. and a Miss R. were subjected at Liverpool in 1883 to a series of experiments in transferring ideas and sensations of every order, the agents being Mr. Guthrie and others. Out of 713 trials there were but 252 cases in which the percipient either got no impression or described the object wrongly. In the remaining 461 cases the success was either complete or partial.

"Miss X." has published (*Proceedings of Society for Psychical Research*, Vol. VI) a long series of telepathic interchange of experiences over a long distance with "Miss D.," corroborated by independent entries in their respective diaries. Of 20 such entries 14 refer to a consciousness on the part of Miss D. that Miss X. was at that hour (the hours are quite irregular) playing a certain definite piece of music.

Miss Wingfield was the subject of a series of number-guessings, where out of 2,624 trials there were 275 successes instead of 29, which was the figure probable on the assumption of "chance." The numbers thought of were the 90 two-digital ones, from 10 to 99. They were drawn at random from a bowl and thought of by the percipient's sister. In a later series of 400 trials with this percipient the completely right guesses were 27 instead of the chance number 4; there were moreover, 21 guesses with the digits reversed, and 162 with a single digit in its right place.

Similar, though less extended and perhaps less conclusive, series of experiments at guessing ideas have been reported in the Society for Psychical Research *Proceedings* by various experimenters—Dessoir, Schmoll and Mabire, W. J. Smith, von Schrenk-Notzing, and Barrett and Gurney. The observations last referred to were those first published.

The subjects were two girls who, four years later when experiments were resumed, were found, when tested in each other's presence, to be cheating by a code of signals. Much has been made of the breakdown of this case. But very many of the earlier successes recorded of these children occurred when they were singly present, and often when only one experimenter knew the thing to be guessed. Collusion under such circumstances can not well be charged, although willingness to cheat rightly casts vague suspicion on all trials done with the percipient concerned, and shows the importance of making all tests under the conditions described as "faultless" a few lines back. Mr. Rawson finally, in Vol. XI of the *Proceedings*, gives a striking series of correct card and diagram guesses.

On telepathy in the hypnotic state there are recorded in the *Proceedings* experiments by Dr. B. Thaw and Prof. and Mrs. H. Sidgwick. The conditions in the latter set seem to have been, on the whole, very careful, though not quite faultless in the technical sense. The agent was the hypnotizer, G. A. Smith. The things to be impressed were usually the numbers (of two digits) on eighty-one lotto-counters, drawn by Prof. Sidgwick from a bag and handed to Mr. Smith to gaze at, while the hypnotized percipient awaited the impression. There were four percipients, with 644 trials made with agent and percipient in the same rooms, and 218 made with them in different rooms. In the former set 131 trials were successful, though the digits were named in reverse order in 14 of these 131 cases. In the latter set there were only 9 successes. The "probable" number of successes by chance would have been in the former set 8, in the latter at most 3. Later, with three of the same percipients and three new ones, Mr. Smith still being agent, Mrs. Sidgwick and Miss Johnson report 252 trials and 27 successes (chance number = 4), with agent and percipient in different rooms. Mr. Smith transferred "mental pictures" to five subjects, successfully in 31 out of 71 trials in one room, in 2 out of 55 in different rooms. The subjects of the mental pictures were such things as "a boy skating," "a baby in a perambulator with nurse," "a mouse in a trap," etc.

Prof. Richet has described (*Proceedings of Society for Psychical Research*, Vol. V) a series of successes in guessing drawings in the hypnotic state; but as he found that the same subjects succeeded 30 times out of 180 trials in guessing the drawing when it was enclosed in an envelope and unknown to any one present, it is doubtful whether telepathy or clairvoyance be the cause of the success. Control experiments showed that "chance" could give as many as 35 percent of good successes at matching pictures made arbitrarily by different persons with others taken at random from a large collection previously prepared. Richet's hypnotic subjects gave, however, 10 percent of good successes in 200 trials, and he concludes the existence of an unknown power.

Thus, to count only systematically pursued experiments, some of which are not mentioned here, there are accounts from more than a dozen competent observers concerning about a score of subjects, all seeming to show a degree of success in guessing very much greater than that which chance would give. Different readers, however, will weigh the evidence differently, according to their prepossessions. Much of it is fragmentary, and in much one or other condition of "faultlessness" in experimenting is violated. The mass, however, is decidedly imposing; and if more and more of this solitary kind of evidence should accumulate, it would probably end by convincing the world.

Meanwhile there are other kinds of telepathy which, illogically perhaps, impress the believing imagination more than high percentages of success in guessing numbers can. Such are cases of the induction of sleep in hypnotic subjects by mental commands given at a distance. Pierre Janet, Richet, Gibert, Ochorowicz, Héricourt, Dufay, Daniex, Tolosa, Latour, and others are the relaters of these observations, of which the most important evidentially are those made on the celebrated somnambulic subject, Madame B., or "Leonie." Out of one series of 25 trials with this woman, there were 18 complete and 4 partial successes. Mr. Ochorowicz vouches for some of these, and gives also a long series in which silent commands were acted out by another hypnotic subject of his own, both he and she being, however, in the same room. The most convincing sort of evidence for thought-transference is given by the sittings of certain "test-mediums," of which the best worked-out case is that of Mrs. Piper, published in the Society for Psychical Research *Proceedings* for 1890, 1892, 1895). This lady shows a profuse intimacy, not so much with the actual passing thoughts of her sitters as with the whole reservoir of their memory or potential thinking; and as the larger covers the less, so the present writer, being as convinced of the reality of the phenomenon in her as he can be convinced of anything in the world, probably makes less exacting demands than he otherwise would on the sort of evidence given for minor grades of the power.

The authors of the word telepathy have used it as a theory whereby to explain "veridical hallucinations" such as would be the apparition of a person at a distance at the time of his death. The theory is that one who is dying or passing through some crisis is for some unknown reason peculiarly able to serve as "agent" and project an impression, and that the telepathic "impact" in such a case produces hallucination. Stated thus boldly the theory sounds most fanciful, but it rests on certain actual analogies. Thus a suggestion made to a suitable subject in the hypnotic trance that at a certain appointed time after his awakening he shall see the operator or other designated person enter the room, will post-hypnotically take effect and be followed at the appointed time by an exteriorized apparition of the person named. Moreover, strange as the fact may appear, there seems evidence, small in amount but good in quality, that one may, by exerting one's will to that effect, cause one's self to appear present to a person at a distance. As many as eight persons worthy of confidence have recently reported successes in this sort of experiment. The writer knows a ninth case, impossible to publish, but where the evidence (as far as taken) is good. Now the committee on the census of hallucinations of the Society for Psychical Research find that the "veridical" ones among them—those, namely, in which the apparition coincides with the death of the person who appears—are 440 times more numerous than they ought to be if they were the result of mere chance. For the particular data and logic by which this figure is obtained, see the report in Vol. X of the Society for Psychical Research *Proceedings*. Of course, if such a conclusion ever be accepted, and if the telepathic theory of such apparitions be credible, the probability that telepathy is the cause of success in the smaller number-guessing cases would be greatly re-enforced. The whole subject, so far as definite observation goes, is still in its earliest infancy.

BIBLIOGRAPHY—J. Ochorowicz, *De la Suggestion Mentale* (Paris, 1887); *Proceedings of the Society for Psychical Research, passim*; F. Podmore, *Apparitions and Thought-Transference* (1894).

8

NOTES ON AUTOMATIC WRITING

Although "The Hidden Self" (Chapter 1) was published a year after "Notes on Automatic Writing" (1889), it can be read as providing its preparatory framework. Unlike "The Hidden Self," however, in which James was most concerned with the psychological processes behind automatic writing, here he is more concerned with its evidential value. Though James doesn't overtly suggest a spirit or mediumship explanation in the article, he hints at the possibility with some of the examples he uses. The question of telepathy is more clearly to the fore, however, as if James found it important to first establish that possibility before considering spirit communication. He returns to the problem in the spiritualistic context in Chapter 20, below, "Mediumships or Possessions."

Though rarely reprinted – perhaps due to so much of it being taken up by anecdotal case summaries – the piece encompasses many features of James's other writings on psychical research, and indeed incorporates thematic elements from the first three sections of this book. It would be equally at home in any of them.

Many communications concerning experiences in automatic writing have been sent in to the Secretary during the past two years, and both he and the undersigned have witnessed the phenomenon in a number of instances. It is unquestionably a field from which a rich harvest of instruction may be hoped; but as professional occupations have prevented that steady experimental study of the matter which it deserves, I will content myself with jotting down a few points which may serve to stimulate the interest of the Society, postponing a more systematic paper to some later date. I must refer the reader to the important papers by Mr. Myers in Nos. VII, VIII, and XI of the London Society's *Proceedings*, for a general introduction to the subject. I regret that the appeal to experiment with the planchette, which was made at the public meeting in the spring of 1887, was followed by insignificant results. Planchettes can be obtained at the toy-shops, or (at cost) by writing to the Secretary of the Society; and, possibly, the remainder of this paper may lead to a little wider trial amongst associates and members.

One phenomenon of which Mr. Hodgson and I have been witnesses is both new and important. *The hand and the arm of the automatic writer are (in certain instances, at least) anaesthetic.* As soon as I read M. Pierre Janet's admirable account of the double personality of his somnambulist, L.,[1] I resolved to look for this symptom in ordinary planchette writers. It will be remembered that the skin of the hysteric L. had been for many years entirely insensible to contact, but that when she took to writing automatically on being waked from the hypnotic trance, the hand which wrote (and which signed all its communications by the name of Adrienne) expressed an intelligence perfectly perceptive of those skin-sensations of which the usual intelligence, expressing itself by word of mouth, was ignorant. Might not, conversely, the usual intelligence of ordinary non-hysteric automatic writers be transiently ignorant of the sensations of the writing hand and arm?

Persons who have written with a planchette are apt to speak of a tingling or prickling in the hands. I have actually tested three automatic writers for anesthesia. In one of them, examined between the acts of writing, no anesthesia was observed, but the examination was superficial. In the two others, both of them men, the anesthesia to pricking and pinching, and possibly to touch, seemed complete. The second of these cases is so interesting that I subjoin the facts in detail.

William L. Smith, of Concord, Mass., student at the Massachusetts Institute of Technology, age 21, perfectly healthy and exceptionally intelligent, whose sincerity it is impossible to suspect, has amused

---

[1] *Revue Philosophique*, XXII, 577; XXIII, 449. Mr. Myers gives an abstract of the case in the third of his articles above referred to, pp. 237-249.

himself on various occasions during the past two years with planchette writing. Of his previous performances more anon. On Jan. 24, 1889, he sat with Mr. Hodgson and myself, with his right hand extended on the instrument, and his face averted and buried in the hollow of his left arm, which lay along the table. Care was taken not to suggest to him the aim of the inquiry.

The planchette began by illegible scrawling. After ten minutes I pricked the back of the right hand several times with a pin—no indication of feeling. Two pricks on the *left* hand were followed by withdrawal, and the question, "What did you do that for?" — to which I replied, "To find whether you were going to sleep." The first legible words which were written after this were, *You hurt me.*

A pencil in the right hand was then tried instead of the planchette. Here again the first legible words were, *No use (?) in trying to spel when you hurt me so.* Next: *Its no use trying to stop me writing by pricking.* These writings were deciphered aloud in the hearing of S., who seemed slow to connect them with the two pin-pricks on his left hand, which alone he had felt.

After some more or less illegible writing (some of it in Greek characters) and questions asked and answered,[2] I pricked the right wrist and fingers several times again quite severely, with no sign of reaction on S.'s part. After an interval, however, the pencil wrote: *Don't you prick me any more.* S. then said, "My right hand is pretty well asleep." I tested the two hands immediately by pinching and pricking, but found no difference between them, *both apparently normal.* S. then said that what he meant by "asleep" was the feeling of "pins and needles" (which an insensible limb has when "waking up").

The last written sentence was then deciphered aloud. S. laughed, having been conscious only of the pricks on his left hand, and said, "It's working those two pin-pricks for all they are worth."

I then asked, "What have I been excited about to-day?" Ans. *Possibly examining.* "No, that was yesterday; try again." Ans. *May be correct dont know possibly sleepin.*[3] "What do you mean by sleeping?" Ans. *I*

---

[2] *Q.* "Who is writing? Is it Smith himself?" *A. YES. Pencil can't go alone.*

[3] What I had in mind was "building-plane." As a matter of fact, however, I had been acutely suffering all day from loss of sleep, and had vainly sought to get a nap in the afternoon. There are claims of lucidity for Mr. Smith's past planchette writing, and this answer may (possibly) not have been a mere coincidence. It is true that I am a chronically bad sleeper, and Mr. S. may have heard of the fact.

don't know (really?) You (distinct figure of a *pin*) *me 19 times*[4] *and think I'll write for you.*

The sitting here ended. It was very inferior in legibility and variety to sittings of the same subject a year previous. Two evenings later we had another sitting. S. had been most of the day in the open air, and had paddled a canoe ten miles. I immediately asked, "Are you still offended at my having pricked you?" Ans. *I'm (?).* "Where did I prick you the other night?" Ans. *On the side of my hand.* "Didn't I prick you anywhere else?" Ans. *No.* "Which hand?" Ans. *This hand.* "Which hand?" Ans. *Right.*

After some remote questions and answers the pencil was changed to the *left* hand, to see if that also would write. It spontaneously wrote a good deal, quite unintelligibly. "Are you angry?" Ans. *Yes.* "Who pricked you? How many times? Tell us all about it." Ans. *19 times on the other hand.* No further writing came on this evening. Shortly after the last answer I pinched four times, severely, the skin of the *left* hand between my nails. S.'s eyes were closed, but his face was visible, and I *thought* I detected a very subtle facial and respiratory reaction upon the pinching. He, however, on being questioned some minutes later, denied that he had been pricked or pinched during this evening. Later still, whilst the left hand still held the pencil, I pinched his *right* hand once, whereupon he started and said he didn't "need to be waked up." No more writing taking place after a quarter of an hour or more, I compared the two hands and found that they had equal and normal sensibility. S. is still ignorant of what interested us in these sittings. He is, unfortunately, too busy to sit again for many weeks.

Here, as the reader will perceive, we have the consciousness of a subject split into two parts, one of which expresses itself through the mouth, and the other through the hand, whilst both are in communication with the ear. The mouth-consciousness is ignorant of all that the hand suffers or does; the hand-consciousness is ignorant of pin-pricks inflicted upon other parts of the body—and of what more remains to be ascertained. If we call this hand-consciousness the automatic consciousness, then we also perceive that the automatic consciousness may transfer itself from the right hand to the left, and carry its own peculiar store of memories with it. The left hand, writing automatically on the second evening, remembered the right hand's experiences on the first, and very likely (though this was not ascertained) knew nothing of its own.

---

[4] I unfortunately hadn't counted the times. Nineteen is a plausible number.

These phenomena remind us of what the lamented Gurney described in his important paper "Peculiarities of Certain Post-hypnotic States," in Part XI of the London Society's *Proceedings*. The facts there, it will be remembered, were these: An order to do something after waking was given to the subject during the trance. Of this order no apparent consciousness remained when the trance was over. But if, before the time of execution arrived, the subject's hand was placed upon a planchette, the writing which came was all about the order, showing that the latter was retained in a split-off portion of the consciousness, which was able to express itself automatically through the hand. This dissociation of the consciousness into mutually exclusive parts is evidently a phenomenon destined, when understood, to cast a light into the abysses of Psychology.

We owe to the kindness of Dr. C. W. Fillmore, of Providence, the report of a case of hystero-epilepsy which illustrates the same phenomenon in an even more extraordinary manner.[5] The record begins in the nineteenth year of the patient's age, and continues for several years. It is filled with every conceivable species of suffering and disorder, but the entries which interest us in the present connection are the following:

> September 17, 1860: Wild with delirium. Tears her hair, pillow-cases, bedclothes, both sheets, night-dress, all to pieces. Her right hand prevents her left hand, by seizing and holding it, from tearing out her hair, but she tears her clothes with her left hand and teeth ...
>
> 29th: Complains of great pain in right arm, more and more intense, when suddenly it falls down by her side. She looks at it in amazement. Thinks it belongs to someone else; positive it is not hers. Sees her right arm drawn around upon her spine. Cut it, prick it, do what you please to it, she takes no notice of it. Complains of great pain in the neck and back, which she now calls her shoulder and arm; no process of reasoning can convince her of the contrary. (To the present time, now nearly five years, the hallucination remains firm. She believes her spine is her right arm, and that her right arm is a foreign object and a nuisance. She believes it to be an arm and a hand, but treats it as if it had intelligence and might keep away from her. She bites it, pounds

---

[5] The report is by the late Dr. Ira Barrows, of Providence. The patient was Miss Anna Winsor. Her mother, brother, and Dr. Wilcox, Dr. B.'s former partner, bear corroborative testimony.

it, pricks it, and in many ways seeks to drive it from her. She calls it "Stump; Old Stump." Sometimes she is in great excitement and tears, pounding "Old Stump." Says "Stump" has got this, that, or the other, that belongs to her.) The history of September is her daily and nightly history till October 25th...

November 12: From eleven to twelve at night sits up, apparently asleep, and writes, with her paper against the wall. After she awakes, seems to be unconscious of what she has written. ...

From November 20 to January 1, 1861: Raving delirium; pulls her hair nearly all out from the top of her head. ... The right hand protects her against the left as much as possible. ...

February 1 to 11: Under the influence of magnetism writes poetry; personates different persons, mostly those who have long since passed away. When in the magnetic state, whatever she does and says is not remembered when she comes out of it. Commences a series of drawings with her right paralyzed hand, "Old Stump." Also writes poetry with it. Whatever "Stump" writes, or draws, or does, she appears to take no interest in; says it is none of hers, and that she wants nothing to do with "Stump" or "Stump's." I have sat by her bed and engaged her in conversation, and drawn her attention in various ways, while the writing and drawing has been uninterrupted. As she had never exhibited any taste for nor taken any lessons in drawing I exhibit here some specimens of her first attempt.[6]

March, 1861: She became blind. ...

January 4, 1862: Is still blind; sees as well with eyes closed as open; keeps them closed much of the time; reads and draws with them closed. Draws in the dark as well as in the light; is clairvoyant. Writes poetry, chiefly with the right hand, and often...while it is dark. The hand-writing differs greatly in different pieces. ...

January 10: When her delirium is at its height, as well as at all other times, her right hand is rational, asking and answering questions in writing; giving directions; trying to prevent her tearing her clothes; when she pulls out her hair it seizes and holds her left hand. When she is asleep, it carries on conversation the same; writes poetry; never sleeps; acts the part of a nurse as far it can; pulls the bedclothes over the patient, if it can reach them, when uncovered; raps on the head-board to awaken her mother (who always sleeps in the room) if anything occurs, as spasms, etc.

---

[6] These specimens we have never received. — W. J.

January, 1863: At night, and during her sleep, "Stump" writes letters, some of them very amusing; writes poetry, some pieces original! Writes "Hasty Pudding," by Barlow, in several cantos, which she had never read; all correctly written, but queerly arranged, as, e.g, one line belonging in one canto would be transposed with another line in another canto. She has no knowledge of Latin or French, yet "Stump" produces the following rhyme of Latin and English:[7]

> Sed tempus recessit, and this was all over,
> Cum illi successit, another gay rover;
> Nam cum navigaret in his own cutter,
> Portentum apparet, which made them all flutter.
>
> Est horridus anguis which they behold,
> Haud dubio sanguis within them ran cold.
> Tringinta pedes his head was upraised,
> Et corporis sedes in secret was placed.
>
> Sic serpens manebat, so says the same joker,
> Et sese ferebat as stiff as a poker;
> Tergura fricabat against the old light-house,
> Et sese liberabat of scaly detritus.
>
> Tunc plumbo percussit thinking he hath him,
> At serpens exsiluit full thirty fathom,
> Exsiluit mare with pain and affright,
> Conatus abnare as fast as he might.
>
> Neque illi secuti? no, nothing so rash,
> Terrore sunt muti he'd made such a splash;
> Sed nunc adierunt the place to inspect,
> Et squamas viderunt, the which they collect.
>
> Quicumque non credat and doubtfully rails,
> Ad locum accedat, they'll show him the scales;
> Quas, sola trophea, they brought to the shore;
> Et causa est ea, they couldn't get more.

---

[7] Does any reader recognize these verses? If so, will he please send them to the Secretary? It is important to ascertain whether their origin were not in the patient's memory.

"Stump" writes both asleep and awake, and the writing goes on while she is occupied with her left hand in other matters. Ask her what she is writing, she replies, "*I* am not writing; that is 'Stump' writing. I don't know what he is writing. I don't trouble myself with 'Stump's' doings." Reads with her book upside down, and sometimes when covered with the sheet. "Stump" produces two bills of fare in French. …

Upon this one subject of her right arm, she is monomaniac. Her right hand and arm are not hers. Attempt to reason with her and she holds up her left arm and says, "This is my left arm. I see and feel my right arm drawn behind me. You say this "Stump" is my right arm. Then I have three arms and hands." In this arm the nerves of sensation are paralyzed, but the nerves of motion preserved. She has no will to move it. She has no knowledge of its motion. This arm appears to have a separate intelligence. When she sleeps, it writes or converses by signs. It never sleeps; watches over her when she sleeps; endeavors to prevent her from injuring herself or her clothing when she is raving. It seems to possess an independent life and, to some extent, foreknowledge.

Miss W. died in January, 1873. The record of her last ten years is not given. It would appear, from certain passages of the record in our possession, that "old Stump" used to write of Miss W. in the third person, as Anna. This seems to be the rule in automatic utterances.

Certain other peculiarities which I have never seen quoted together deserve mention. Thus the planchette-writer often tends to fall into a drowsy condition whilst writing, and to become abstracted from the outer world. Sometimes he even passes into a state of genuine sleep or trance—I have no data thus far for distinguishing which. The writing is often preceded by peculiar sensations in the arm, and the latter is apt to be animated by involuntary spasmodic movements before the writing regularly begins.

I was witness a year ago, in Mr. Smith's case, of a phenomenon which has been described since Braid's time as "exaltation of the muscular sense," but, so far as I know, only recorded of hypnotic subjects.[8] Mr. Smith wrote on large sheets of brown wrapping-paper, his right arm extended, his face on a level with the table, buried in the hollow of his left elbow—a position which made vision of the surface of the paper a physical impossibility. Nevertheless, two or three times in my presence on one evening, after covering a sheet with writing (the pencil never

---

[8] See, for example, Carpenter's *Mental Physiology*, §128.

being raised, so that the words ran into each other), he returned to the top of the sheet and proceeded downwards, dotting each *i* and crossing each *t* with absolute precision and great rapidity. On another evening, whilst sitting in the same position, he drew the entire outline of a grotesque human figure in such a way that the pencil ended at the point where it began, and that it is now impossible to tell, from inspection of the perfectly continuous outline, just where the point in question lay. Such feats would seem quite impossible to one in the normal waking state.

Another often noted idiosyncrasy of these writings is the *freakiness* of their execution. Mirror-script, spelling backwards, writing from right to left, and even beginning at the right-hand lower corner of the page and inscribing every word with its last letter first, etc., till the top is reached, are among the peculiarities of the automatic pencil. Mr. Myers has tried to assimilate some of these traits to what is observed in aphasia—with what success, later inquiry alone can show.

Another remarkable point is that two persons can often make a planchette or a bare pencil write automatically when neither can succeed alone. The explanation of this is hard to find. The individuals themselves will sometimes say, "One of us gives the force, the other the intelligence." Certain it is that perfectly determinate combinations of individuals are often required for success. The more physiological explanation is that the automatic freedom is interfered with by conscious attention to the performance, and that when two persons work together each thinks that the other is the source of movement, and lets his own hand freely go. We sadly need more discriminating observations on this as well as other points.

Of course, the great *theoretic* interest of these automatic performances, whether speech or writing, consists in the questions they awaken as to the boundaries of our individuality. One of their most constant peculiarities is that the writing and speech announce themselves as from a personality other than the natural one of the writer, and often convince *him*, at any rate, that his organs are played upon by someone not himself. This foreignness in the personality reaches its climax in the demoniacal possession which has played so great a part in history, and which, in our country, seems replaced by the humaner phenomenon of trance-mediumship, with its Indian or other outlandish "control," giving more or less optimistic messages from the "summer-land." So marked is it in all the extreme instances that we may say that the *natural and presumptive* explanation of the phenomenon is unquestionably the popular or "spiritualistic" one, of "control" by another intelligence. It is only when we put the cases into a series, and see how insensibly those at the upper extreme shade down at the lower extreme into what is unquestionably the work of the individual's own mind in an abstracted state, that more complex and would-be "scientific" ways of conceiving the matter force themselves upon us. The whole subject is at present a perfect puzzle on the theoretic side. And even on the phenomenal side we need more abundant proof than we have yet received that the content of the automatic communications may transcend the possible information of the individual through whose hand they come. To interest the reader in these more difficult phases of the subject I will append as illustrations some of the cases which we have received. The first is from Mr. Sidney Dean, of Warren, R.I., member of Congress from Connecticut from 1855 to 1859, who has been all his life a robust and active journalist, author, and man of affairs. He has for many years been a writing subject, and has a large collection of manuscript automatically produced.

> Some of it (we writes us) is in hieroglyph, or strange compounded arbitrary characters, each series possessing a seeming unity in general design or character, followed by what purports to be a translation or rendering into mother English. I never attempted the seemingly impossible feat of copying the characters. They were cut with the precision of a graver's tool, and generally with a single rapid stroke of the pencil. Many languages, some obsolete and passed from history, are professedly given. To see them would satisfy you that no one could copy them except by tracing.[9]
>
> These, however, are but a small part of the phenomena. The "automatic" has given place to the *impressional*, and when the work is in progress I am in the normal condition, and seemingly two minds, intelligences, persons, are practically engaged. The writing is in my own hand but the dictation not of my own mind and will, but that of

---

[9] I should say that I have seen some of these curious hieroglyphs by Mr. D., which professed to be Chinese. They bore no outward resemblance to what I have learned to know as Chinese characters. I owe to the kindness of Colonel Bundy some four or five other *soi-disant* specimens of ancient languages, automatically written, which I have had examined by my colleagues conversant with Sanskrit, Hebrew, Assyrian, Arabic, and Persian, as well as by a Japanese student who knew Chinese. None of the characters were in any instance recognized. — W. J.

another, upon subjects of which I can have no knowledge and hardly a theory; and I, myself, consciously criticize the thought, fact, mode of expressing it, etc., while the hand is recording the subject-matter and even the words impressed to be written. If *I* refuse to write the sentence, or even the word, the impression instantly ceases, and my willingness must be mentally expressed before the work is resumed, and it is resumed at the point of cessation, even if it should be in the middle of a sentence. Sentences are commenced without knowledge of mine as to their subject or ending. In fact, I have never known in advance the subject of disquisition.

There is in progress now, at uncertain times, not subject to my will, a series of twenty-four chapters upon the scientific features of life, moral, spiritual, eternal. Seven have already been written in the manner indicated. These were preceded by twenty-four chapters relating generally to the life beyond material death, its characteristics, etc. Each chapter is signed by the name of some person who has lived on earth—some with whom I have been personally acquainted, others known in history. ... I know nothing of the alleged authorship of any chapter until it is completed and the name impressed and appended. ...[10] I am interested not only in the reputed authorship—of which I have nothing corroborative—but in the philosophy taught, of which I was in ignorance until these chapters appeared. From my standpoint of life—which has been that of biblical orthodoxy—the philosophy is new, seems to be reasonable, and is logically put. I confess to an inability to successfully controvert it to my own satisfaction.

It is an intelligent *ego* who writes, or else the influence assumes individuality, which practically makes of the influence a personality. It is *not* myself; of that I am conscious at every step of the process. I have also traversed the whole field of the claims of "unconscious cerebration," so called, so far as I am competent to critically examine it, and it fails, as a theory, in numberless points, when applied to this strange work through me. It would be far more reasonable and satisfactory for me to accept the silly hypothesis of reincarnation— the old doctrine of metempsychosis—as taught by some spiritualists

---

[10] I have seen and read three of these chapters. They are fluent, scholarly, and philosophical enough, but to my mind have a curious resemblance in style to other inspirational productions which I have read, and doubtfully attain to real originality. One of them, signed Louis Agassiz, was, both in thought and diction, wholly unlike the utterances during life of my lamented teacher. — W. J.

today, and to believe that I lived a former life here, and that once in a while it dominates my intellectual powers, and writes chapters upon the philosophy of life, or opens a post-office for spirits to drop their effusions, and have them put into English script. No; the easiest and most natural solution to me is to admit the claim made, i.e., that it is a decarnated intelligence who writes. But *who?* that is the question. The names of scholars and thinkers who once lived are affixed to the most un grammatical and weakest of *bosh*. ...

It seems reasonable to me—upon the hypothesis that it is a person using another's mind or brain—that there must be more or less of that other's style or tone incorporated in the message, and that to the unseen personality, i.e., the power which impresses, the thought, the fact, or the philosophy, and not the style or tone, belongs. For instance, while the influence is impressing my brain with the greatest force and rapidity, so that my pencil fairly flies over the paper to record the thoughts, I am conscious that, in many cases, the vehicle of the thought, i.e., the language, is very natural and familiar to me, as if, somehow, *my* personality as a writer was getting mixed up with the message. And, again, the style, language, everything, is entirely foreign to my own style.

Another gentleman, Mr. John N. Arnold, of 19 College street, Providence, RI, describes his experience as follows:

I make my mind as negative as possible, place myself in the attitude of writing, with pencil and paper, and in about two or three minutes I feel a sensation at the elbow as if a galvanic battery had touched it. The thrill continues down the forearm till it reaches the hand, which quickly doubles over towards the thumb, and then back, with a strong tension, several times. When quiet, it begins to write. The power that writes sometimes tells the truth, but oftener lies. For instance, an influence which called itself Lydia, my wife's sister, wrote that Rose (my wife) had been raising blood. I replied I thought not. Lydia insisted, and, upon reaching home, I found she was correct. Again, she wrote that a lady friend was dead. I contradicted the Automat, as I had seen the lady but a few hours before. Lydia seemed hurt to think I doubted her, and strongly asserted that the lady was dead. In a few hours I ascertained the falsity of Lydia's vehement assertion by meeting the lady in question. I got so little satisfaction from the power that I gave it up, and of late can only get names, but no communications, except yes or no, in answer to my questions.

In a second communication Mr. Arnold adds:

> The pencil was always held in my right hand. I never had any mirror-writing. I sometimes guessed what was coming, but never knew. For instance, many words begin with the first two or three letters the same, as *"pre*suming," *"pre*fix." I would sometimes guess, after the Automat finished the *e* in such a word; but generally was mistaken, even when the context would indicate my word to be the proper one.
>
> It is at least ten years (and it may be more) since the writing about my wife. I had no reason to think my wife had had hæmoptysis. She had had an attack in 1860, when we went to Macon, Ga, but not since; so that I was surprised when the Automat wrote with such confidence and persistency, and said that when I got home I should see that it was telling the truth. When I reached home I questioned my wife about it. She seemed very much astonished, and wanted to know how I got my information, as she had taken pains to conceal it from me, fearing it would cause me alarm. I have just asked my wife about this affair, and she seems to remember it substantially as I do. I have never tried answering mental questions put by another; in fact, the Automat and I got disgusted with one another years ago. We had a falling out, and haven't been on good terms since. The Auto got tired with my lack of patience, and I got tired with the Auto's lack of truthfulness.
>
> I am glad to answer any questions about this matter, and when you get a theory that will fit this problem, please write me. I don't mean unconscious cerebration, astral light, or spirit friends; but something new, something that will fit tight and snug all around and won't have to be taken in at the back, or let out in the arm-size, and won't go all to pieces like Don Quixote's pasteboard helmet when the Damascus blade of logic, reason, and common-sense descends upon it.

An isolated case of apparent clairvoyance, like that which this gentleman reports, had of course better be treated as an accidental coincidence. But there are other cases harder so to treat—cases where some sort of telepathy appears to be involved. But telepathy seems always doomed to be baffling. The telepathic explanation of the cases I have in mind is neither disproved nor established with the fulness that is desirable. As an illustration of what I mean, take Mr. W. L. Smith's case again. It was first made known to us in November, 1887, by a letter from one of his neighbors, Miss ––, who wrote as follows:

After reading the reports on Automatic Writing published by the English SPR, I determined to try my own power and those of my friends. Accordingly my friend W. L. S. and I each made a planchette. ... The successful writer was S. himself, and with him we have obtained more remarkable results than I have ever seen reported. It is worthwhile to notice that he had never seen a planchette before he made his according to my direction, and had never seen writing done with one until he made his first attempt in my presence, so that the possibility of unconscious deception, which might have existed in the case of a person who had already amused himself with a planchette, was out of the question with him. The question of conscious deception may be set aside at once; yet, appreciating that experiments whose fairness depends on the honesty of any person lose their scientific value, we took pains so far as possible to avoid everything which might have been suspicious with unknown writers.

Our first attempt, though only partially successful, so far exceeded our expectations, that we were much encouraged.

After relating three attempts at answering mental questions which seem to have been failures the account goes on:

At the fourth experiment, a repetition of the third, with a different card, the suit and number were immediately and correctly written. As in these cases there had been a possibility of thought-transfer, the next experiment was differently arranged.

The pack was carefully shuffled *by me*, and held under a table, both my hand and W.'s being in contact with it; neither of us could see the pack. I then faced the top card, again asking mentally for the suit and number of the card faced. The planchette immediately wrote the word *which*. We were about to consider the trial a failure when it occurred to me that I might have faced two cards. I found, on examining the pack, that this was not so; but, still without suggestion from W., I looked further, and found a second card in the middle of the pack, which I had unconsciously faced in shuffling.

I mention this in detail because it was the first instance of a writing unexpected by either W. or myself. At several succeeding experiments the planchette correctly wrote suit and number of cards turned up out of sight of everyone, until we became tired of that test and gave it up.

A series of questions, the answers to which were unknown to any one present, seemed to furnish a fair test for the powers of the planchette. At first the questions were asked aloud; in all cases they were put without suggestion by W.

I will describe two experiments as instances of trials of this kind. During these two experiments we sat in the dark, and yet the answers were legibly written.

My first question was, "What is the name on the visiting card which lies at the top of the cards in the hall?"

The planchette did not write immediately; during the time while we waited for an answer I involuntarily formed an idea of the name which I expected, and feared that thought-transfer would come in for a share of consideration if the answer should be correctly written. At last I heard the motion of the pencil; when it ceased we took the paper to the light and found the words *Upside down. After* reading this, we examined the card-plate, and found as an explanation of planchette's answer, the top card turned *upside down* on the pile.

Now, not only had S. no means of knowing that the top card was upside down, but no one else in the house knew it until after the writing by planchette; I had even a distinct idea of a certain name in my mind during the whole of the experiment. Furthermore, and most remarkable of all, the hall where the card-plate stood was unlighted, so that when we went to examine the card we were quite unable to say whether or not there was a name upon the card until we had carried the plate into the next room.

This fact reminded us of the power we had already seen in planchette to read the suit and number of playing-cards, held under the table so as to be out of the range of possible, as well as actual, vision.

We put the same question, "What is the name on the card which lies at the top on the card-plate?" a second time, the cards having been rearranged by a third person, who himself did not know what card he had placed at the top. The planchette wrote, *"Miss L. P. H.--"*; the name on the card proved to be Miss Lillian C. H. --. This partial mistake struck us as interesting, but we could find no explanation for it, as the card-plate stood in a lighted room during this experiment, where it would have seemed much easier for planchette to see it than in the first trial.

Although these questions were put without the slightest suggestion from W., he had been told before each experiment what inquiry had been made. From this time on we took pains to keep from him all knowledge, not only of the answer, but of the question asked. The question was either asked mentally or written on paper, and kept, with great care, out of his sight, except in a few instances, which I will mark with an asterisk in the following descriptions. Although deception was out of the question, we tried to perform all experiments with as great strictness as if the writer had been unknown to us, and it is only in the starred cases that there existed the *possibility* of W.'s seeing the question.

In the following four experiments the *answers* to the questions asked were known to one or more persons in the room, but not to S.:

1. Q. Is Miss H. going away Tuesday?
A. *Miss H. is no consequence to me. I don't know.*
2. Q. What did her uncle do in Paris?
A. *How should I know you or he did in Paris, or all France (sic), I wasn't there.*

(Mr. F. said he had been thinking, when the question was asked, of a friend who had been with him in Paris.)

3. Q. What sort of a voyage home did he have?
A. *Fair. If you keep that question to yourself there is no chance for thought transfer.*

(This was not written at once, which was explained by the planchette as due to the fact that the question had been asked mentally, and by only one person. It was one of a few cases of mirror-writing.)

4. Q. On what steamer did J. A. come home?
A *J. A. has been way off like Mr. F. I am not everywhere.*

(This was interesting, as W.'s acquaintance with Mr. F. was limited to the evening in which the latter had been present at a planchette writing, and during which, as may be seen from the second and third questions above, Mr. F.'s visit to Paris was mentioned.)

In the following six experiments the answers to the questions asked were known to persons present at the writing, and would have been known to W. if he had known what question was proposed. Accordingly, our care was exceedingly great in all these cases to keep the question out of sight. It is worth notice that in no case was the answer exactly what was expected by those who knew what inquiry had been made.

1. Q. Who wrote the play of *Hamlet*?
A. *I'd give a good deal to know that myself.*
2. Q. Can Mr. F. make planchette write?
A. *He can if he tries hard enough old man Bacon and gets some one to help at first.*

(Before and after the words "old man Bacon" were what might have been meant for parentheses. As the words had no meaning where they were written, we naturally referred them to the question immediately preceding, "Who wrote the play of *Hamlet*?" where they certainly seemed appropriate.)

*3. Q. What letters correspond to the notes

A. *Gace.*
*4. Q. Add 4905, 3641 and 9831.
A. *17377.*

(Planchette first copied the quantities to be added, making, by the way, a mistake in copying; this mistake, however, did not appear in the addition, though a mistake does appear in a column where the copy was correct.)

5. Q. How far is the earth from the sun?
A. *192,310,009 kill.*

(This is curious, as everyone who had known what question had been asked was expecting the answer in miles. W., however, always uses the metric system.)

6. Q. Who wrote *Childe Harold*?
A. *Byron, not drunk when he did it.*

Here would seem to be excellent evidence of mental questions answered and of telepathic or clairvoyant replies given. Sometime after this account was received I had the opportunity to sit with Mr. S. and the friends with whom the former successes had occurred. There were several other persons present as well. Writing came in profusion, bold and legible, but nothing that could be construed as telepathic. Many questions were written by the ladies with whom the former successes had occurred, out of S.'s sight, but were either not answered, or answered so vaguely that it was not certain that the particular question had been grasped. The questions were written across the table from Mr. S. Considering various hyperæsthetic possibilities, such questions should always be prepared outside of the room. Twice, early in 1888, Mr. S. sat for the Secretary and myself, when questions were secretly written, but in no instance pertinently answered. These negative results are, of course, not incompatible with the positive ones previously obtained, for if telepathy exist, it is certainly of fitful occurrence, even in a given individual. But they lend, at least, no strength to the first report; and, as luck will always have it, farther sittings with us (except the two recorded at the outset of this paper) have been made impossible to the subject by family wishes and his busy life.

Another similarly baffling case is given me by Mr. C., who graduated in 1888 at Harvard College, whom I know intimately, and whose sincerity I cannot doubt. Mr. C, it should be said, is himself the subject of certain automatic phenomena, with which, however, this narrative has naught to do. He told me of the following experience, either one or two days after it happened, and then wrote out the account which follows:

> It was on the evening of November 2. The company consisted of four ladies and two gentlemen. In the course of conversation a chance remark turned our thoughts upon psychological matters. Almost everyone had some strange thing to relate, but no one would acknowledge belief in any supernatural power.
>
> After speaking of various reports of mind-reading and hypnotic experiments I said, in a half-serious, half-joking way, "Suppose we try something of the sort."
>
> The suggestion being favored, the daughter of the house, a girl of nineteen or twenty years of age, seated herself by a table, with pencil and paper. She seemed to think it was all foolery, but was amiable enough to contribute all she could to possible success, and, shading her eyes with her hand, she made herself as passive as possible.
>
> On my part, I stood up at the opposite side of the table, about three feet removed, and fixed my mind upon a certain word, and (wishing to select one that would be most remote from her mind) I took "hell." With almost no hesitation in beginning, the girl made the letters, one after another, with easy legibleness (though the handwriting was neither hers nor mine).
>
> Surprised at the success of the experiment, I felt interested to continue, and now determined to test it to the satisfaction of others. Accordingly, I went for a moment into the hall with one of the company, and there said to her that my next word should be "omen." Returning to the room, the same success attended as before, except that the "e" was, in its smallness, out of proportion to the other letters, and the line between "o" and "m" was too long, because of a slip of the hand.

The experiment continued in like manner till some ten or a dozen words were written, of which I now remember (besides the above two, "hell" and "omen") "word," "four," "moon."

The person to whom each time I announced my intended word was of a disposition entirely to be relied on as free from either serious or facetious tricks, though, for that matter, I do not see how collusion with the "Subject" was possible without being noticed.

The paper on which the words were written I wanted to take, but as the young lady wished to keep it I said nothing. On inquiring for it a few days later, it could not be found.

On the third day after (November 5), I again went to the house to see if more might not be done. Certain other interests, however, being emphasized in my mind, I did not find myself able to exert so strong a will as on the previous occasion. Whether because of this or not, I cannot judge; but the results were more meagre, but two words being successfully written, "music" and "girl." Upon my thinking of one word, "orange," my "subject" wrote all the letters, but in wrong order, thus: "georan."

An additional fact that I noticed this time (and I think it was true of the first evening's experiments) was, that when I stood at the right side of the girl she wrote downwards, and when I stood opposite her she wrote upwards.

The rest of the trials, which were of lines and diagrams imagined by me, resulted in nothing but undecipherable scrawls.

Concerning the feelings of myself and of the "Subject" there is but this to say: that the girl had a headache the next day after the experiment (to which, being unaccustomed to headaches, she ascribed it), and no effect after the second. Upon me there was no after effect either time, except that after the first experiment, and on the same night, I felt as one does after giving strained attention to one thing.

The lady who did the writing, three other ladies, and a gentleman who witnessed the first evening's performance, endorsed, on Nov. 16, Mr. C.'s statement as a "true report"; but I am not at liberty in this case to publish any names. On Dec. 2, Mr. C. added this postscript:

> I omitted to say with regard to the second series of trials, that "music," "girl," and "orange" (the three words which the girl wrote) were the only *words* that I tried.

Concerning the first evening's experiments, my memory enables me to add, that besides the words already mentioned as being successfully written, my subject wrote with remarkable plainness this figure [a spiral], and also its reverse (though not so promptly).

Yet one further fact, perhaps worth noting: On this first evening I twice (possibly three times) let my thoughts stray whithersoever they would, while my subject and the onlookers supposed that I was exercising my intent upon some particular word. The results in these instances were nothing; unrelated pencil-marks as rambling as my thoughts, though, of course, in no way resembling them.

A few days after this I spent an evening at the subject's house with C. Nothing of interest occurred, though we tried to get results similar to those of the first occasion. The subject wrote a very little, automatically; but no sign whatever of telepathy appeared. C., I found, had stood (on the successful occasion) where he could see the movement of the young lady's hand as it wrote. The hypothesis must of course be considered, that he may have guided it by unconscious indications, like those given in the "willing game" to the blindfold subject. The indications must in this instance have been reduced to changes in his respiration. If such indications were given, they were at any rate ineffectual when I was there, and also on three later occasions, on which, with the same *modus operandi*, Mr. C. reports that he only got total or partial failure. The sitting first reported remains thus a unique occurrence, not to be distinctly classified as yet.

The great desideratum is to get cases which can be examined continuously. Little can be done without the help of associates of the Society. I publish these incomplete notes, making no mention of much of our collected material, in order to show how important is the field, and how great the need of its assiduous cultivation.

9

REPORT OF THE COMMITTEE ON HYPNOTISM (EXCERPT)

As seen earlier, some of James's writings show how certain phenomena were originally seen as having possible "paranormal" origins before they were understood as being purely psychological. This blurring of boundaries is evident by the very fact that this 1889 "Report of the Committee on Hypnotism" was originally published in the *Proceedings of the American Society for Psychical Research*.

The article is primarily a review of progress in the psychological study of hypnotic states, though characteristically, at the end of the article James relates the phenomenon to psychical research. Only that section is reprinted here. It is interesting that, as with his article on automatic writing (Chapter 7) he discusses the relationship between hypnotism and telepathy specifically, rather than hypnotism and mediumship.

There was no sign of any sort of clairvoyance in either of the two advanced subjects above mentioned, nor, as tested by card guessing, in Mrs. P., the medium, when in the hypnotic condition. A very good student subject, discovered by one of his comrades, was reported, on what seemed not bad evidence, to have named in his trance objects hidden from his sight; but, in the two sittings we had with him, nothing of the sort occurred. Indeed, on the second of these occasions, he was with difficulty kept entranced at all.

The only quite mysterious case of perception we found was with another subject, who in either six or seven different trials picked out from a heap of silver and copper change, consisting of from fourteen to twenty-two pieces, the one coin which had been contributed by his operator to the heap. He never made a false guess on the evenings when these successes occurred; and the only reason he could give for his choice was either that the coin *felt* as if it were the right one, or that it "felt heavy." The coins were of course arranged out of his sight; and in some of the later trials, though not in the whole series, express care was taken to see whether he might not have been guided to his choice by the right coin being *warmer* than the rest, but with a negative result. On *one* evening he altogether failed in this experiment. With handkerchiefs he was less uniformly successful. We shall continue these experiments, so as to ascertain, if possible, the nature of the clue which determined the subject's choice.

A direct difference in the effects of upward and downward passes, independent of suggestion or expectation, has always been part of the orthodox "magnetic" creed. But the recent flood of "scientific" literature on the subject is almost mute on this point. Dr. J. K. Mitchell of Philadelphia, a contemporary of Braid, whose caution, clearness, and cool head ought ere now to have secured for him a prominent name in the history of hypnotism,[1] admitted that the different effects of upward and downward passes were the only sign of a direct physical influence of operator upon subject which he was able to find. Our own experiments verified the difference in question in cases too numerous to be plausibly ascribed to accident. The young men upon whom the passes were made knew nothing of what we were seeking to test, and as often as not answered wrongly when asked later if they knew the direction in which the passes had been made. Yet in five or six individuals, upward passes, the first time they were tried, awoke the patient, or restored his hand, arm, etc., to its natural state, whilst downward passes had a precisely opposite effect. It is a curious thing to see the face of a man whose eyes and mouth have been shut tight by suggestion, and over whose face the operator makes passes in an upward direction on the

---

[1] See his *Five Essays,* edited by Dr. S. Weir Mitchell, Philadelphia (1859).

right side, whilst he makes downward passes on the left. On being told to open their eyes and whistle, two or three such patients have opened upon us only the right eye, and whistled out of the right corner of their mouth. Others showed no difference whatever in their reaction to the different passes. The matter must be prosecuted further. Obviously, so long as it is under dispute, experiments, to prove anything, must be made with ignorant subjects, and must succeed the first time they are tried.

Besides the observations we have recorded, we verified most of the now classical and familiar phenomena of trance. A few curious observations on the *rapport* between operator and subject, and on the influence of magnets, had better be treated as coincidences for the present, because not found in the subject at different times. Our experience has impressed upon us the variability of the same subject's trance from one day to another. It may occur that a phenomenon met with one day, but not repeated, and therefore accounted a mere coincidence, is really due to a particular phase of the trance, realized on that occasion, but never again when sought for. To decide definitely between these alternatives, in the case of any special phenomenon, would obviously require many sittings and consume much time.

10

THE CONSCIOUSNESS OF LOST LIMBS (EXCERPT)

As with the previous chapter, this one concerns a subject that would today be considered the domain of conventional psychology, though was originally published in the *Proceedings of the American Society for Psychical Research* (in its first issue, from 1887). It deals with what is now called phantom limb syndrome, an accepted neurophysiological phenomenon.

Based on a survey of amputees conducted by James himself, he learned little from the results and expressed disappointment in the project. Among his findings was that thinking about the lost limb often caused the individual to feel its absence. Some said they could still wiggle their toes, or reported feeling heat, cold, or the movement of air in their lost limb. "One man writes that whenever he walks through puddles and wets his sound foot, his lost foot feels wet too." He concluded that "phantasms of lost legs and arms are to the mental organism just what rudimentary organs are to the bodily organism. They have no longer any real relations with the environment, being mere vestiges of something which formerly had real relations."

The article mainly seeks to understand the phenomenon in terms of anatomical trauma relating to amputation alongside psychological factors. As he himself acknowledged, the piece was not an important contribution to the study of the syndrome, though his brief closing remarks relating the phenomenon to psychical research are worth reprinting here.

My final observations are on a matter which ought to interest students of "psychic research." Surely if there be any distant material object with which a man might be supposed to have clairvoyant or telepathic relations, that object ought to be his own cut-off arm or leg. Accordingly, a very widespread belief will have it, that when the cut-off limb is maltreated in any way, the man, no matter where he is, will feel the injury. I have nearly a score of communications on this point, some believing, more incredulous. One man tells of experiments of warming, etc., which the doctor in an adjoining room made on the freshly cut-off leg, without his knowledge, and of which his feelings gave him no suspicion. Of course, did such telepathic *rapport* exist, it need not necessarily be found in every case. But in none of the cases of my collection in which the writers seek to prove it does their conclusion inspire confidence. All (with perhaps one exception which, unfortunately, I have lost) are vaguely told; and, indeed, amongst all the pains which come and go in the first weeks of amputation, it would be strange if some did not coincide with events happening to the buried or "pickled" limb. One man writes me that he has dug up his buried leg eight times, and changed its position. He asks me to advise him whether to dig it up again, saying he "dreads to."

11

REVIEW OF *TELEPATHIC DREAMS EXPERIMENTALLY INDUCED* BY G. B. ERMACORA

William James wrote at least three reviews of books dealing with telepathy. Two of them are largely redundant with discussions found in previous articles here, though one is of interest due to the relative obscurity of the book and its unusual approach. It was written by an Italian physicist, Giovanni Battista Ermacora, and is an early work on telepathy in dreams – prefiguring the modern classic study *Dream Telepathy* by Montague Ullmann, Stanley Krippner, and Alan Vaughan[1] by nearly 80 years.

Telepathic Dreams Experimentally Induced. G. B. Ermacora. *Proceedings of the Society for Psychical Research* Vol. XI, pp. 235-308.

This is a startling experimental record of a new genus of thought transference. The personages are: Dr. Ermacora; the Signora Maria, a young woman with trances and automatic writing in which she

---

[1] Montague Ullman, Stanley Krippner, & Alan Vaughan (2023 rev. ed.) *Dream Telepathy: The Landmark ESP Experiments*. Santa Fe: Afterworlds Press.

manifests a secondary personality alleging itself to be a spirit named Elvira; Angelina, Maria's cousin, a child in her fifth year; and, finally, the Signora Annetta, Maria's mother. The two ladies and the child live together at Padua, and Dr. Ermacora is a familiar visitor at the house. A certain spontaneous dream of Angelina's, in which she seemed to see the so-called Elvira, led Dr. E. to try systematically whether he could determine Angelina's dreams by ordering "Elvira" to appear to her in sleep and make her dream according to his prescription. The experiments made were seventy in number and almost everyone succeeded. Dr. Ermacora, for reasons that he does not give, was unable to isolate Angelina from the two ladies, so the physical possibility was not precluded of Siga. Maria telling the child every night, after the details of the dream had been dictated in the evening, what she must report next morning. He considers it morally impossible, however, that the ladies should willfully play a trick on him; and believing that Signora Maria, if she coached Angelina at all, could only do so whilst herself asleep, he habitually locked and sealed Angelina into a separate room, and got Signora Annetta to sleep with Signora Maria, so as to detect any possible somnambulism. This nevertheless was not reported. He moreover prescribed dreams, the nature of whose details was incommunicable verbally, such as dreams of persons shown in photograph to Maria-Elvira, and afterwards identified in photograph by the child as having been seen in dreams; or dreams of instruments pictured in manufacturers' catalogues, and similarly discriminated in Maria's absence by the child from amongst other figures of instruments that contained the same mechanical elements and would have had to be described in the same words. The child's accounts also made it clear that the suggestion, whatever it was, must have been in optical, and not in verbal terms; for she often gave circumstances of the dream in words of her own limited experience that differed from the names used in prescribing the dream – "dog" for lamb, e.g. (she had never seen a lamb); "hail" for snow; "dark place down stairs" for cellar (she had never been in a cellar); "tramway" for ship (the steamboats at Venice which was the child's home are known as tramways) etc.

Dr. E.'s conclusion is that there was communication between the subliminal selves of Angelina and Maria. It is clear, in spite of the precautions taken, that much of the evidence hinges on the honesty of Siga. Maria and her mother, which Dr. Ermacora says it is impossible for him to doubt. I, knowing Dr. E. personally, and having been present at one of his experiments, do not doubt his honesty. He is a trained physicist, author of a thick book on electricity, and possesses an unusual experience of "psychic" phenomena, and a shrewd mind in comparing hypotheses. The editors do not doubt my honesty, or they will not print this report. But the facts are so unprecedented that the whole chain of honesties will seem a weak one, and the "rigorously scientific" mind will exercise its natural privilege, and doubtless promptly and authoritatively dismiss the narrative as "rot."

12

REVIEW OF *PHANTASMS OF THE LIVING* BY EDMUND GURNEY, FREDERIC W. H. MYERS, AND FRANK PODMORE

*P**hantasms of the Living*, one of the key early classics of psychical research, was largely the work of the psychologist and philosopher Edmund Gurney. That James was much impressed with this herculean effort we have already seen in Chapter 2, "What Psychical Research Has Accomplished." As seen elsewhere in this book, he also cited the work in many of his other writings on psychical research (as well as in *The Principles of Psychology*) and saw it as one of the evidential foundations upon which the new science should be built.

Phantasms of the Living. By Edmund Gurney, Frederic W. H. Myers, and Frank Podmore. 2 vols. London: Trübner, 1886.

This is a most extraordinary work – fourteen hundred large and closely printed pages by men of the rarest intellectual qualifications, for the purpose of setting on its legs again a belief which the common consent of the 'enlightened' has long ago relegated to the rubbish-heap of old wives' tales. In any reputable department of science the qualities displayed in these volumes would be reckoned superlatively good. Untiring zeal in collecting facts, and patience in seeking to make them accurate; learning, of the solidest sort, in discussing them; in theorizing, subtlety and originality, and, above all, fairness, for the work absolutely reeks with candor – this combination of characters is assuredly not found in every bit of so-called scientific research that is published in our day.

The book hardly admits of detailed criticism, so much depends on the minutiae of the special cases reported: so I will give a broad sketch of its contents. The title, *Phantasms of the Living*, expresses a theory on which the recorded facts are strong, but of which the latter are of course independent. The "facts" are instances of what are commonly called "apparitions." Collected for the Society of Psychical Research, their sifting and cataloguing is a laborious piece of work which has a substantive value, whatever their definitive explanation may prove to be. Very roughly speaking, there are reported in the book about seven hundred cases of sensorial phantasms which seem vaguely or closely connected with some distant contemporaneous event. The event, in about one-half of the cases, was someone's death. In addition to these cases, Mr. Gurney has collected about six hundred hallucinations seemingly irrelevant to any actual event, and thus has certainly a wider material to work upon than anyone who has yet studied the subject of phantasms. Of course, the rationalistic way of interpreting the coincidence of so large a number with a death or other event, is to call it chance. Such a large number of "veridical" phantasms occurring by chance would, however, imply an enormous total number of miscellaneous phantasms occurring all the while in the community. Mr. Gurney finds (to take the visual cases alone) that among 5,705 persons, interrogated at random, only 23 visual hallucinations had occurred in the last twelve years. And combining by the calculus of probabilities such data as the population drawn upon for the coincidence-cases, the adult population of the country, the number of deaths in the country within twelve years, etc., he comes to the conclusion that the odds against the chance occurrence of as many first-hand and well-attested veridical visual phantasms as his collection embraces, is as a trillion of trillions of trillions to 1. Of course, the data are extremely rough; and, in particular, the census of phantasms occurring at large in the community ought to be much wider than it is. But the veridical phantasms have, furthermore, many peculiarities. They are more apt to be visual than auditory. Casual hallucinations are oftener auditory. The person appearing is almost always recognized; not so in casual hallucinations. They tend to coincide with a particular form of outward event, viz., death. These and other features seem to make of them a natural group of phenomena.

The next best rationalistic explanation of them is that they are fictions, willful or innocent; and that Messrs. Gurney, Myers, and Podmore are victims, partly of the tendency to hoax, but mainly of the false memories and mythopoetic instincts of mankind. These possibilities do not escape our authors, but receive ample consideration at their hands. Nothing, in fact, is more striking than the zeal with which they cross-examine the witnesses; nothing more admirable than the labor they spend in testing the accuracy of the stories, so far as can be done by ransacking old newspapers for obituaries and the like. If a story contains a fire burning in a grate – *presto* the Greenwich records are searched to see whether the thermometer warranted a fire on that day; if it contains a medical practitioner, the medical register is consulted to make sure he is correct; etc. But obviously a hoax might keep all such accessories true, and a story true as to the main point might have grown false as to dates and accessories. It therefore comes back essentially to the investigator's instinct, or nose, as one might call it, for good and bad evidence. A born dupe will go astray, with every precaution; a born judge will keep the path, with few. *Saturday reviewers* will dispose of the work in the simplest possible way by treating the authors as born dupes. "Scientists" who prefer offhand methods will do the same. Other readers will be baffled, many convinced. The present writer finds that some of the cases accounted strong by the authors strike him in the reading as weak, while scruples shown by them in other cases seem to him fanciful. This is the pivot of the whole matter; for I suppose the improbability of the phantasms being veridical by chance, will, if the *stories* are true, be felt by everyone. Meanwhile it must be remembered, that, so far as expertness in judging of truth comes from training, no reader can possibly be as expert as the authors. The way to become expert in a matter is to get lots of experience of that particular matter. Neither a specialist in nervous diseases, nor a criminal lawyer, will be expert in dealing with these stories until he has had Messrs. Gurney's, Myers's, and Podmore's special education. Then his pathology, or his familiarity with false evidence, may also serve him in good stead. But in him, or in them, "gumption" will, after all, be the basis of superiority. How much of it the authors have, the future alone can decide.

One argument against the value of the evidence they rely on is drawn from the history of witchcraft. Nowhere, it is said (as by Mr. Lecky in his *Rationalism* [*History of the Rise and Influence of the Spirit of Rationalism in Europe*, 1865]), is better-attested evidence for facts; yet the evidence is now utterly discredited, and the facts, then apparently so plenty, occur no more. Mr. Gurney considers this objection, and comes to an extremely interesting result. After "careful search through about 260 books on the subject (including the principal ones of the sixteenth, seventeenth, and eighteenth centuries) and a large number of contemporary records of trials," he affirms that the only facts of witchcraft for which there is any good evidence whatever are those neuropathic phenomena (trance, anesthesia, hysteria, "suggestion," etc.) which, so far from being now discredited, are more than ever ascertained; while the marvels like conveyance through the air, transformation into animals, etc., do not rest on a single first-hand statement made by a person not "possessed" or under torture.

The authors' theory of veridical phantasms is that they are caused by thought-transference. The ghost theory and the "astral-form" theory are criticized as unsatisfactory (ghosts of clothes, phantasms not seen by all present, etc.). Thought-transference has been once for all established as a *vera causa*. Why not assume that even the impressions announcing death were made during the last moments of the dying person's life?

Where the apparition is to several witnesses, this explanation has to be much strained; and, in spite of Messrs. Myers's and Gurney's ingenuity, I can hardly feel as if they had made out a very plausible case. But any theory helps the analysis of facts; and I do not understand that Messrs. Gurney and Myers hold their telepathic explanation to have at present much more than this provisional sort of importance.

I have given my impression of the ability of the work. My impression of its success is this: the authors have placed a matter which, previous to them, had been handled so loosely as not to compel the attention of scientific minds, in a position which makes inattention impossible. They have established a presumption, to say the least, which it will need further statistical research either to undo or to confirm. They have at the same time made further statistical research easy; for their volumes will certainly stimulate the immediate registration and publication, on a large scale, of cases of hallucinations (both veridical and casual) which but for them would have been kept private. The next twenty-five years will then probably decide the question. Either a flood of confirmatory phenomena, caught in the act, will pour in, in consequence of their work; or it will *not* pour in – and then we shall legitimately enough explain the stories here preserved as mixtures of odd coincidence with fiction. In the one case Messrs. Gurney and Myers will have made an epoch in science, and will take rank among the immortals as the first effective prophets of a doctrine whose ineffectual prophets have been many. In the other case they will have made as great a wreck and misuse of noble faculties as the sun is often called to look down upon. The prudent bystander will be in no haste to prophesy; or, if he prophesy, he will hedge. I may be lacking in prudence; but I feel that I ought to describe the total effect left at present by the book on my mind. It is a strong suspicion that its authors will prove to be on the winning side. It will surprise me after this if neither "telepathy" nor "veridical hallucinations" are among the beliefs which the future tends to confirm.

13

A SUGGESTION ABOUT MYSTICISM

In this essay, written in 1910, James introduces the notion of extended consciousness to explain mystical experiences. As with some of his other ideas, in various interpretations this one remains current in conceptualizations about psychic phenomena.

Though rarely reprinted, the essay is an important piece of James's thinking on the metaphysics of psychical research, serving to connect his interests in the subject with religion and extraordinary experiences. He articulated this line of thought in a 1902 letter to the Cambridge philosopher James Ward. Concerning the "supernormal cognitions" of Mrs. Piper and other psychic phenomena, he wrote, "The relation of it all to religion is through mysticism. I can't ignore the vital prominence of that sort of experience in the religious life."[1] The examples he cites, however, are typically concerned more with telepathy than with survival.

Although James states at the beginning that he is writing from the perspective of an outsider, a large part of the essay is taken up with descriptions of his own unusual experiences in order to illustrate his ideas. The essay is perhaps the closest he came to making a personal statement on the subject, and it may be no coincidence that it was written only six months before his death.

* * *

---

[1] Letter from William James to James Ward, July 29, 1902. In Robert Barton Perry (1935) *The Thought and Character of William James*, Vol. II. Boston: Little Brown, 650.

Much interest in the subject of religious mysticism has been shown in philosophic circles of late years. Most of the writings I have seen have treated the subject from the outside, for I know of no one who has spoken as having the direct authority of experience in favor of his views. I also am an outsider, and very likely what I say will prove the fact loudly enough to readers who possibly may stand within the pale. Nevertheless, since between outsiders one is as good as another, I will not leave my suggestion unexpressed.

The suggestion, stated very briefly, is that states of mystical intuition may be only very sudden and great extensions of the ordinary "field of consciousness." Concerning the causes of such extensions I have no suggestion to make; but the extension itself would, if my view be correct, consist in an immense spreading of the margin of the field, so that knowledge ordinarily transmarginal would become included, and the ordinary margin would grow more central. Fechner's "wave-scheme" will diagrammatize the alteration, as I conceive it, if we suppose that the wave of present awareness, steep above the horizontal line that represents the plane of the usual "threshold," slopes away below it very gradually in all directions. A fall of the threshold, however caused, would, under these circumstances, produce the state of things which we see on an unusually flat shore at the ebb of a spring tide. Vast tracts usually covered are then revealed to view, but nothing rises more than a few inches above the water's bed, and great parts of the scene are submerged again, whenever a wave washes over them.

Some persons have naturally a very wide, others a very narrow, field of consciousness. The narrow field may be represented by an unusually steep form of the wave. When by any accident the threshold lowers, in persons of this type—I speak here from direct personal experience—so that the field widens and the relations of its center to matters usually subliminal come into view, the larger panorama perceived fills the mind with exhilaration and sense of mental power. It is a refreshing experience; and—such is now my hypothesis—we only have to suppose it to occur in an exceptionally extensive form, to give us a mystical paroxysm, if such a term be allowed.

A few remarks about the field of consciousness may be needed to give more definiteness to my hypothesis. The field is composed at all times of a mass of present sensation, in a cloud of memories, emotions, concepts, etc. Yet these ingredients, which have to be named separately, are not separate, as the conscious field contains them. Its form is that of a much-at-once, in the unity of which the sensations, memories, concepts, impulses, etc., coalesce and are dissolved. The present field as a whole came continuously out of its predecessor and will melt into its successor as continuously again, one sensation-mass passing into another sensation-mass and giving the character of a gradually changing *present* to the experience, while the memories and concepts carry time-coefficients which place whatever is present in a temporal perspective more or less vast.

When, now, the threshold falls, what comes into view is not the next mass of *sensation*; for sensation requires new physical stimulations to produce it, and no alteration of a purely mental threshold can create these. Only in case the physical stimuli were already at work subliminally, preparing the next sensation, would whatever sub-sensation was already prepared reveal itself when the threshold fell. But with the memories, concepts, and conational states, the case is different. Nobody knows exactly how far we are "marginally" conscious of these at ordinary times, or how far beyond the "margin" of our present thought transmarginal consciousness of them may exist.[2] There is at any rate no definite bound set between what is central and what is marginal in consciousness, and the margin itself has no definite bound *a parte foris* [on the outside]. It is like the field of vision, which the slightest movement of the eye will extend, revealing objects that always stood there to be known. My hypothesis is that a movement of the threshold downwards will similarly bring a mass of subconscious memories, conceptions, emotional feelings, and perceptions of relation, etc., into view all at once; and that if this enlargement of the nimbus that surrounds the sensational present is vast enough, while no one of the items it contains attracts our attention singly, we shall have the conditions fulfilled for a kind of consciousness in all essential respects like that termed mystical. It will be transient, if the change of threshold is transient. It will be of reality, enlargement, and illumination, possibly rapturously so. It will be of unification, for the present coalesces in it with ranges of the remote quite out of its reach under ordinary circumstances; and the sense of *relation* will be greatly enhanced. Its form will be intuitive or

---

[2] Transmarginal or subliminal, the terms are synonymous. Some psychologists deny the existence of such consciousness altogether (A. H. Pierce, for example, and Münsterberg apparently). Others, e.g., Bergson, make it exist and carry the whole freight of our past. Others again (as Myers) would have it extend (in the "telepathic" mode of communication) from one person's mind into another's. For the purposes of my hypothesis I have to postulate its existence; and once postulating it, I prefer not to set any definite bounds to its extent.

perceptual, not conceptual, for the remembered or conceived objects in the enlarged field are supposed not to attract the attention singly, but only to give the sense of a tremendous *muchness* suddenly revealed. If they attracted attention separately, we should have the ordinary steep-waved consciousness, and the mystical character would depart.

Such is my suggestion. Persons who *know* something of mystical experience will no doubt find in it much to criticize. If any such shall do so with definiteness, it will have amply served its purpose of helping our understanding of mystical states to become more precise.

The notion I have tried (at such expense of metaphor) to set forth was originally suggested to me by certain experiences of my own, which could only be described as very sudden and incomprehensible enlargements of the conscious field, bringing with them a curious sense of cognition of real fact. All have occurred within the past five years; three of them were similar in type; the fourth was unique.

In each of the three like cases, the experience broke in abruptly upon a perfectly commonplace situation and lasted perhaps less than two minutes. In one instance I was engaged in conversation, but I doubt whether the interlocutor noticed my abstraction. What happened each time was that I seemed all at once to be reminded of a past experience; and this reminiscence, ere I could conceive or name it distinctly, developed into something further that belonged with it, this in turn into something further still, and so on, until the process faded out, leaving me amazed at the sudden vision of increasing ranges of distant fact of which I could give no articulate account. The mode of consciousness was perceptual, not conceptual—the field expanding so fast that there seemed no time for conception or identification to get in its work. There was a strongly-exciting sense that my knowledge of past (or present?) reality was enlarging pulse by pulse, but so rapidly that my intellectual processes could not keep up the pace. The *content* was thus entirely lost to retrospection—it sank into the limbo into which dreams vanish as we gradually awake. The feeling—I won't call it belief—that I had had a sudden *opening*, had seen through a window, as it were, distant realities that incomprehensibly belonged with my own life, was so acute that I cannot shake it off today.

This conviction of fact-revealed, together with the perceptual form of the experience and the inability to make articulate report, are all characters of mystical states. The point of difference is that in my case certain special directions only, in the field of reality, seemed to get suddenly uncovered, whereas in classical mystical experiences it appears rather as if the whole of reality were uncovered at once. *Uncovering* of some sort is the essence of the phenomenon, at any rate, and is what, in the language of the Fechnerian wave-metaphor, I have used the expression "fall of the threshold" to denote.

My fourth experience of uncovering had to do with dreams. I was suddenly intromitted into the cognizance of a pair of dreams that I could not remember myself to have had, yet they seemed somehow to connect with me. I despair of giving the reader any just idea of the bewildering confusion of mind into which I was thrown by this, the most intensely peculiar experience of my whole life. I wrote a full memorandum of it a couple of days after it happened, and appended some reflections. Even though it should cast no light on the conditions of mysticism, it seems as if this record might be worthy of publication, simply as a contribution to the descriptive literature of pathological mental states. I let it follow, therefore, as originally written, with only a few words altered to make the account more clear.

"San Francisco, Feb. 14th 1906. – The night before last, in my bed at Stanford University, I woke at about 7:30 a.m., from a quiet dream of some sort, and whilst gathering my waking wits, seemed suddenly to get mixed up with reminiscences of a dream of an entirely different sort, which seemed to telescope, as it were, into the first one, a dream very elaborate, of lions, and tragic. I concluded this to have been a previous dream of the same sleep; but the apparent mingling of two dreams was something very queer, which I had never before experienced.

"On the following night (Feb. 12-13) I awoke suddenly from my first sleep, which appeared to have been very heavy, in the middle of a dream, in thinking of which I became suddenly confused by the contents of two other dreams that shuffled themselves abruptly in between the parts of the first dream, and of which I couldn't grasp the origin. Whence come *these dreams*? I asked. They were close to *me*, and fresh, as if I had just dreamed them; and yet they were far away *from the first dream*. The contents of the three had absolutely no connection. One had a cockney atmosphere, it had happened to someone in London. The other two were American. One involved the trying on of a coat (was this the dream I seemed to wake from?) the other was a sort of nightmare and had to do with soldiers. Each had a wholly distinct emotional atmosphere that made its individuality discontinuous with that of the others. And yet, in a moment, as these three dreams alternately telescoped into and out of each other, and I seemed to myself to have been their common dreamer, they seemed quite as distinctly *not* to have been dreamed in succession, in that one sleep. *When*, then? Not on a previous night, either. *When*, then, and *which* was the one out of which I had just awakened? *I could no longer tell*: one was as close to me as the others, and yet they entirely repelled each other, and I seemed thus to belong to three different dream-systems at once, no one of which would connect itself either with the others or with my waking life. I began to feel curiously confused and scared, and tried to wake myself up wider, but I seemed already wide-awake. Presently cold shivers of dread ran over me: *am I getting into other people's dreams?* Is this a "telepathic" experience? Or an invasion of double (or treble) personality? Or is it a thrombus in a cortical artery? and the beginning of a general mental "confusion" and disorientation which is going on to develop who knows how far?

"Decidedly I was losing hold of my "self," and making acquaintance with a quality of mental distress that I had never known before, its nearest analogue being the sinking, giddying anxiety that one may have when, in the woods, one discovers that one is really "lost." Most human troubles look towards a terminus. Most fears point in a direction, and concentrate towards a climax. Most assaults of the evil one may be met by bracing oneself against something, one's principles, one's courage, one's will, one's pride. But in this experience all was diffusion from a center, and foothold swept away, the brace itself disintegrating all the faster as one needed its support more direly. Meanwhile vivid perception (or remembrance) of the various dreams kept coming over me in alternation. Whose? *whose?* WHOSE? Unless I can *attach* them, I am swept out to sea with no horizon and no bond, getting *lost*. The idea aroused the "creeps" again, and with it the fear of again falling asleep and renewing the process. It had begun the previous night, but then the confusion had only gone one step, and had seemed simply curious. *This* was the second step—where might I be after a third step had been taken? My teeth chattered at the thought.

"At the same time I found myself filled with a new pity towards persons passing into dementia with *Verwirrtheit* [confusion], or into invasions of secondary personality. We regard them as simply *curious*; but what *they* want in the awful drift of their being out of its customary self, is any principle of steadiness to hold on to. We ought to assure them and reassure them that we will stand by them, and recognize the true self in them to the end. We ought to let them know that we are with *them* and not (as too often we must seem to them) a part of the world that but confirms and publishes their deliquescence.

"Evidently, I was in full possession of my reflective wits; and whenever I thus objectively thought of the situation in which I was, my anxieties ceased. But there was a tendency to relapse into the dreams and reminiscences, and to relapse vividly; and then the confusion recommenced, along with the emotion of dread lest it should develop farther.

"Then I looked at my watch. Half-past twelve! Midnight, therefore. And this gave me another reflective idea. Habitually, on going to bed, I fall into a very deep slumber from which I never naturally awaken until after two. I never awaken, therefore, from a midnight dream, as I did tonight, so of midnight dreams my ordinary consciousness retains no recollection. My sleep seemed terribly heavy as I woke tonight. Dream states carry dream memories—why may not the two succedaneous dreams (whichever two of the three *were* succedaneous) be memories of *twelve o'clock dreams of previous nights*, swept in, along with the just-fading dream, into the just-waking system of memory? Why, in short, may I not be tapping, in a way precluded by my ordinary habit of life, *the midnight stratum* of my past experiences?

"This idea gave great relief—I felt now as if I were in full possession of my *anima rationalis* [rational animal, or human nature]. I turned on my light, resolving to read myself to sleep. But I didn't read, I felt drowsy instead, and, putting out the light, soon was in the arms of Morpheus.

"I woke again two or three times before daybreak with no dream-experiences, and finally, with a curious, but not alarming, confusion between two dreams, similar to that which I had had the previous morning, I awoke to the new day at seven.

"Nothing peculiar happened the following night, so the thing seems destined not to develop any further."[3]

---

[3] I print the rest of my memorandum in the shape of a note:

"Several ideas suggest themselves that make the observation instructive.

"First, the general notion, now gaining ground in mental medicine, that certain mental maladies may be foreshadowed in dream-life, and that therefore the study of the latter may be profitable.

"Then the specific suggestion, that states of "confusion," loss of personality, *apraxia*, etc., so often taken to indicate cortical lesion or degeneration of dementic type, may be very superficial functional affections. In my own case the confusion was *foudroyante*—a state of consciousness unique and unparalleled in my sixty-four years of the world's experience; yet it alternated

The distressing confusion of mind in this experience was the exact opposite of mystical illumination, and equally unmystical was the definiteness of what was perceived. But the exaltation of the sense of relation was mystical (the perplexity all revolved about the fact that the three dreams *both did and did not belong in the most intimate way together*); and the sense that *reality was being uncovered* was mystical in the highest degree. To this day I feel that those extra dreams were dreamed in reality, but when, where, and by whom, I cannot guess.

In the *Open Court* for December, 1909, Mr. Frederick Hall narrates a fit of ether-mysticism which agrees with my formula very well. When one of his doctors made a remark to the other, he chuckled, for he realized that these friends "believed they saw real things and causes, but they *didn't*, and I did. ... I was where the causes *were* and to see them required no more mental ability than to recognize a color as blue. ... The knowledge of how little (the doctors) actually did see, coupled with their evident feeling that they saw all there was, was funny to the last degree. ... They knew as little of the real causes as does the child who, viewing a passing train and noting its revolving wheels, supposes that they, turning of themselves, give to coaches and locomotive their momentum. Or imagine a man seated in a boat, surrounded by dense fog, and out of the fog seeing a flat stone leap from the crest of one wave to another. *If he had always sat thus*, his explanations must be very crude as compared with those of a man whose eyes could pierce fog, and who saw upon the shore the boy skipping stones. In some such way the remarks of the two physicians seemed to me like the last two "skips" of a stone thrown from my side. ... All that was essential in the remark I knew before it was made. Thus to discover convincingly and for

---

quickly with perfectly rational states, as this record shows. It seems, therefore, merely as if the threshold between the rational and the morbid state had, in my case, been temporarily lowered, and as if similar confusions might be very near the line of possibility in all of us.

"There are also the suggestions of a telepathic entrance into someone else's dreams, and of a doubling up of personality. In point of fact I don't know now "who" had those three dreams, or which one "I" first woke up from, so quickly did they substitute themselves back and forth for each other, discontinuously. Their discontinuity was the pivot of the situation. My sense of it was as "vivid" and "original" an experience as anything Hume could ask for. And yet they kept telescoping!

"Then there is the notion that by waking at certain hours we may tap distinct strata of ancient dream-memory."

myself, that the things which are unseen are those of real importance, this was sufficiently stimulating."

It is evident that Mr. Hall's marginal field got enormously enlarged by the ether, yet so little defined as to its particulars that what he perceived was mainly the thoroughgoing causal integration of its whole content. That this perception brought with it a tremendous feeling of importance and superiority is a matter of course.

I have treated the phenomenon under discussion as if it consisted in the uncovering of tracts of *consciousness*. Is the consciousness already there waiting to be uncovered? and is it a veridical revelation of reality? These are questions on which I do not touch. In the subjects of the experience the "emotion of conviction" is always strong, and sometimes absolute. The ordinary psychologist disposes of the phenomenon under the conveniently "scientific" head of *petit mal* [absence seizure], if not of "bosh" or "rubbish." But we know so little of the noetic value of abnormal mental states of any kind that in my opinion we had better keep an open mind and collect facts sympathetically for a long time to come. We shall not *understand* these alterations of consciousness either in this generation or in the next.

PART III

MEDIUMSHIP

14

REPORT OF THE COMMITTEE ON MEDIUMISTIC PHENOMENA

What follows are James's first published comments on the mediumship of Mrs. Leonora Piper, published in the 1886 *Proceedings of the American Society for Psychical Research*. He is characteristically cautious, and his application of his psychological training in testing Piper's hypnotizability makes for fascinating reading. James had already concluded that Piper was "in possession of a power as yet unexplained" – a conviction he seems to have held for the rest of his life.

The Committee on Mediumistic Phenomena has no definitely concluded piece of work to offer. An account of what has been done during the year, however, with a few reflections, may not be out of place.

My own time was chiefly divided between two mediums—one a trance-medium, whom, at her request, I shall call Mrs. P.; the other, Miss Helen Berry, whose public "materializing" manifestations are reputed to be among the best of their class.

Concerning Miss Berry, there is little to say. Test conditions against fraud are not habitually offered at her seances. On one occasion it was granted to [Unitarian minister] Mr. [Minot J.] Savage to sit behind the cabinet, others being in front, whilst I explored it after the mediums entrance, and found no confederate concealed. A trap-door seemed out of the question. In a minute two forms emerged from the cabinet. But this was our first sitting, and for certain reasons we cannot call the experiment satisfactory until we have an opportunity of taking part in it again. The real test of the Berry's genuineness is supposed to be the resemblance of the forms to deceased friends of the sitters, and the character of what they say. A large amount of testimony can be collected from sitters as to the unmistakable identity of the forms with their dead wives, husbands, brothers, etc.

I visited twelve seances, and took with me, or sent, personal friends enough to have, in all, first-hand reports of thirty-five visits, embracing sixteen or seventeen seances. No spirit form came directly to any one of us, so we offer no opinion regarding the phenomena.

To turn to the much simpler and more satisfactory case of Mrs. P. This lady can at will pass into a trance condition, in which she is "controlled" by a power purporting to be the spirit of a French doctor, who serves as intermediary between the sitter and deceased friends. This is the ordinary type of trance-mediumship at the present day. I have myself witnessed a dozen of her trances, and have testimony at first hand from twenty-five sitters, all but one of whom were virtually introduced to Mrs. P. by myself.

Of five of the sittings we have verbatim stenographic reports. Twelve of the sitters, who in most cases sat singly, got nothing from the medium but unknown names or trivial talk. Four of these were members of the society, and of their sittings verbatim reports were taken.

Fifteen of the sitters were surprised at the communications they received, names and facts being mentioned at the first interview which it seemed improbable should have been known to the medium in a normal way. The probability that she possessed no clue as to the sitter's identity was, I believe, in each and all of these fifteen cases, sufficient. But of only one of them is there a stenographic report; so that, unfortunately for the medium, the evidence in her favor is, although more abundant, less exact in quality than some of that which will be counted against her.

Of these fifteen sitters, five, all ladies, were blood relatives, and two (I myself being one) were men connected by marriage with the family to which they belonged. Two other connections of this family are included in the twelve who got nothing. The medium showed a most startling intimacy with this family's affairs, talking of many matters known to no one outside, and which *gossip* could not possibly have conveyed to her ears. The details would prove nothing to the reader, unless printed *in extenso*, with full notes by the sitters. It reverts, after all, to personal conviction. My own conviction is not evidence, but it seems fitting to record it. I am persuaded of the medium's honesty, and of the genuineness of her trance; and although at first disposed to think that the "hits" she made were either lucky coincidences, or the result of knowledge on her part of who the sitter was and of his or her family affairs, I now believe her to be in possession of a power as yet unexplained.

The most promising way of investigating phenomena like this seems to be that of learning a great deal about one "subject," who, of course, ought to be a good specimen of the class. Hitherto we have heard a little about a great many subjects. Stenographic reports are expensive, but they seem indispensable for a conclusive discussion of the facts. They do away with doubts about the veracity of the sitter's memory; and they enable us to make a comparison of different sittings, which without them is hardly possible at all. Questions arise as to the irrelevant names and facts which almost every sitting to some extent contains. Are they improvisations of the moment? Are they in themselves right and coherent, but addressed to the wrong sitter? Or are they vestiges of former sittings, now emerging as part of the automatism of the medium's brain? A reading of the stenographic reports already taken makes it probable that, for some of them at least, this last explanation is correct. "Spirits" originally appearing to me have appeared in the sittings of others who knew nothing either of their persons or their names.

What science wants is a *context* to make the trance phenomena continuous with other physiological and psychological facts. Curious to ascertain whether there were continuity between the medium-trance and the ordinary hypnotic trance, I made some observations *ad hoc* upon Mrs. P. My first two attempts to hypnotize her were unsuccessful. Between the second time and the third, I suggested to her "control" in the medium-trance that he should make her a mesmeric subject for me. He agreed. (A suggestion of this sort made by the operator in one hypnotic trance would probably have some effect on the next.) She became partially hypnotized on the third trial; but the effect was so slight that I ascribe it rather to the effect of repetition than to the suggestion made. By the fifth trial she had become a pretty good hypnotic subject, as far as muscular phenomena and automatic imitations of speech and gesture go; but I could not affect her consciousness, or otherwise get her beyond this point. Her condition in this semi-hypnosis is very different from her medium-trance. The latter is characterized by great muscular unrest, even her ears moving vigorously in a way impossible to her in her waking state. But in hypnosis her muscular relaxation and weakness are extreme. She often makes several efforts to speak ere her voice becomes audible; and to get a strong contraction of the hand, for example, express manipulation and suggestion must be practiced. The automatic imitations I spoke of are in the first instance very weak, and only become strong after repetition. Her pupils contract in the medium-trance. Suggestions to the "control" that he should make her recollect after the trance what she had been saying were accepted, but had no result. In the hypnotic trance such a suggestion will often make the patient remember all that has happened.

No sign of thought-transference—as tested by card and diagram-guessing—has been found in her, either in the hypnotic condition just described, or immediately after it; although her "control" in the medium-trance has said that he would bring them about. So far as tried (only twice), no right guessing of cards in the medium-trance. She was twice tried with epistolary letters in the medium-trance—once indicating the contents in a way rather surprising to the sitter; once failing. In her normal waking state she made one hundred and twenty-seven guesses at playing-cards looked at by me—I sometimes touching her, sometimes not. Suit right (first guess) thirty-eight times—an excess of only six over the "probable" number of thirty-two—obviously affording no distinct evidence of thought-transference. Trials of the "willing game," and attempts at automatic writing, gave similarly negative results. So far as the evidence goes, then, her medium-trance seems an isolated feature in her psychology. This would of itself be an important result if it could be established and generalized, but the record is obviously too imperfect for confident conclusions to be drawn from it in any direction. Being compelled by other work to abandon the subject for the present, these notes are published merely as a suggestion of lines of inquiry which others may be better fitted than myself to carry out.

If a good trance subject could be obtained for the society at the outset of her or his career, and kept from doing miscellaneous work until patiently and thoroughly observed and experimented on, with stenographic reports of trances, and as much attention paid to failures and errors as to successes, I am disposed to think that the results would in any event be of scientific value, and would be worth the somewhat high expense which they necessarily would entail. If the friends of spiritualism would contribute money for the thorough carrying out of any such scheme, they would probably do as much as by any one thing could be done to bring about the "recognition" of trance-mediumship by scientific men.

As for the other kinds of mediumistic phenomena, I have during the past year been very much struck by the *volume* of evidence which can be collected in their favor. But the mere volume of evidence is of no account unless it can be proved that the evidence is likely to be of the ordinary human sort, bad and good mixed together in the usual proportion. If it is possible that it is unusually bad in *quality*, the quantity of it is of little account. Now, that there *are* reasons for believing its quality to be in these matters below the average, no one familiar with the facts can doubt. Only the establishment of one or two absolutely and coercively proven cases—of materialization, for example—will show that the hearsay evidence for *that* phenomenon may be mixed. And only *then* can the volume of evidence already extant on the subject be taken into account by one who has no direct personal experience on which to rely. The ordinary disbeliever rules out all hearsay evidence in advance. The believer accepts far too much of it, because he knows that some of it is good. The committee of the society should first devote itself to the very exact and complete study of a few particular cases. These may consume much labor and time. But if, after studying them, it should reach favorable conclusions, it would do vastly more to make the vaguer testimony already extant influential with the society as a whole than it could do by discussing such testimony now.

15

A RECORD OF OBSERVATIONS OF CERTAIN PHENOMENA OF TRANCE

This piece was written at the request of Fredric Myers, who wanted James's further perspectives on the mediumship of Leonora Piper. It takes the form of a letter to Myers and was published in the *Proceedings of the Society for Psychical Research* for 1890, as Part III of the extensive and detailed reports on the Piper case by Sir Oliver Lodge and Walter Leaf.[1] The report by Richard Hodgson, to which James refers in this letter, was actually not published until 1892.[2] It gives further details of Hodgson's and James's investigations of Piper's mediumship.

In the letter, we can discern a further evolution of James's thinking in relation to psychical research. Though his scientific skepticism remains, gone are the attempts to understand mediumship by reference to hypnotism or other comparatively mundane phenomena.

---

[1] "A Record of Observations of Certain Phenomena of Trance" in *Proceedings of the Society for Psychical Research* 6 (1890). The sections by each author are as follows: Frederic Myers, 436-442; Oliver Lodge, 443-557, 647-650; Walter Leaf, 558-646; William James, 651–659.

[2] Richard Hodgson's report, also titled "A Record of Observations of Certain Phenomena of Trance," may be found in *Proceedings of the Society for Psychical Research* (1892) 8, 1-167.

Instead, the question is whether Piper's abilities are a form of telepathy ("thought-transference") or genuine communication with souls of the dead. It is also the first time he advanced his "cosmic reservoir" theory. James quoted at some length from his "Report of the Committee on Mediumistic Phenomena," presented in the previous chapter. The duplicated passages have been omitted here.

Dear Mr. Myers,

You ask for a record of my own experiences with Mrs. Piper, to be incorporated in the account of her to be published in your *Proceedings*. I regret to be unable to furnish you with any direct notes of sittings beyond those which Mr. Hodgson will have already supplied. I admit that in not having taken more notes I was most derelict, and can only cry *peccavi* [*mea culpa*]. The excuse (if it be one) for my negligence was that I wished primarily to satisfy *myself* about Mrs. Piper; and feeling that as evidence for others no notes but stenographic notes would have value, and not being able to get these, I seldom took any. I still think that as far as influencing public opinion goes, the bare fact that So-and-so and So-and-so have been convinced by their personal experience that "there is something in mediumship" is the essential thing. Public opinion follows leaders much more than it follows evidence. Professor Huxley's bare "endorsement" of Mrs. Piper, e.g., would be more effective than volumes of notes by such as I. Practically, however, I ought to have taken them, and the sight of your more scientific methods makes me doubly rue my sins.

Under the circumstances, the only thing I can do is to give you my present state of belief as to Mrs. Piper's powers, with a simple account from memory of the steps which have led me to it.

I made Mrs. Piper's acquaintance in the autumn of 1885. My wife's mother, Mrs. Gibbens, had been told of her by a friend, during the previous summer, and never having seen a medium before, had paid her a visit out of curiosity. She returned with the statement that Mrs. P. had given her a long string of names of members of the family, mostly Christian names, together with facts about the persons mentioned and their relations to each other, the knowledge of which on her part was incomprehensible without supernormal powers. My sister-in-law went the next day, with still better results, as she related them. Amongst other things, the medium had accurately described the circumstances of the writer of a letter which she held against her forehead, after Miss G. had given it to her. The letter was in Italian, and its writer was known to but two persons in this country.

(I may add that on a later occasion my wife and I took another letter from this same person to Mrs. P., who went on to speak of him in a way which identified him unmistakably again. On a third occasion, two years later, my sister-in-law and I being again with Mrs. P., she reverted in her trance to these letters, and then gave us the writer's name, which she said she had not been able to get on the former occasion.)

But to revert to the beginning. I remember playing the *esprit fort* [person of strong character] on that occasion before my feminine relatives, and seeking to explain by simple considerations the marvelous character of the facts which they brought back. This did not, however, prevent me from going myself a few days later, in company with my wife, to get a direct personal impression. The names of none of us up to this meeting had been announced to Mrs. P., and Mrs. J. and I were, of course, careful to make no reference to our relatives who had preceded. The medium, however, when entranced, repeated most of the names of "spirits" whom she had announced on the two former occasions and added others. The names came with difficulty, and were only gradually made perfect. My wife's father's name of Gibbens was announced first as Niblin, then as Giblin. A child Herman (whom we had lost the previous year) had his name spelled out as Herrin. I think that in no case were both Christian and surnames given on this visit. But the *facts predicated* of the persons named made it in many instances impossible not to recognize the particular individuals who were talked about. We took particular pains on this occasion to give the Phinuit control no help over his difficulties and to ask no leading questions. In the light of subsequent experience I believe this not to be the best policy. For it often happens, if you give this trance personage a name or some small fact for the lack of which he is brought to a standstill, that he will then start off with a copious flow of additional talk, containing in itself an abundance of "tests."

My impression after this first visit was that Mrs. P. was either possessed of supernormal powers, or knew the members of my wife's family by sight and had by some lucky coincidence become acquainted with such a multitude of their domestic circumstances as to produce the startling impression which she did. My later knowledge of her sittings and personal acquaintance with her has led me absolutely to reject the latter explanation, and to believe that she has supernormal powers.

I visited her a dozen times that winter, sometimes alone, sometimes with my wife, once in company with the Rev. M. J. Savage. I sent a large number of persons to her, wishing to get the results of as many first sittings as possible. I made appointments myself for most of these people, whose names were in no instance announced to the medium. In the spring of 1886 I published a brief "Report of the Committee on Mediumistic Phenomena" in the *Proceedings of the American Society for Psychical Research* [...].

I dropped my inquiries into Mrs. Piper's mediumship for a period of about two years, having satisfied myself that there was a genuine mystery there, but being over-freighted with time-consuming duties, and feeling that any adequate circumnavigation of the phenomena would be too protracted a task for me to aspire just then to undertake. I saw her once, half accidentally, however, during that interval, and in the spring of 1889 saw her four times again. In the fall of 1889 she paid us a visit of a week at our country house in New Hampshire, and I then learned to know her personally better than ever before, and had confirmed in me the belief that she is an absolutely simple and genuine person. No one, when challenged, can give "evidence" to others for such beliefs as this. Yet we all live by them from day to day, and practically I should be willing now to stake as much money on Mrs. Piper's honesty as on that of anyone I know, and am quite satisfied to leave my reputation for wisdom or folly, so far as human nature is concerned, to stand or fall by this declaration.

As for the explanation of her trance phenomena, I have none to offer. The *primâ facie* theory, which is that of spirit-control, is hard to reconcile with the extreme triviality of most of the communications. What real spirit, at last able to revisit his wife on this earth, but would find something better to say than that she had changed the place of his photograph? And yet that is the sort of remark to which the spirits introduced by the mysterious Phinuit are apt to confine themselves. I must admit, however, that Phinuit has other moods. He has several times, when my wife and myself were sitting together with him, suddenly started off on long lectures to us about our inward defects and outward shortcomings, which were very earnest, as well as subtile morally and psychologically, and impressive in a high degree. These discourses, though given in Phinuit's own person, were very different in style from his more usual talk, and probably superior to anything that the medium could produce in the same line in her natural state. Phinuit himself, however, bears every appearance of being a fictitious being. His French, so far as he has been able to display it to me, has been limited to a few phrases of salutation, which may easily have had their rise in the medium's "unconscious" memory; he has never been able to understand *my* French; and the crumbs of information which he gives about his earthly career are, as you know, so few, vague, and unlikely sounding as to suggest the romancing of one whose stock of materials for invention is excessively reduced. He is, however, as he actually shows himself, a definite human individual, with immense tact and patience, and great desire to please and be regarded as infallible. With respect to the rough and slangy style which he so often affects, it should be said that the Spiritualistic tradition here in America is all in favor of the "spirit-control" being a grotesque and somewhat saucy personage. The *Zeitgeist* has always much to do with shaping trance phenomena, so that a "control" of that temperament is what one would naturally expect. Mr. Hodgson will already have informed you of the similarity between Phinuit's name and that of the "control" of the medium at whose house Mrs. Piper was first entranced. The most remarkable thing about the Phinuit personality seems to me the extraordinary tenacity and minuteness of his memory. The medium has been visited by many hundreds of sitters, half of them, perhaps, being strangers who have come but once. To each Phinuit gives an hourful of disconnected fragments of talk about persons living, dead, or imaginary, and events past, future, or unreal. What normal waking memory could keep this chaotic mass of stuff together? Yet Phinuit does so; for the chances seem to be, that if a sitter should go back after years of interval, the medium, when once entranced, would recall the minutest incidents of the earlier interview, and begin by recapitulating much of what had then been said. So far as I can discover, Mrs. Piper's waking memory is not remarkable, and the whole constitution of her trance memory is something which I am at a loss to understand. But I will say nothing more of Phinuit, because, aided by our friends in France, you are already systematically seeking to establish or disprove him as a former native of this world.

Phinuit is generally the medium of communication between other spirits and the sitter. But two other *soi-disant* [self-styled] spirits have, in my presence, assumed direct "control" of Mrs. Piper. One purported to be the late Mr. E. The other was an aunt of mine who died last year in New York. I have already sent you the only account I can give of my earliest experiences with the "E. control." The first messages came through Phinuit, about a year ago, when, after two years of non-intercourse with Mrs. Piper, she lunched one day at our house and gave my wife and myself a sitting afterwards. It was bad enough; and I confess that the human being in me was so much stronger than the man of science that I was too disgusted with Phinuit's tiresome twaddle even to note it down. When later the phenomenon developed into pretended direct speech from E. himself I regretted this, for a complete record would have been useful. I can now merely say that neither then, nor at any other time, was there to my mind the slightest inner verisimilitude in the personation. But the failure to produce a more plausible E. speaks directly in favor of the non-participation of the medium's *conscious* mind in the performance. She could so easily have coached herself to be more effective.

Her trance talk about my own family shows the same innocence. The skeptical theory of her successes is that she keeps a sort of detective bureau open upon the world at large, so that whoever may call is pretty sure to find her prepared with facts about his life. Few things could have been easier, in Boston, than for Mrs. Piper to collect facts about my own father's family for use in my sittings with her. But although my father, my mother, and a deceased brother were repeatedly announced as present, nothing but their bare names ever came out, except a hearty message of thanks from my father that I had "published the book." I *had* published his *Literary Remains*; but when Phinuit was asked "what book?" all he could do was to spell the letters L, I, and say no more. If it be suggested that all this was but a refinement of cunning, for that such skillfully distributed reticences are what bring most credit in to a medium, I must deny the proposition *in toto*. I have seen and heard enough of sittings to be sure that a medium's trump cards are promptitude and completeness in her revelations. It is a mistake in general (however it may occasionally, as now, be cited in her favor) to keep back anything she knows. Phinuit's stumbling, spelling, and otherwise imperfect ways of bringing out his facts is a great drawback with most sitters, and yet it is habitual with him.

The aunt who purported to "take control" directly was a much better personation, having a good deal of the cheery strenuousness of speech of the original. She spoke, by the way, on this occasion, of the condition of health of two members of the family in New York, of which we knew nothing at the time, and which was afterwards corroborated by letter. We have repeatedly heard from Mrs. Piper in trance things of which we were not at the moment aware. If the supernormal element in the phenomenon be thought-transference it is certainly not that of the sitter's *conscious* thought. It is rather the reservoir of his potential knowledge which is tapped; and not always *that*, but the knowledge of some distant living person, as in the incident last quoted. It has sometimes even seemed to me that too much intentness on the sitter's part to have Phinuit say a certain thing acts as a hindrance.

Mrs. Blodgett, of Holyoke, Mass., and her sister, devised, before the latter died, what would have been a good test of actual spirit return. The sister, Miss H. W., wrote upon her deathbed a letter, sealed it, and gave it to Mrs. B. After her death no one living knew what words it contained. Mrs. B., not then knowing Mrs. Piper, entrusted to me the sealed letter, and asked me to give Mrs. Piper some articles of the deceased sister's personal apparel, to help her to get at its contents. This commission I performed. Mrs. P. gave correctly the full name (which even I did not know) of the writer, and finally, after a delay and ceremony which occupied several weeks on Phinuit's part, dictated what purported to be a copy of the letter. This I compared with the original (of which Mrs. B. permitted me to break the seal); but the two letters had nothing in common, nor were any of the numerous domestic facts alluded to in the medium's letter acknowledged by Mrs. Blodgett to be correct. Mrs. Piper was equally unsuccessful in two later attempts which she made to reproduce the contents of his document, although both times the revelation purported to come direct from its deceased writer. It would be hard to devise a better test than this would have been, had it immediately succeeded, for the exclusion of thought-transference from living minds.

My mother-in-law, on her return from Europe, spent a morning vainly seeking for her bankbook. Mrs. Piper, on being shortly afterwards asked where this book was, described the place so exactly that it was instantly found. I was told by her that the spirit of a boy named Robert F. was the companion of my lost infant. The F.'s were cousins of my wife living in a distant city. On my return home I mentioned the incident to my wife, saying, "Your cousin did lose a baby, didn't she? but Mrs. Piper was wrong about its sex, name, and age." I then learned that Mrs. Piper had been quite right in all those particulars, and that mine was the wrong impression. But, obviously, for the source of revelations such as these, one need not go behind the sitter's own storehouse of forgotten or unnoticed experiences. Miss X.'s experiments in crystal-gazing prove how strangely these survive. If thought-transference be the clue to be followed in interpreting Mrs. Piper's trance utterances (and that, as far as my experience goes, is what, far more than any supra-mundane instillations, the phenomena *seem* on their face to be) we must admit that the "transference" need not be of the conscious or even the unconscious thought of the sitter, but must often be of the thought of some person far away. Thus, on my mother-in-law's second visit to the medium she was told that one of her daughters was suffering from a severe pain in her back on that day. This altogether unusual occurrence, unknown to the sitter, proved to be true. The announcement to my wife and brother of my aunt's death in New York before we had received the telegram (Mr. Hodgson has, I believe, sent you an account of this) may, on the other hand, have been occasioned by the sitters' conscious apprehension of the event. This particular incident is a "test" of the sort which one readily quotes; but to my mind it was far less convincing than the innumerable small domestic matters of which Mrs. Piper incessantly talked in her sittings with members of my family. With the affairs of my wife's maternal kinsfolk in particular her acquaintance in trance was most intimate. Some of them were dead, some in California, some in the State of Maine. She characterized them all, living as well as deceased, spoke of their relations to each other, of their likes and dislikes, of their as yet unpublished practical plans, and hardly ever made a mistake, though, as usual, there was very little system or continuity in anything that came out. A *normal* person, unacquainted with the family, could not possibly have said as much; one acquainted with it could hardly have avoided saying more.

The most convincing things said about my own immediate household were either very intimate or very trivial. Unfortunately the former things cannot well be published. Of the trivial things, I have forgotten the greater number, but the following, *raræ nantes*, may serve as samples of their class: She said that we had lost recently a rug, and I a waistcoat. (She wrongly accused a person of stealing the rug, which was afterwards found in the house.) She told of my killing a gray-and-white cat, with ether, and described how it had "spun round and round" before dying. She told how my New York aunt had written a letter to my wife, warning her against all mediums, and then went off on a most amusing criticism, full of *traits vifs* [sharp remarks], of the excellent woman's character. (Of course no one but my wife and I knew the existence of the letter in question.) She was strong on the events in our nursery, and gave striking advice during our first visit to her about the way to deal with certain "tantrums" of our second child, "little Billy-boy," as she called him, reproducing his nursery name. She told how the crib creaked at night, how a certain rocking chair creaked mysteriously, how my wife had heard footsteps on the stairs, etc., etc. Insignificant as these things sound when read, the accumulation of a large number of them has an irresistible effect. And I repeat again what I said before, that, taking everything that I know of Mrs. P. into account, the result is to make me feel as absolutely certain as I am of any personal fact in the world that she knows things in her trances which she cannot possibly have heard in her waking state, and that the definitive philosophy of her trances is yet to be found. The limitations of her trance information, its discontinuity and fitfulness, and its apparent inability to develop beyond a certain point, although they end by rousing one's moral and human impatience with the phenomenon, yet are, from a scientific point of view, amongst its most interesting peculiarities, since where there are limits there are conditions, and the discovery of these is always the beginning of explanation.

This is all that I can tell you of Mrs. Piper. I wish it were more "scientific." But, *valeat quantum* [for what it's worth]! it is the best I can do.

16

REVIEW OF *A FURTHER RECORD OF OBSERVATIONS OF CERTAIN PHENOMENA OF TRANCE* BY RICHARD HODGSON

As mentioned in the introduction to the previous chapter, Richard Hodgson published his own contribution to the investigations into Mrs. Piper's mediumship two years after those of Lodge, Leaf, and James.[1] Six years later, he published his follow-up, *A Further Record of Observations of Certain Phenomena of Trance*. James reviewed this second report of Hodgson's for the *Psychological Review* in 1898. As well as being a valuable summary of the report, the review is of special interest for James's own assessment of the case in the last two paragraphs. His increasing conviction of the reality of psychic phenomena is evident in his confident and even tone, and in his somewhat sardonic remarks aimed at materialist critics.

A Further Record of Observations of Certain Phenomena of Trance, Richard Hodgson. *Proceedings of Society for Psychical Research*, Part XXXIII, Feb. 1898, Vol. XIII, pp. 284-583.

---

[1] Richard Hodgson (1892) "A Record of Observations of Certain Phenomena of Trance," *Proceedings of the Society for Psychical Research* 8, 1-167.

A continuation of the case of the test-medium, Mrs. Piper, already reported on in previous *Proceedings*. The present account is based on the results of 500 more sittings, about 130 of which were with unnamed strangers introduced to Mrs. Piper, for the first time. The almost exclusive "control" up to 1892 was a personality named Phinuit, concerning whose earthly identity no evidence has turned up. Since 1892, however, the principal control has, until a year ago, purported to be the spirit of G. P., a young literary man recently dead in New York. The most striking feature of the present report is the expressed opinion of Dr. Hodgson, that the communications of G. P., as well as of others, now seem to him more naturally explicable on the hypothesis of spirit-return than on any other hypothesis. This conversion to spiritism of so critical an investigator, until lately disinclined to any such conclusion, marks, of course, the passage of a "critical point" in the history of the Society for Psychical Research, as well as in Dr. Hodgson's own career.

The phenomenon, briefly described, is as follows: The medium waits passively for the trance to come on, which it now does quietly, though formerly there was a good deal of respiratory disturbance and muscular twitching. "Phinuit" used to communicate entirely by speech, but G. P. early manifested himself by seeking to write on a pad placed on the medium's head. He now writes on the table. "Phinuit" may talk whilst the hand is writing on other subjects, often under controls different from G. P., and purporting to be deceased friends of sitters. After two hours, more or less, the communications grow "weak" and confused, and Mrs. Piper emerges from the trance, often with an expression of fear or distress, and usually with incoherent expressions on her lips, which Dr. Hodgson ascribes to her own subliminal consciousness, as distinguished from her consciousness under complete control. These intermediary and fragmentary expressions he considers to be also worthy of study.

The remarkable feature of the trances is the supernormal knowledge which the medium in a majority of cases displays of her sitter's private affairs. This knowledge is incoherent, fragmentary and, as a rule, of unimportant matters. The communications most convincing to those who received them could, out of deference to the natural dislike to publicity of sitters, not be printed at all, so that the evidence now offered to the reader is by no means "full-strength." Dr. Hodgson gives copious specimens of it, however, such as it is, in most of its varieties, including complete failures amongst the rest. It is intolerably tedious and incoherent reading; and one can but admire, along with the pertinacity of the reporter and his scrupulous accuracy, the manner in which his memory retains the threads of cross-connection among the parts of the system, and is able to bring points in one sitting to the illustration of points in another. Certainly there never before was such a conjunction of a good medium with a thorough investigator—and in this respect the report marks an epoch in our knowledge of trance-states.

Dr. Hodgson considers that the hypothesis of fraud cannot be seriously entertained. I agree with him absolutely. The medium has been under observation, much of the time under close observation, as to most of the conditions of her life, by a large number of persons, eager, many of them, to pounce upon any suspicious circumstance, for fifteen years. During that time *not only has there not been one single suspicious circumstance remarked, but not one suggestion has ever been made from any quarter* which might tend positively to explain how the medium, living the apparent life she leads, could possibly collect information about so many sitters by natural means. The "scientist," who is confident of "fraud" here, must remember that in science as much as in common life a hypothesis must receive some positive specification and determination before it can be profitably discussed; and a fraud which is no assigned kind of fraud, but simply "fraud" at large, fraud *in abstracto*, can hardly be regarded as a specially scientific explanation of specific concrete facts. In the concrete here, there is *no* sign *whatever* that the medium when awake has any curiosity about persons, least of all about persons whom she has never met.

No, Mrs. Piper's trances are phenomena *sui generis*. Mr. Hodgson, admitting the element of supernormal knowledge in them as a fact, weighs against each other as two theories of its origin, first the supposition of telepathy from the sitters' and other living minds, and second, spirit-communication. He finds the latter theory to offer on the whole the least resistance, since a minute discussion of the points of success and failure shows that they fall into the simpler systematic order if we connect them with the departed personalities from which they profess to proceed. G. P., for instance (with one exception, which Mr. Hodgson explains), always recognized his old acquaintances (30 in number) when anonymously introduced as sitters, and rightly called them by name, but similarly recognized no one else. Obviously, such selection round G. P. as a center would be less simply explicable were the medium tapping the consciousnesses of the sitters for their names, than were an independent personality with G. P.'s actual mundane memories a factor of the case. Again, the very confusion of many communicators, identified by sitters, and their inability to bring out more than a few rudimentary facts about themselves, points rather to a genuine spirit-presence obstructed in its means, than to telepathy from the sitters, whose minds, full of other facts relevant to the case, might apparently be drawn upon for them as easily as for those already given. In brief: "There are various selections of information given in connection with various communicators which are intelligible if regarded as made by the communicators themselves, but for which there is no satisfactory explanation to be found by referring them to Mrs. Piper's personality. With one class of *deceased* persons Mrs. Piper's supposed telepathic percipience fails; with another class it succeeds; and it fails and succeeds apparently in accordance with what we should expect from the minds of the deceased, and not in accordance with what we should expect from the minds of living persons acting upon Mrs. Piper's percipient personality" (p. 393). The case is a matter of balancing probabilities based on minute comparisons of detail, and Mr. Hodgson is far from ascribing certainty to the spiritistic conclusion which he adopts.

Mr. Hodgson fails to mention one feature of the case which may make for the spirit-hypothesis, and which will probably have struck other readers besides myself. No one can be conversant with his investigation of the Piper case without admiring the great grasp of memory of details which the investigator exhibits. And yet Mr. Hodgson's memory is as nothing compared with Mrs. Piper's, who, with hundreds of sitters, many appearing only a few times, at years of interval, and conversing of inconceivably paltry personal details, seems never to fail to make connection again, or to take up the conversation just where it was left. Mr. Hodgson's memory covers fewer years, and taking and transcribing the notes of the sittings, as he does, and consulting and comparing the records *ad libitum* [as much as required], he has a great advantage over Mrs. Piper. Yet he would be quite incapable of resuming conversation with former sitters as she does in her trance. Mrs. Piper's trance-memory, then, is no ordinary human memory; and we have to explain its singular perfection either as the natural endowment of her solitary subliminal self, or as a collection of distinct memory-systems, each with a communicating "spirit," as its vehicle. The choice obviously cannot be made off-hand.

If I may be allowed a personal expression of opinion at the end of this notice, I would say that the Piper phenomena are the most absolutely baffling thing I know. Of the various applicable hypotheses, each seems more unnatural than the rest. Any definitely known form of fraud seems out of the question; yet undoubtedly, could it be made probable, fraud would be by far the most satisfying explanation, since it would leave no further problems outstanding. The spirit-hypothesis exhibits a vacancy, triviality and incoherence of mind painful to think of as the state of the departed; and coupled therewithal a pretension to impress one, a disposition to "fish" and face round, and disguise the essential hollowness, which are, if anything, more painful still. Mr. Hodgson has to resort to the theory that, although the communicants probably are spirits, they are in a semi-comatose or sleeping state while communicating, and only half aware of what is going on, while the habits of Mrs. Piper's neural organism largely supply the definite form of words, etc., in which the phenomenon is clothed. Then there is the theory that the "subliminal" extension of Mrs. Piper's own mind masquerades in this way, and plays these fantastic tricks before high heaven, using its preternatural powers of cognition and memory for the basest of deceits. Many details make for this view, which also falls well into line with what we know of automatic writing and similar subliminal performances in the public at large. But what a ghastly and grotesque sort of appendage to one's personality is this, from any point of view: the humbugging and masquerading extra-marginal self is as great a paradox for psychology as the comatose spirits are for pneumatology. Finally, we may fall back on the notion of a sort of floating mind-stuff in the world, infra-human, yet possessed of fragmentary gleams of superhuman cognition, unable to gather itself together except by taking advantage of the trance states of some existing human organism, and there enjoying a parasitic existence which it prolongs by making itself acceptable and plausible under the improvised name of a "spirit control." On any of these theories our "classic" human life, as we may call it, seems to connect itself with an environment so "romantic" as to baffle all one's habitual sense of teleology and moral meaning. And yet there seems no refuge for one really familiar with the Piper phenomenon (or, doubtless, with others that are similar) from admitting one or other, perhaps even all of these fantastic prolongations of mental life into the unknown.

The world is evidently more complex than we are accustomed to think it, the "absolute world-ground," in particular, being farther off (as Mr. F. C. S. Schiller has well pointed out) than it is the wont either of the usual empiricisms or of the usual idealisms to think it. This being the case, the "scientific" sort of procedure is evidently Mr. Hodgson's, with his dogged and candid exploration of all the details of so exceptional a concrete instance; and not that of the critics who, refusing to come to any close quarters with the facts, survey them at long range and summarily dispose of them at a convenient distance by the abstract name of fraud.

17

MRS. PIPER, "THE MEDIUM"

Following the publication of Hodgson's *A Further Record of Observations of Certain Phenomena of Trance*, James's fellow psychologist-turned-antagonist J. McKeen Cattell (see Chapter 4) published a somewhat disparaging critique in an 1898 issue of the journal *Science*[1], of which Cattell himself was editor. James rose to Hodgson's defense, but also to his own, having taken umbrage at some of Cattell's remarks. Cattell began by dismissing the entire contents of the thirteen volumes published by the SPR up to that time as "trivial," before criticizing Hodgson's work with Mrs. Piper in particular. After once again quoting James's famous "white crow" remark, Cattell wrote:

> It is Professor James who gives dignity and authority to psychical research in America, and if he has selected a crucial case it deserves consideration. The difficulty has been that proving innumerable mediums to be frauds does not disprove the possibility (though it greatly reduces the likelihood) of one medium being genuine. But here we have the "white crow" selected by Professor James from all the pie bald crows exhibited by the Society.

---

[1] Cattell, J. McKeen (1889) "Mrs. Piper, 'the Medium.'" *Science* 7, 534-35. His rejoinder may be found on pp. 641-42.

Cattell then quoted comments from five scientists who had attended sittings with Mrs. Piper: J. Mark Baldwin, John Trowbridge, N.S. Shaler, J.M. Peirce, and S. Weir Mitchell. All of them were highly critical of her mediumship and had witnessed little or nothing of evidential value. They highlighted the many errors Mrs. Piper had made, the incoherence of what she said, and the irrelevance and lack of truth in her statements. The following is James's reply to Cattell.

To the Editor of *Science*: Your reference to my name in the editorial note in *Science* for April 15th, entitled 'Mrs. Piper, the Medium,' justifies me in making some remarks of my own in comment on your remarks upon Mr. Hodgson's report of her case. Any hearing for such phenomena is so hard to get from scientific readers that one who believes them worthy of careful study is in duty bound to resent such contemptuous public notice of them in high quarters as would still further encourage the fashion of their neglect.

I say any hearing; I don't say any fair hearing. Still less do I speak of fair treatment in the broad meaning of the term. The scientific mind is by the pressure of professional opinion painfully drilled to fairness and logic in discussing orthodox phenomena. But in such mere matters of superstition as a medium's trances it feels so confident of impunity and indulgence whatever it may say, provided it be only contemptuous enough, that it fairly revels in the un- trained barbarians' arsenal of logical weapons, including all the various sophisms enumerated in the books.

Your own comments seem to me an excellent illustration of this fact. If one wishes to refute a man who asserts that some A's are B's, the ordinary rule of logic is that one must not show that some *other* A's are *not* B's—one must show him either that those first A's themselves are not B's, or else that no A possibly can be a B. Now Mr. Hodgson comes forward asserting that many of Mrs. Piper's trances show supernatural knowledge. You thereupon pick out from his report five instances in which they showed nothing of the kind. You thereupon wittily remark, "We have piped into you and ye have not danced," and you sign your name with an air of finality, as if nothing more in the way of refutation were needful and as if what earlier in the article you call "the trivial character of the evidence...taken under the wing of the Society" were now sufficiently displayed.

If, my dear sir, you were teaching Logic to a class of students, should you, or should you not, consider this a good instance by which to illustrate the style of reasoning termed "irrelevant conclusion," or *ignoratio elenchi*, in the chapter on fallacies? I myself think it an extraordinarily perfect instance.

And what name should you assign to the fallacy by which you quote one of those five sitters as saying that he himself got nothing from the medium "but a few preposterous compliments," whilst you leave unquoted the larger part of his report, relating the inexplicable knowledge which the medium showed of the family affairs of his wife, who accompanied him to the sitting? I am not sure that the logic books contain any technical name for the fallacy here, but in legal language it is sometimes called *suppressio veri*, sometimes something still less polite. At any rate, you will admit on reflection that to use the conclusion of that sitter's report alone, as you did, was to influence your readers' minds in an unfair way.

I am sure that you have committed these fallacies with the best of scientific consciences. They are fallacies into which, of course, you would have been in no possible danger of falling in any other sort of matter than this. In our dealings with the insane the usual moral rules don't apply. Mediums are scientific outlaws, and their defendants are quasi-insane. Any stick is good enough to beat dogs of that stripe with. So in perfect innocence you permitted yourself the liberties I point out.

Please observe that I am saying nothing of the merits of the *case*, but only of the merits of your forms of controversy which, alas, are typical. The case surely deserves opposition more powerful from the logical point of view than your remarks; and I beg such readers of *Science* as care to form a reasonable opinion to seek the materials for it in the *Proceedings of the Society for Psychical Research*, Part XX XIII (where they will find a candid report based on 500 sittings since the last report was made), rather than in the five little negative instances which you so triumphantly cull out and quote.

Truly yours,
William James

***

In his brief rejoinder, Cattell reiterated some of the points he'd already made and concluded:

> I wrote the note with reluctance and only because I believe that the Society for Psychical Research is doing much to injure

psychology. The authority of Professor James is such that he involves other students of psychology in his opinions unless they protest. We all acknowledge his leadership, but we cannot follow him into the quagmires.

The discussion did not end there, however, for James felt compelled to write a personal letter to Cattell in reply:

I have read your brief retort and live. Your state of prejudice is so absolute, that quite naively and unconsciously you perpetrate acts of insolence quite as remarkable as your lapses of logic, as if I were some minor or child making a nuisance in the psychological neighborhood. You surely would not adopt that tone in regard to any other difference of scientific opinion, least of all where the adversary had 15 years first-hand acquaintance with the facts and you had never seen them.

No! my dear fellow, it is as I say, all the virtues have to be drilled into us afresh in each special matter, and the day for psychical research has not yet come. Understanding the conditions, I don't care personally a rap for the treatment, or think the less well as human beings of the treaters—yourself included. As you smile indulgently at me, so I, dear Cattell, at you. He smiles best who smiles last, and my prophetic soul is in no doubt about that. ... On re-reading I can see that my first two pages suggest temper (the word insolence etc.). Nothing could less be the case. I fairly delight in you, my dear boy, as a first-class specimen.

18

REPORT ON MRS. PIPER'S HODGSON-CONTROL (EXCERPTS)

Following Richard Hodgson's death in 1905, Mrs. Piper allegedly began to receive communications from him – and indeed claimed that he had become one of her "controls." As Hodgson had been a friend of James, and a fellow investigator of Piper's mediumship, it was natural for James to look into the case. The result was a 110-page report that was published in the 1909 *Proceedings of the Society for Psychical Research*. James was clearly ambivalent about the results of his investigation, as expressed in a letter to Thomas Sergeant Perry[1], an American editor, scholar, and literary critic:

> It is a hedging sort of an affair. ... The truth is that the 'case' is a particularly poor one for testing Mrs. Piper's claim to bring back spirits. It is leakier than any other case, and intrinsically, I think, no stronger than many of her other good cases. ...

Despite these misgivings, James did find certain aspects of the case to be evidential, though he remained cautious due to the fact that the

---

[1] Letter to Thomas Sergeant Perry, 29 January 1909. In William James (coll. 1920) *The Letters of William James*. H. James (ed.) London: Longmans Green, 319-20.

Hodgson-control did not fully correspond to the Hodgson he had known in life. The case seemed to strengthen his feeling that while there was "proof," it was not incontrovertible, and could be interpreted in various ways.

Much of the *PSPR* report is taken up with many pages of verbatim transcripts of sittings with Mrs. Piper, alongside detailed analyses of the pros and cons of the evidential value of the events of eleven sittings (and can make for frankly tedious reading, as James himself acknowledged). The extracts that follow are James's introduction, general assessments, observations, and conclusions (with section titles added to facilitate reading). In them we see James the philosopher strongly emerging, as he observes his own role *as* observer, explores the relationship between subjective feeling and hard evidence, and speculates on the kind of metaphysical system that might explain the various dimensions of Mrs. Piper's mediumship.

Introduction

Richard Hodgson died suddenly upon December 20th, 1905. On December 28th a message purporting to come from him was delivered in a trance of Mrs. Piper's, and she has hardly held a sitting since then without some manifestation of what professed to be Hodgson's spirit taking place. Hodgson had often during his lifetime laughingly said that if he ever passed over and Mrs. Piper was still officiating here below, he would control her better than she had ever yet been controlled in her trances, because he was so thoroughly familiar with the difficulties and conditions on this side. Indeed he was; so that this would seem *prima facie* a particularly happy conjunction of spirit with medium by which to test the question of spirit return.

I have collated 69 of the American sittings (the latest being that of January 1st, 1908) in which the professed R. H. has appeared (his communications forming possibly a sixth of the total bulk of the records), and a few remarks as to my own relation to the phenomenon would seem a good introduction to what follows. I have no space for twice-told tales, so I will assume that my readers are acquainted, to some degree at any rate, with previously printed accounts of Mrs. Piper's mediumship.[2] I

---

[2] Chief among these are Hodgson's reports in Vols. VIII and XIII of the S.P.R. *Proceedings*, Mrs. Sidgwick's discussion in Vol. XV, Hyslop's long account in Vol. XVI, and his briefer one in his book *Science and a Future Life*.

had myself had no sitting with Mrs. Piper and had hardly seen her for some nine years, but for most of that time I had been kept informed of what was going on by reading the typed records, furnished me by my friend Hodgson, of all the trances of which report was taken, and for which the sitters had not asked secrecy to be observed. The "Control" most frequently in evidence in these years has been the personage calling himself "Rector." Dr. Hodgson was disposed to admit the claim to reality of Rector and of the whole Imperator-Band of which he is a member, while I have rather favored the idea of their all being dream-creations of Mrs. Piper, probably having no existence except when she is in trance, but consolidated by repetition into personalities consistent enough to play their several roles. Such at least is the dramatic impression which my acquaintance with the sittings has left on my mind. I can see no contradiction between Rector's being on the one hand an improvised creature of this sort, and his being on the other hand the extraordinarily impressive personality which he unquestionably is. He has marvelous discernment of the inner states of the sitters whom he addresses, and speaks straight to their troubles as if he knew them all in advance. He addresses you as if he were the most devoted of your friends. He appears like an aged and, when he speaks instead of writing, like a somewhat hollow-voiced clergyman, a little weary of his experience of the world, endlessly patient and sympathetic, and desiring to put all his tenderness and wisdom at your service while you are there. Critical and fastidious sitters have recognized his wisdom, and confess their debt to him as a moral adviser. With all due respect to Mrs. Piper, I feel very sure that her own waking capacity for being a spiritual adviser, if it were compared with Rector's, would fall greatly behind.

As I conceive the matter, it is on this mass of secondary and automatic personality of which of late years Rector has been the center, and which forms the steady background of Mrs. Piper's trances, that the supernormal knowledge which she unquestionably displays is flashed. Flashed, grafted, inserted—use what word you will—the trance-automatism is at any rate the intermediating condition, the supernormal knowledge comes as if from beyond, and the automatism uses its own forms in delivering it to the sitter. The most habitual form is to say that it comes from the spirit of a departed friend. The earliest messages from "Hodgson" have been communicated by "Rector," but he soon spoke in his own name, and the only question which I shall consider in this paper is this: *Are there any unmistakable indications in the messages in question that something that we may call the "spirit" of*

Hodgson was probably really there? We need not refine yet upon what the word "spirit" means and on what spirits are and can do. We can leave the meaning of the word provisionally very indeterminate—the vague popular notion of what a spirit is is enough to begin with.

Sources other than R. H.'s surviving spirit for the veridical communications from the Hodgson-control may be enumerated as follows:

(1) Lucky chance-hits.

(2) Common gossip.

(3) Indications unwarily furnished by the sitters.

(4) Information received from R. H., during his lifetime, by the waking Mrs. P. and stored up, either supraliminally or subliminally, in her memory.

(5) Information received from the living R. H., or others, at sittings, and kept in Mrs. Piper's trance-memory, but out of reach of her waking consciousness.

(6) "Telepathy," i.e. the tapping of the sitter's mind, or that of some distant living person, in an inexplicable way.

(7) Access to some cosmic reservoir, where the memory of all mundane facts is stored and grouped around personal centers of association.

Let us call the first five of these explanations "natural," and the last two "supernatural" or "mystical." It is obvious that no mystical explanation ought to be invoked so long as any natural one remains at all plausible. Only after the first five explanations have been made to appear improbable, is it time for the telepathy-theory and the cosmic-reservoir theory to be compared with the theory of R. H.'s surviving spirit.

The total amount of truthful information communicated by the R. H. control to the various sitters is copious. He reminds them, for the most part, of events—usually unimportant ones—which they and the living R. H. had experienced together. Taking any one of these events singly, it is never possible in principle to exclude explanations number 1 and 4. About number 3, a complete record of the sitting ought generally to decide. Number 2 is often excluded either by the trivial or by the intimate nature of the case. Number 5 would be easily settled if the records of the sittings of the living Hodgson with Mrs. Piper were complete and accessible. They are supposed, for the past ten or twelve years at least, to exist in complete form. But parts of them are in Hodgson's private cipher, and they are now so voluminous that it would be rash to say of any recent message from Hodgson, so long as the matter of it might conceivably have been talked of at any previous trance of Mrs. Piper's, that no record of such talk exists. It might exist without having yet been found.

Add, to these several chances that any communication of fact by the Hodgson-control may have had a natural source, the further consideration that Mrs. Piper had known H. well for many years, and one sees that her subliminal powers of personation would have had an unusually large amount of material to draw upon in case they wished to get up a make-believe spirit of Hodgson. So far, then, from his particular case being an unusually good one by which to test the claim that Mrs. Piper is possessed during her trances by the spirits of our departed friends, it would seem to be a particularly poor one for that purpose. I have come to the conclusion that it is an exceptionally poor one. Hodgson's familiarity when in the flesh with the difficulties at this end of the line has not made him show any more expertness as a spirit than other communicators have shown; and for his successes there are far more naturalistic explanations available than is the case with the other spirits who have professed to control Mrs. Piper.

So much for generalities, and so much for my own personal equation, for which my various hearers will make their sundry kinds of allowance. But before taking up the messages in detail, a word more about the fourth of the naturalistic explanations which I have instanced (conversations, that is, between Mrs. Piper and Hodgson when alive) is in order. Abstractly, it seems very plausible to suppose that R. H. (who systematically imposed on himself the law of never mentioning the content of any trance in her waking presence) might have methodically adopted a plan of entertaining her on his visits by reciting all the little happenings of his days, and that it is this chronicle of small beer, stored in her memory, that now comes out for service in simulating his spirit-identity.

In the concrete, however, this is not a highly probable hypothesis. Everyone who knew Hodgson agrees that he was little given to anecdotical small change, unless the incident were comic or otherwise of an impressive order, and that his souvenirs of fact were usually of a broad and synthetic type. He had had a "splendid time" at such a place, with a "glorious" landscape, swim, or hill-climb, but no further detail. Gifted with great powers of reserve by nature, he was professionally schooled to secretiveness; and a decidedly incommunicative habit in the way of personal gossip had become a second nature with him—especially towards Mrs. Piper. For many years past he had seen her three times weekly (except during the months of her summer vacation) and had had to transcribe the record afterwards. The work was time-consuming, and he found it excessively fatiguing. He had economized energy upon it by adopting for many years past a purely business tone with the medium, entering, starting the trance, and leaving when it was over, with as few unnecessary words as possible. Great *brusquerie* was among the excellent R. H.'s potentialities, and for a while the amount of it displayed towards Mrs. P. led to a state of feeling on her part which a *New York Herald* reporter once took advantage of to exploit publicly. R. H. was remonstrated with, and was more considerate afterwards. It may well be that Mrs. Piper had heard one little incident or another, among those to be discussed in the following report, from his living lips, but that any large mass of these incidents are to be traced to this origin, I find incredible.

Preliminary Conclusions

(1) The case is an exceptionally bad one for testing spirit- return, owing to the unusual scope it gives to naturalistic explanations.

(2) The phenomena it presents furnish no knock-down proof of the return of Hodgson's spirit.

(3) They are well compatible, however, with such return, provided we assume that the Piper-organism not only transmits with great difficulty the influences it receives from beyond the curtain, but mixes its own automatic tendencies most disturbingly therewith. Hodgson himself used to compare the conditions of spirit-communication to those of two distant persons on this earth who should carry on their social intercourse by employing each of them a dead-drunk messenger.

(4) Although this Hodgson-case, taken by itself, yields thus only a negative, or at the best a baffling conclusion, we have no scientific right to take it by itself, as I have done. It belongs with the whole residual mass of Piper-phenomena, and they belong with the whole mass of cognate phenomena elsewhere found. False personation is a ubiquitous feature in this total mass. It certainly exists in the Piper-case; and the great question there is as to its limits. If, when lavish allowance has been made for this strange tendency in our subliminal life, there should still appear a balance of probability (which in this case can only mean a balance of simplicity) in the view that certain parts of

the Piper-communications really emanate from personal centers of memory and will, connected with lives that have passed away; if, I say, this balance of probability should appear decisively anywhere in the mass, then the rest of the mass will have to be interpreted as at least possibly similarly caused. I admire greatly Hodgson's own discussion of the Piper-case in Volume XIII of our *Proceedings*, especially in sections 5 and 6, where, taking the whole mass of communication into careful account, he decides for this spiritist interpretation. I know of no more masterly handling anywhere of so unwieldy a mass of material; and in the light of his general conclusions there, I am quite ready to admit that my own denials in this present paper may be the result of the narrowness of my material, and that possibly R. H.'s spirit has been speaking all the time, only my ears have been deaf. It is true that I still believe the "Imperator-band" to be fictitious entities, while Hodgson ended by accepting them as real; but as to the general probability of there being real communicators somewhere in the mass I cannot be deaf to Hodgson's able discussion, or fail to feel the authority which his enormous experience gave to his opinion in this particular field.

(5) I therefore repeat that if ever our growing familiarity with these phenomena should tend more and more to corroborate the hypothesis that "spirits" play some part in their production, I shall be quite ready to undeafen my ears, and to revoke the negative conclusions of this limited report. The facts are evidently complicated in the extreme, and we have as yet hardly scratched the surface of them. But methodical exploration has at last seriously begun, and these earlier observations of ours will surely be interpreted one day in the light of future discoveries which it may well take a century to make. I consequently disbelieve in being too "rigorous" with our criticism of anything now in hand, or in our squeezing so evidently vague a material too hard in our technical forceps, at the present stage. What we need is more and more observations. Quantity will probably have to supplement quality in the material. When we have the facts in sufficient number, we may be sure that they will cast plenty of explanatory backward light. We can therefore well afford to play a waiting game.

Participation Experience and the Scientific Method

One who takes part in a good sitting has usually a far livelier sense, both of the reality and of the importance of the communication, than one who merely reads the record. Active relations with a thing are required to bring the reality of it home to us, and in a trance-talk the sitter actively cooperates. When you find your questions answered and your allusions understood; when allusions are made that you think you understand, and your thoughts are met by anticipation, denial, or corroboration; when you have approved, applauded, or exchanged banter, or thankfully listened to advice that you believe in; it is difficult not to take away an impression of having encountered something sincere in the way of a social phenomenon. The whole talk gets warmed with your own warmth, and takes on the reality of your own part in it; its confusions and defects you charge to the imperfect conditions, while you credit the successes to the genuineness of the communicating spirit. Most of us also, when sitters, react more, prick our ears more, to the successful parts of the communication. These consequently loom more in our memory, and give the key to our dramatic interpretation of the phenomenon. But a sitting that thus seemed important at the time may greatly shrink in value on a cold re-reading; and if read by a non-participant, it may seem thin and almost insignificant.[3]

Somewhat similar fluctuations are noticed in the reality-feeling which the records may awaken at different times in one and the same reader. When I first undertook to collate this series of sittings and make the present report, I supposed that my verdict would be determined by pure logic. Certain minute incidents, I thought, ought to make for spirit-return or against it in a "crucial" way. But watching my mind work as it goes over the data, convinces me that exact logic plays only a preparatory part in shaping our conclusions here; and that the decisive

---

[3] A striking example of this was furnished me lately by a manuscript which a friend sent me. She had been one of Mrs. Piper's most assiduous clients. Her conversations with a certain spirit-control had been copious, fluent and veridical, and to herself so comforting and elevating, that she had epitomized them in this manuscript which, she thought, ought to be published. Strictly evidential matter was ruled out from it as too minute or private, and what remained was ethical and human matter only. Never having known the communicator, and reading passively and critically, I felt bound to dissuade from publication. I could not believe that readers would find in the communications a twentieth part of the importance which their receiver had found in them. The vital heat was absent, and what remained was ashes. I may well have been wrong in this opinion, but the incident brought vividly home to my own mind the contrast between the inside view of the sitter, and the outside one of the mere critic.

vote, if there be one, has to be cast by what I may call one's general sense of dramatic probability, which sense ebbs and flows from one hypothesis to another—it does so in the present writer at least— in a rather illogical manner. If one sticks to the detail, one may draw an anti-spiritist conclusion; if one thinks more of what the whole mass may signify, one may well incline to spiritist interpretations.

This was the shape in which I myself left the matter in my recent preliminary report. I said that spirit-return was not proved by the Hodgson-control material, taken by itself, but that this adverse conclusion might possibly be reversed if the limited material were read in the light of the total mass of cognate phenomena. To say this is to say that the proof still baffles one. It still baffles me, I have to confess; but whether my subjective insufficiency or the objective in- sufficiency (as yet) of our evidence be most to blame for this, must be decided by others.

The common-sense rule of presumption in scientific logic is never to assume an unknown agent where there is a known one, and never to choose a rarer cause for a phenomenon when a commoner one will account for it. The usual is always more probable, and exceptional principles should be invoked only when the use of ordinary ones is impossible. Fraud is a form of human agency both known and common, though much less common than cynics suppose; "personation" is unquestionably common in the whole realm of our subconscious operations; "telepathy" seems fairly established as a fact, though its frequency is still questionable; accidental coincidences occur, however rarely; but "spirits" of any grade, although they are indeed matters of tradition, seem to have shown themselves (so far as concrete evidence for them goes) nowhere except in the specific phenomena under investigation. Our rule of presumption should lead us then to deny spirits and to explain the Piper-phenomena by a mixture of fraud, subconscious personation, lucky accident, and telepathy, whenever such an explanation remains possible. Taking these Hodgson-records in detail, and subjecting their incidents to a piecemeal criticism, such an explanation does seem practically possible everywhere; so, as long as we confine ourselves to the mere logic of presumption, the conclusion against the spirits holds good.

But the logic of presumption, safe in the majority of cases, is bound to leave us in the lurch whenever a real exception confronts us; and there is always a bare possibility that any case before us may be such an exception. In the case at present before us the exceptional possibility is that of "spirits" really having a finger in the pie. The records are fully compatible with this explanation, however explicable they may be without it. Spirits may cooperate with all the other factors, they may indeed find that harnessing the other factors in their service is the only way open to them for communicating their wishes. The lower factors may, in fact, be to a spirit's wishes what the physical laws of a machine are to its maker's and user's aims. A spectator, confining his attention to a machine's parts and their workings, and finding everything there explicable by mechanical push and pull, may be tempted to deny the presence of any higher actuation. Yet the particular pushes and pulls which the form of that machine embodies, would not be there at all without a higher *meaning which the machine expresses*, and which it works out as a human purpose. To understand the parts of the machine fully, we must find the human purpose which uses all this push and pull as its means of realization. Just so the personation, fishing, guessing, using lucky hits, etc., in Mrs. Piper, may be, as it were, the mechanical means by which "spirits" succeed in making her living organism express their thought, however imperfectly.

As soon, therefore, as we drop our routine rule of presumption, and ask straight for truth and nothing but truth, we find that *the whole question is as to whether the exceptional case con- fronts us*. This is a question of probabilities and improbabilities. Now in every human being who in cases like this makes a decision instead of suspending judgment, the sense of probability depends on the forms of dramatic imagination of which his mind is capable. The explanation has *in any event* to be dramatic. Fraud, personation, telepathy, spirits, elementals, are all of them dramatic hypotheses. If your imagination is incapable of conceiving the spirit-hypothesis at all, you will just proclaim it "impossible" (as my colleague Münsterberg does, *Psychology and Life*, p. 130), and thus confess yourself incompetent to discuss the alternative seriously.

I myself can perfectly well imagine spirit-agency, and I find my mind vacillating about it curiously. When I take the phenomena piecemeal, the notion that Mrs. Piper's subliminal self should keep her sitters apart as expertly as it does, remembering its past dealings with each of them so well, not mixing their communications more, and all the while humbugging them so profusely, is quite compatible with what we know of the dream-life of hypnotized subjects. Their consciousness, narrowed to one suggested kind of operation, shows remarkable skill in that operation. If we suppose Mrs. Piper's dream-life once for all to have had the notion suggested to it that it must personate spirits to sitters, the fair degree of virtuosity it shows need not, I think, surprise us. Nor need the exceptional memory shown surprise us, for memory seems extraordinarily strong in the subconscious life. But I find that when I ascend from the details to the whole meaning of the phenomenon, and especially when I connect the Piper-case with all the other cases I know of automatic writing and mediumship, and with the whole record of spirit-possession in human history, the notion that such an immense current of experience, complex in so many ways, should spell out absolutely nothing but the words "intentional humbug" appears very unlikely. The notion that so many men and women, in all other respects honest enough, should have this preposterous monkeying self annexed to their personality seems to me so weird that the spirit-theory immediately takes on a more probable appearance. The spirits, if spirits there be, must indeed work under incredible complications and falsifications, but at least if they are present, some honesty is left in a whole department of the universe which otherwise is run by pure deception. The more I realize the quantitative massiveness of the phenomenon and its complexity, the more incredible it seems to me that in a world all of whose vaster features we are in the habit of considering to be *sincere* at least, however brutal, this feature should be wholly constituted of insincerity.

If I yield to a feeling of the dramatic improbability of this, I find myself interpreting the details of the sittings differently. I am able, while still holding to all the lower principles of interpretation, to imagine the process as more complex, and to share the feeling with which Hodgson came at last to regard it after his many years of familiarity, the feeling which Prof. Hyslop shares, and which most of those who have good sittings are promptly inspired with. I can imagine the spirit of R. H. talking to me through inconceivable barriers of obstruction, and forcing recalcitrant or only partly consilient processes in the Medium to express his thoughts, however dimly.

This is as candid an account of my own personal equation as I can give. I exhibited it in my treatment of special incidents in the preliminary report, and the reader will make allowance for it in what is to follow. In the end he must draw his conclusions for himself; I can only arrange the material.

Final Conclusions

These eleven incidents sound more like deliberate truth-telling, whoever the truth-teller be, than like lucky flukes. On the whole they make on me the impression of being supernormal. I confess that I should at this moment much like to know (although I have no means of knowing) just how all the documents I am exhibiting in this report will strike readers who are either novices in the field, or who consider the subject in general to be pure "rot" or "bosh." It seems to me not impossible that a bosh-philosopher here or there may get a dramatic impression of there being something genuine behind it all. Most of those who remain faithful to the "bosh"-interpretation would, however, find plenty of comfort if they had the entire mass of records given them to read. Not that I have left things out (I certainly have tried not to!) that would, if printed, discredit the detail of what I cite, but I have left out, by not citing the whole mass of records, so much mere mannerism, so much repetition, hesitation, irrelevance, unintelligibility, so much obvious groping and fishing and plausible covering up of false tracks, so much false pretension to power, and real obedience to suggestion, that the stream of veridicality that runs throughout the whole gets lost as it were in a marsh of feebleness, and the total dramatic effect on the mind may be little more than the word "humbug." The really significant items disappear in the total bulk. "Passwords," for example, and sealed messages are given in abundance, but can't be found. (I omit these here, as some of them may prove veridical later.) Preposterous Latin sentences are written, e.g. "Rebus merica este fecrum"—or what reads like that (April 4th, 1906). Poetry gushes out, but how can one be sure that Mrs. Piper never knew it? The weak talk of the Imperator-band about *time* is reproduced, as where R. H. pretends that he no longer knows what "seven minutes" mean (May 14th, 1906). Names asked for can't be given, etc., etc.[4] All this mass of diluting material, which can't be reproduced in abridgment, has its inevitable dramatic effect; and if

---

[4] For instance, on July 2nd, the sitter asks R. H. to name some of his cronies at the Tavern Club. Hodgson gives six names, only five of which belonged to the Tavern Club, and those five were known to the controls already. None of them, I believe, were those asked for, namely, "names of the men he used to play pool with or go swimming with at Nantasket." Yet, as the sitter (Mr. Dorr) writes, "He failed to realize his failure."

one tends to *hate* the whole phenomenon anyhow (as I confess that I myself sometimes do) one's judicial verdict inclines accordingly.

Nevertheless, I have to confess also that the more familiar I have become with the records, the less *relative significance* for my mind has all this diluting material tended to assume. The active cause of the communications is on any hypothesis a will of some kind, be it the will of R. H.'s spirit, of lower supernatural intelligences, or of Mrs. Piper's subliminal; and although some of the rubbish may be deliberately willed (certain hesitations, misspellings, etc., in the hope that the sitter may give a clue, or certain repetitions, in order to gain time) yet the major part of it is suggestive of something quite different—as if a will were there, but a will to say something which the machinery fails to bring through. Dramatically, most of this "bosh" is more suggestive to me of dreaminess and mind-wandering than it is of humbug. Why should a "will to deceive" prefer to give incorrect names so often, if it can give the true ones to which the incorrect ones so frequently approximate as to suggest that they are meant? True names impress the sitter vastly more. Why should it so multiply false "passwords" ("Zeivorn," for example) and stick to them? It looks to me more like aiming at something definite, and failing of the goal. Sometimes the control gives a message to a distant person quite suddenly, as if for some reason a resistance momentarily gave way and let pass a definite desire to give such a message. Thus on October 1 7th, "Give my love to Carl Putnam," a name which neither Mrs. Piper nor the sitter knew, and which popped in quite irrelevantly to what preceded or followed. A definite will is also suggested when R. H. sends a message to James Putnam about his "watch stopping." He sends it through several sitters and sticks to it in the face of final denial, as if the phrase covered, however erroneously, some distinct "intention to recall," which ought not to be renounced.

That a "will to personate" is a factor in the Piper-phenomenon, I fully believe, and I believe with unshakeable firmness that this will is able to draw on supernormal sources of information. It can "tap," possibly the sitter's memories, possibly those of distant human beings, possibly some cosmic reservoir in which the memories of earth are stored, whether in the shape of "spirits" or not. If this were the only will concerned in the performance, the phenomenon would be humbug pure and simple, and the minds tapped telepathically in it would play an entirely passive role—that is, the telepathic data would be fished out by the personating will, not forced upon it by desires to communicate, acting externally to itself.

But it is possible to complicate the hypothesis. Extraneous "wills to communicate" may contribute to the results as well as a "will to personate," and the two kinds of will may be distinct in entity, though capable of helping each other out. The will to communicate, in our present instance, would be, on the *prima facie* view of it, the will of Hodgson's surviving spirit; and a natural way of representing the process would be to suppose the spirit to have found that by pressing, so to speak, against "the light," it can make fragmentary gleams and flashes of what it wishes to say mix with the rubbish of the trance-talk on this side. The two wills might thus strike up a sort of partnership and reinforce each other. It might even be that the "will to personate" would be comparatively inert unless it were aroused to activity by the other will. We might imagine the relation to be analogous to that of two physical bodies, from neither of which, when alone, mechanical, thermal, or electrical activity can proceed, but if the other body be present, and show a difference of "potential," action starts up and goes on apace.

Conceptions such as these seem to connect in schematic form the various elements in the case. Its essential factors are done justice to; and, by changing the relative amounts in which the rubbish-making and the truth-telling wills contribute to the resultant, we can draw up a table in which every type of manifestation, from silly planchet-writing up to Rector's best utterances, finds its proper place. Personally, I must say that, although I have to confess that no crucial proof of the presence of the "will to communicate" seems to me yielded by the Hodgson-control taken alone, and in the sittings to which I have had access, yet the total effect in the way of dramatic probability of the whole mass of similar phenomena on my mind, is to make me believe that a "will to communicate" *is* in some shape there. I cannot demonstrate it, but practically I am inclined to "go in" for it, to bet on it and take the risks.

The question then presents itself: In what shape is it most reasonable to suppose that the will thus postulated is actually there? And here again there are various pneumatological possibilities, which must be considered first in abstract form. Thus the will to communicate may come either from permanent entities, or from an entity that arises for the occasion. R. H.'s spirit would be a permanent entity; and inferior parasitic spirits ("daimons," elementals, or whatever their traditional names might be) would be permanent entities. An improvised entity might be a limited process of consciousness arising in the cosmic reservoir of earth's memories, when certain conditions favoring systematized activity in particular tracts thereof were fulfilled. The conditions in that case might be conceived after the analogy of what happens when two poles of different potential are created in a mass of matter, and cause a current of electricity, or what not, to pass through an intervening tract of space until then the seat of rest.

To consider the case of permanent entities first, there is no *a priori* reason why human spirits and other spiritual beings might not either co-operate at the same time in the same phenomenon, or alternately produce different manifestations. *Prima facie*, and as a matter of "dramatic" probability, other intelligences than our own appear on an enormous scale in the historic mass of material which Myers first brought together under the title of Automatisms. The refusal of modern "enlightenment" to treat "possession" as a hypothesis to be spoken of as even possible, in spite of the massive human tradition based on concrete experience in its favor, has always seemed to me a curious example of the power of fashion in things scientific. That the demon-theory (not necessarily a devil-theory) will have its innings again is to my mind absolutely certain. One has to be "scientific" indeed, to be blind and ignorant enough to suspect no such possibility. But if the liability to have one's somnambulistic or automatic processes participated in and interfered with by spiritual entities of a different order ever turn out to be a probable fact, then not only what I have called the will to communicate, but also the will to *personate* may fall outside of the medium's own dream-life. The humbugging may not be chargeable to her all alone, centers of consciousness lower than hers may take part in it, just as higher ones may occasion some of the more inexplicable items of the veridical current in the stream.

The plot of possibilities thus thickens; and it thickens still more when we ask how a will which is dormant or relatively dormant during the intervals may become consciously reanimated as a spirit-personality by the occurrence of the medium's trance. A certain theory of Fechner's helps my own imagination here, so I will state it briefly for my reader's benefit.

Fechner in his *Zend-Avesta*[5] and elsewhere assumes that mental and physical life run parallel, all memory-processes being, according to him, coordinated with material processes. If an act of yours is to

---

[5] *Zend-Avesta*, 2nd edition, 1901, §§ XXI and following. Compare also Elwood Worcester: *The Living Word*, New York, Moffett, Yard & Co., 1908, Part II: and Wm. James, *A Pluralistic Universe*, Longmans, Green & Co., 1909. Lecture iv.

be consciously remembered hereafter, it must leave traces on the material universe such that when the *traced parts of the said universe systematically enter into activity together* the act is consciously recalled. During your life the traces are mainly in your brain; but after your death, since your brain is gone, they exist in the shape of all the records of your actions which the outer world stores up as the effects, immediate or remote, thereof, the cosmos being in some degree, however slight, made structurally different by every act of ours that takes place in it.[6] Now, just as the air of the same room can be simultaneously used by many different voices for communicating with different pairs of ears, or as the ether of space can carry many simultaneous messages to and from mutually attuned Marconi-stations, so the great continuum of material nature can have certain tracts within it thrown into emphasized activity whenever activity begins in any part or parts of a tract in which the potentiality of such systematic activity inheres. The bodies (including of course the brains) of Hodgson's friends who come as sitters, are naturally parts of the material universe which carry some of the traces of his ancient acts. They function as receiving stations, and Hodgson (at one time of his life at any rate) was inclined to suspect that the sitter himself acts "psychometrically," or by his body being what, in the trance-jargon, is called an "influence," in attracting the right spirits and eliciting the right communications from the other side. If, now, *the rest of the system of physical traces* left behind by Hodgson's acts were by some sort of mutual induction throughout its extent, thrown into gear and made to vibrate all at once, by the presence of such human bodies to the medium, we should have a Hodgson-system active in the cosmos again, and the "conscious aspect" of this vibrating system might be Hodgson's spirit redivivus, and recollecting and willing in a certain momentary way. There seems fair evidence of the reality of psychometry; so that this scheme covers the main phenomena in a vague general way. In particular, it would account for the "confusion" and "weakness" that are such prevalent features: the system of physical

---

[6] "It is Handel's work, not the body with which he did the work, that pulls us half over London. There is not an action of a muscle in a horse's leg upon a winter's night as it drags a carriage to the Albert Hall but what is in connection with, and part outcome of, the force generated when Handel sat in his room at Gopsall and wrote the Messiah. ... This is the true Handel who is more a living power among us one hundred and twenty-two years after his death than during the time he was amongst us in the body." Samuel Butler, in the *New Quarterly*, I. 303, March, 1908.

traces corresponding to the given spirit would then be only imperfectly aroused. It tallies vaguely with the analogy of energy finding its way from higher to lower levels. The sitter, with his desire to receive, forms, so to speak, a drainage-opening or sink; the medium, with her desire to personate, yields the nearest lying material to be drained off; while the spirit desiring to communicate is shown the way by the current set up, and swells the latter by its own contributions.

It is enough to indicate these various possibilities, which a serious student of this part of nature has to weigh together, and between which his decision must fall. His vote will always be cast (if ever it be cast) by the sense of the dramatic probabilities of nature which the sum total of his experience has begotten in him. *I myself feel as if an external will to communicate were probably there*, that is, I find myself doubting, in consequence of my whole acquaintance with that sphere of phenomena, that Mrs. Piper's dream-life, even equipped with "telepathic" powers, accounts for all the results found. But if asked whether the will to communicate be Hodgson's, or be some mere spirit-counterfeit of Hodgson, I remain uncertain and await more facts, facts which may not point clearly to a conclusion for fifty or a hundred years.

My report has been too rambling in form, and has suffered in cordiality of tone from having to confine itself to the face-value of the Hodgson-material taken alone. The content of that material is no more veridical than is a lot of earlier Piper-material, especially in the clays of the old Phinuit control.[7] And it is, as I began by saying, vastly more leaky and susceptible of naturalistic explanation than is anybody of Piper-material recorded before. Had I been reviewing the entire Piper-phenomenon, instead of this small section of it, my tone would probably give much less umbrage to some of its spiritistic friends who are also valued friends of mine.

---

[7] See, in proof of this assertion, Hodgson's and Hyslop's previous reports.

19

PHYSICAL PHENOMENA AT A PRIVATE CIRCLE

This article, from the 1909 *Journal of the American Society for Psychical Research*, is essentially a brief investigation, lacking any of the in-depth analysis or philosophical speculation of the previous chapters. Though little more than a footnote in the annals of psychical research, it is interesting to read how, despite seeing inexplicable physical phenomena with his own eyes, James still retained his ambiguity regarding interpretation – sticking to both his scientific skepticism and his open-minded rationality that could not simply ignore evidence.

A fortnight ago I heard that, at a private circle of spiritualists in a New England town, a table had been bodily lifted from the floor with no contact but that of fingers to its upper surface. The rarity of the case induced me to make a visit to the town in question, where I have had three sittings with the circle and from whence I now write.

The circle is composed of solid citizens of the town and their wives or sisters. They have sat weekly for a couple of years, and impressed me as perfectly sincere and earnest in their quest of facts. They use a four-cornered and four-legged table of wood, thirteen pounds in weight, on the center of which a revolving disc twenty inches in diameter, bearing an alphabet, has been pivoted. The disc revolves with a minimum of friction, and an index hand, pivoted independently, points to the letters and spells messages. The sitters' fingers may be placed on the edges of the table an inch below the disc or on the disc itself. To avoid too much pressure on the rotating disc, a ring or rail of thick brass wire has been adjusted to the corners of the table, surrounding the disc at four inches' distance, on which the wrists of those present may rest while they lay their fingertips on the disc. This ring slides with a moderate friction through four brass collars which sustain it, and which themselves are sustained by brass stems screwed to the angles of the table. The disc and the ring are thus concentric. (I go into these details about the ring, for reasons which will appear presently.)

For nearly three years nothing happened at this circle but answers to questions by tipping, and messages spelt out by the disc. No one present seemed to be exclusively the medium, though one lady, absent from town at the time of my visit, was considered to have the most "power."

I

Of the first physical phenomenon I got only oral testimony. This was the fact on two occasions, in the autumn of 1907, of explosive sounds as "loud as a pistol shot," seeming to occur each time in the room where the sitting was being held. On one occasion the sound was repeated seven times. On the other, the sitting being held in a house a couple of miles distant from the first one, it occurred but once. It was entirely unexpected and unexplained, seems to have startled everyone very much, and all present believed that it was spiritual.

II

The second physical phenomenon obtained by the circle was the following: I copy the account from the diary of the circle's proceedings, under date of November 24th, 1907.

> At this meeting we at first took large center table, placed ordinary finger-bowls on table, one for each person, and partly filled with water. Mrs. M.'s bowl moved with just her fingers in the water, not touching the bowl in any way. Made intelligent movements, moving towards Mr. R. when asked. Other bowls also moved, but fingers had to be in contact with them in some manner.

The five witnesses have signed their names to this record for me. They say that the bowl "waltzed round the edge of the table," that they had tried the experiment on other evenings, but that this was the only attempt that succeeded.

III

The next phenomenon of the kind which happened is given in the following account which I wrote down from the oral testimony of seven of the eight witnesses, and to which all but the absent one have appended their signatures, though they are willing to have these printed.

> On the night of November 19th, 1908, we, the undersigned, were having a sitting round the table used for many months in our experiments. [The table I have described above.—W. J.]
> On the occasion in question our fingertips were all resting on the top of the disc, so that they could not possibly exert any lifting force whatever on the table. The hands of Mrs. B. alone were in the air, a few inches above the center of the disc. After some of the usual tiltings of the table, with two or three of the legs off the ground, *it rose gently and with all four legs off the ground to the height of six inches or more*, to the great surprise of all of us, and remained in the air two or three seconds, subsiding slowly to the ground.
> Some said that the sensation of resistance to their fingers was as if the table were supported by a spiral spring.
> Immediately after this a message was spelt out, ordering Mrs. B. to join her hands above the table with those of Mr. D. The same phenomenon was then repeated twice over, the table rising the last time to what seemed to be ten inches from the floor." [Here follow the signatures.]

IV

My own first visit was on Thursday, Dec. 3, 1908. (Thursday is the night on which the circle habitually sits.) Eight persons, counting myself, were present, three women, five men.

We sat at first with our fingers on the solid table beneath the disc, and various tippings came. Then, with our wrists or palms on the ring and our fingers on the disc various messages were spelt.

Mrs. B., whose fifth sitting it was, had her fingers automatically jerked away whenever she placed them on the disc. This had happened previously; and, during the previous lifting of the table on Nov. 19th, she had held her hands in the air some inches above the disc. She kept them in that situation on this present occasion whenever we made attempts to have the table lifted. Such attempts were several times repeated, but with no success.

On the controls then being asked whether they could not *make the disc rotate* without contact, they spelt "no."

Suddenly, while we were sitting with our wrists on the brass ring and our fingers on the disc, which turned and spelled, *we perceived that the ring or rail itself was moving.* It had never done this on any previous evening. The phenomenon was consequently unexpected, and seemed to strike all present with surprise.

Someone immediately suggested that all wrists should be lifted, and then, in brilliant light, and no one's hands in any way in contact with the rail, our fingers, however, resting on the disc, we all distinctly saw the rail or ring *slide slowly and for several inches through the collars, as if spontaneously.*

We then stuck a mark upon the ring to make its motion more obvious, and repeated five or six times the experiment, the same result ensuing, though more slightly each time. It always took the contact of our wrists to start the rail, but *its motion continued when the contact ceased*. This was not from its acquired momentum, for we ascertained that the friction of the collars which held the rail stopped instantly every motion imparted voluntarily by the hand.

On the succeeding Saturday and Sunday evenings, we sat again (one of the ladies being absent), but nothing but the usual tilting of the table and spelling of messages occurred.

So much for the "record," which all present have signed. It will be observed that all the phenomena reported (save the movements of the finger bowl) were unexpected and startling to the spectators. The explosions and the table's rising seem to have been eminently so, and to have made a great impression.

On December 3rd, when the ring revolved, the conditions of observation were perfect, the light (from an electric chandelier just overhead) being brilliant, and the phenomena being slow enough, and often enough repeated, to leave my own mind in no doubt at the time as to what was witnessed. I was quite convinced that I saw that no hand was on the ring while it was moving. The maximum length of its path under these circumstances was fully six inches. With this conviction that I saw all there was to see, I have to confess that I am surprised that the phenomenon affected me emotionally so little. I may add, as a psychological fact, that now, after four days' interval, my mind seems strongly inclined not to "count" the observation, as if it were too exceptional to have been probable. I have only once before seen an object moved "paradoxically," and then the conditions were unsatisfactory. But I have supposed that if I could once see the same thing "satisfactorily," the levee by which scientific opinion protects nature would be cracked for me, and I should be as one watching an incipient overflow of the Mississippi of the supernatural into the fields of orthodox culture. I find, however, that I look on nature with unaltered eyes today, and that my orthodox habits tend to extrude this would-be levee-breaker. It forms too much of an exception.

Nevertheless, in the somewhat scandalously divided state of opinion about Eusapia Paladino, I think that every approach to similar phenomena observed anywhere ought to be recorded. It may be that the frequency rather than the quality of the records, will establish their "case."

20

THE CONFIDENCES OF A "PSYCHICAL RESEARCHER"

W ritten for the popular publication *American Magazine* in 1909, this article marked James's formal end to his serious involvement with psychical research. It was composed quickly as he was completing his Hodgson-control report (Chapter 17), and it is probable that articulating his thoughts for a popular audience helped him to formulate his final conclusions, and vice versa. Indeed, there is some overlap between the two pieces, though presented for very different audiences. In the present article, James gives himself freer rein to say what he really thinks and lets his metaphysical speculations run free in ways that recall his more widely accepted philosophical writings (as will be seen in section V of this book). The description given to the article by the magazine editor was: "In which the author, after twenty-five years of 'dabbling' in 'Psychics,' states his conclusions, goes on record, and describes the field wherein he thinks the greatest scientific conquests of the coming generation will be achieved."

The article seems intended to be James's last word on the subject, and indeed when it was reprinted in the collection *Memories and Studies* edited by his son Henry, it was retitled "Final Impressions of a Psychical Researcher."

The article was "illustrated with crayon portraits by William Oberhardt" depicting mediums and psychical researchers discussed by James. They are included below, reprinted for the first time.

The late Professor Henry Sidgwick was celebrated for the rare mixture of ardor and critical judgment which his character exhibited. The liberal heart which he possessed had to work with an intellect which acted destructively on almost every particular object of belief that was offered to its acceptance. A quarter of a century ago, scandalized by the chaotic state of opinion regarding the phenomena now called by the rather ridiculous name of "psychic"—phenomena of which the supply reported seems inexhaustible, but which scientifically trained minds mostly refuse to look at—he established, along with Professor Barrett, Frederic Myers and Edmund Gurney, the Society for Psychical Research. These men hoped that if the material were treated rigorously and, as far as possible, experimentally, objective truth would be elicited, and the subject rescued from sentimentalism on the one side and dogmatizing ignorance on the other. Like all founders, Sidgwick hoped for a certain promptitude of result; and I heard him say, the year before his death, that if anyone had told him at the outset that after twenty years he would be in the same identical state of doubt and balance that he started with, he would have deemed the prophecy incredible. It appeared impossible that that amount of handling evidence should bring so little finality of decision.

Can We "Communicate with Spirits?"

My own experience has been similar to Sidgwick's. For twenty-five years I have been in touch with the literature of psychical research, and have had acquaintance with numerous "researchers." I have also spent a good many hours (though far fewer than I ought to have spent) in witnessing (or trying to witness) phenomena. Yet I am theoretically no "further" than I was at the beginning; and I confess that at times I have been tempted to believe that the Creator has eternally intended this department of nature to remain *baffling*, to prompt our curiosities and hopes and suspicions all in equal measure, so that, although ghosts and clairvoyances, and raps and messages from spirits, are always seeming to exist and can never be fully explained away, they also can never be susceptible of full corroboration.

The peculiarity of the case is just that there are so many sources of possible deception in most of the observations that the whole lot of them *may be* worthless, and yet that in comparatively few cases can aught more fatal than this vague general possibility of error be pleaded against the record. Science meanwhile needs something more than bare possibilities to build upon; so your genuinely scientific inquirer—I don't mean your ignoramus "scientist"—has to remain unsatisfied. It is hard to believe, however, that the Creator has really put any big array of phenomena into the world merely to defy and mock our scientific tendencies; so my deeper belief is that we psychical researchers have been too precipitate with our hopes, and that we must expect to mark progress not by quarter-centuries, but by half-centuries or whole centuries.

I am strengthened in this belief by my impression that just at this moment a faint but distinct step forward is being taken by competent opinion in these matters. "Physical phenomena" (movements of matter without contact, lights, hands and faces "materialized," etc.) have been one of the most baffling regions of the general field (or perhaps one of the least baffling *prima facie*, so certain and great has been the part played by fraud in their production); yet even here the balance of testimony seems slowly to be inclining towards admitting the supernaturalist view. Eusapia Paladino, the Neapolitan medium, has been under observation for twenty years or more. Schiaparelli, the astronomer, and Lombroso were the first scientific men to be converted by her performances. Since then innumerable men of scientific standing have seen her, including many "psychic" experts. Everyone agrees that she cheats in the most barefaced manner whenever she gets an opportunity. The Cambridge experts, with the Sidgwicks and Richard Hodgson at their head, rejected her *in toto* on that account. Yet her credit has steadily risen, and now her last converts are the eminent psychiatrist, Morselli, the eminent physiologist, Botazzi, and our own psychical researcher, Carrington, whose book on *The Physical Phenomena of Spiritualism* (*against* them rather!) makes his conquest strategically important. If Mr. Podmore, hitherto the prosecuting attorney of the SPR so far as physical phenomena are concerned, becomes converted also, we may indeed sit up and look around us. Getting a good health bill from "Science," Eusapia will then throw retrospective credit on Home and Stainton Moses, Florence Cook (Prof. Crookes's medium), and all similar wonder-workers. The balance of *presumptions* will be changed in favor of genuineness being possible at least, in all reports of this particularly crass and low type of supernatural phenomenon.

EUSAPIA PALADINO

The Neapolitan Medium, under observation for twenty years, who has convinced Schiaparelli and Lombroso of her genuineness, and who cheats in a barefaced manner whenever she gets an opportunity

CESARE LOMBROSO

The famous criminologist who originated the theory that there is a definite criminal type, the born criminal, that may be distinguished from other men by physical stigmata. He is Paladino's most distinguished convert

GIOVANNI SCHIAPARELLI

The Italian astronomer who discovered the so-called "canals" in Mars, and who is a well-known psychical researcher

Scientists Who Cheat

Not long after Darwin's *Origin of Species* appeared I was studying with that excellent anatomist and man, Jeffries Wyman, at Harvard. He was a convert, yet so far a half-hesitating one, to Darwin's views; but I heard him make a remark that applies well to the subject I now write about. When, he said, a theory gets propounded over and over again, coming up afresh after each time orthodox criticism has buried it, and each time seeming solider and harder to abolish, you may be sure that there is truth in it. Oken and Lamarck and Chambers had been triumphantly dispatched and buried, but here was Darwin making the very same heresy seem only more plausible. How often has "Science" killed off all spook philosophy, and laid ghosts and raps and "telepathy" away underground as so much popular delusion. Yet never before were these things offered us so voluminously, and never in such authentic-seeming shape or with such good credentials. The tide seems steadily to be rising, in spite of all the expedients of scientific orthodoxy. It is hard not to suspect that here may be something different from a mere chapter in human gullibility. It may be a genuine realm of natural phenomena.

Falsus in uno, falsus in omnibus, once a cheat, always a cheat, such has been the motto of the English psychical researchers in dealing with mediums. I am disposed to think that, as a matter of policy, it has been wise. Tactically it is far better to believe much too little than a little too much; and the exceptional credit attaching to the row of volumes of the SPR's *Proceedings*, is due to the fixed intention of the editors to proceed very slowly. Better a little belief tied fast, better a small investment *salted down*, than a mass of comparative insecurity.

But, however wise as a policy the SPR's maxim may have been, as a test of truth I believe it to be almost irrelevant. In most things human the accusation of deliberate fraud and falsehood is grossly superficial. Man's character is too sophistically mixed for the alternative of "honest or dishonest" to be a sharp one. Scientific men themselves will cheat—at public lectures—rather than let experiments obey their well-known tendency towards failure. I have heard of a lecturer on physics, who had taken over the apparatus of the previous incumbent, consulting him about a certain machine intended to show that, however the peripheral parts of it might be agitated, its center of gravity remained immovable. "It *will* wobble," he complained.

"Well," said the predecessor, apologetically, "to tell the truth, whenever *I* used that machine I found it advisable to *drive a nail* through the center of gravity." I once saw a distinguished physiologist, now dead, cheat most shamelessly at a public lecture, at the expense of a poor rabbit, and all for the sake of being able to make a cheap joke about its being an "American rabbit"—for no other, he said, could survive such a wound as he pretended to have given it.

A Confession by Professor James

To compare small men with great, I have myself cheated shamelessly. In the early days of the Sanders Theater at Harvard, I once had charge of a heart on the physiology of which Prof. Newell Martin was giving a popular lecture. This heart, which belonged to a turtle, supported an index-straw which threw a moving shadow, greatly enlarged, upon the screen, while the heart pulsated. When certain nerves were stimulated, the lecturer said, the heart would act in certain ways which he described. But the poor heart was too far gone and, although it stopped duly when the nerve of arrest was excited, that was the final end of its life's tether. Presiding over the performance, I was terrified at the fiasco, and found myself suddenly acting like one of those military geniuses who on the field of battle convert disaster into victory. There was no time for deliberation; so, with my forefinger under a part of the straw that cast no shadow, I found myself impulsively and automatically imitating the rhythmical movements which my colleague had prophesied the heart would undergo. I kept the experiment from failing; and not only saved my colleague (and the turtle) from a humiliation that but for my presence of mind would have been their lot, but I established in the audience the true view of the subject. The lecturer was stating this; and the misconduct of one half-dead specimen of heart ought not to destroy the impression of his words. "There is no worse lie than a truth misunderstood," is a maxim which I have heard ascribed to a former venerated President of Harvard. The heart's failure would have been misunderstood by the audience and given the lie to the lecturer. It was hard enough to make them understand the subject anyhow; so that even now as I write in cool blood I am tempted to think that I acted quite correctly. I was acting for the *larger* truth, at any rate, however automatically; and my sense of this was probably what prevented the more pedantic and literal part of my conscience from checking the action of my sympathetic finger. To this day the memory of that critical emergency has made me feel charitable towards all mediums who make phenomena come in one way when they won't come easily in another. On the principles of the SPR, my conduct on that one occasion ought to discredit everything I ever do, everything for example, I may write in this article—a manifestly unjust conclusion.

A Shallow State of Public Opinion

Fraud, conscious or unconscious, seems ubiquitous throughout the range of physical phenomena of spiritism, and false pretense, prevarication and fishing for clues are ubiquitous in the mental manifestations of mediums. If it be not everywhere fraud simulating reality, one is tempted to say, then the reality (if any reality there be) has the bad luck of being fated everywhere to simulate fraud. The suggestion of humbug seldom stops, and mixes itself with the best manifestations. Mrs. Piper's control, "Rector," is a most impressive personage, who discerns in an extraordinary degree his sitter's inner needs, and is capable of giving elevated counsel to fastidious and critical minds. Yet in many respects he is an arrant humbug—such he seems to me at least—pretending to a knowledge and power to which he has no title, nonplussed by contradiction, yielding to suggestion, and covering his tracks with plausible excuses. Now the non-"researching" mind looks upon such phenomena simply according to their face-pretension and never thinks of asking what they may signify below the surface. Since they profess for the most part to be revealers of spirit life, it is either as being absolutely that, or as being absolute frauds, that they are judged. The result is an inconceivably shallow state of public opinion on the subject. One set of persons, emotionally touched at hearing the names of their loved ones given, and consoled by assurances that they are "happy," accept the revelation, and consider spiritualism "beautiful." More hard-headed subjects, disgusted by the revelation's contemptible contents, outraged by the fraud, and prejudiced beforehand against all "spirits," high or low, avert their minds from what they call such "rot" or "'bosh" entirely. Thus do two opposite sentimentalisms divide opinion between them! A good expression of the "scientific" state of mind occurs in Huxley's *Life and Letters*.

"I regret," he writes, "that I am unable to accept the invitation of the Committee of the Dialectical Society. ... I take no interest in the subject. The only case of 'Spiritualism' I have ever had the opportunity of examining into for myself was as gross an imposture as ever came under my notice. But supposing these phenomena to be genuine—they do not interest me. If anybody would endow me with the faculty of listening to the chatter of old women and curates in the nearest provincial town, I should decline the privilege, having better things to do. And if the folk in the spiritual world do not talk more wisely and sensibly than their friends report them to do, I put them in the same category. The only good that I can see in the demonstration of the 'Truth of Spiritualism' is to furnish an additional argument against suicide. Better live a crossing-sweeper, than die and be made to talk twaddle by a 'medium' hired at a guinea a *Seance*."[1]

Obviously, the mind of the excellent Huxley has here but two whole-souled categories, namely revelation or imposture, to apperceive the case by. Sentimental reasons bar revelation out, for the messages, he thinks, are not romantic enough for that; fraud exists anyhow; therefore the whole thing is nothing but imposture. The odd point is that so few of those who talk in this way realize that they and the spiritists are using the same major premise and differing only in the minor. The major premise is: "Any spirit-revelation must be romantic." The minor of the spiritist is: "This is romantic"; that of the Huxleyan is: "this is dingy twaddle"—whence their opposite conclusions!

MRS. PIPER

One of the most notable living mediums. Her control, "Rector," is a most impressive personage, who discerns in an extraordinary degree his sitter's inner needs, and is capable of giving elevated counsel to fastidious and critical minds

---

[1] T.H. Huxley, *Life and Letters*, I, 240.

One Way of Interpreting Certain Phenomena

Meanwhile the first thing that anyone learns who attends seriously to these phenomena is that their causation is far too complex for our feelings about what is or is not romantic enough to be spiritual to throw any light upon it. The causal factors must be carefully distinguished and traced through series, from their simplest to their strongest forms, before we can begin to understand the various resultants in which they issue. Myers and Gurney began this work, the one by his serial study of the various sorts of "automatism," sensory and motor, the other by his experimental proofs that a split-off consciousness may abide after a post-hypnotic suggestion has been given. Here we have subjective factors; but are not transsubjective or objective forces also at work? Veridical messages, apparitions, movements without contact, seem *prima facie* to be such. It was a good stroke on Gurney's part to construct a theory of apparitions which brought the subjective and the objective factors into harmonious co-operation. I doubt whether this telepathic theory of Gurney's will hold along the whole line of apparitions to which he applied it, but it is unquestionable that some theory of that mixed type is required for the explanation of all mediumistic phenomena; and that when all the psychological factors and elements involved have been told off—and they are many—the question still forces itself upon us: Are these all, or are there indications of any residual forces acting on the subject from beyond, or of any "metapsychic" faculty (to use Richet's useful term), exerted by him? This is the problem that requires real expertness, and this is where the simple sentimentalisms of the spiritist and scientist leave us in the lurch completely.

"Psychics" form indeed a special branch of education, in which experts are only gradually becoming developed. The phenomena are as massive and wide-spread as is anything in Nature, and the study of them is as tedious, repellent and undignified. To reject it for its unromantic character is like rejecting bacteriology because *penicillium glaucum* grows on horse-dung and *bacterium termo* lives in putrefaction. Scientific men have long ago ceased to think of the dignity of the materials they work in. When imposture has been checked off as far as possible, when chance coincidence has been allowed for, when opportunities for normal knowledge on the part of the subject have been noted, and skill in "fishing" and following clues unwittingly furnished by the voice or face of bystanders have been counted in, those who have the fullest acquaintance with the phenomena admit that in good mediums *there is a residuum of knowledge displayed* that can only be called supernormal: the medium taps some source of information not open to ordinary people. Myers used the word "telepathy" to indicate that the sitter's own thoughts or feelings may be thus directly tapped. Mrs. Sidgwick has suggested that if living minds can be thus tapped telepathically, so possibly may the minds of spirits be similarly tapped—if spirits there be. On this view we should have one distinct theory of the performances of a typical test-medium. They would be all originally due to an odd *tendency to personate*, found in her dream life as it expresses itself in trance. [Most of us reveal such a tendency whenever we handle a "ouija-board" or a "planchet," or let ourselves write automatically with a pencil.] The result is a "control," who purports to be speaking; and all the resources of the automatist, including his or her trance-faculty of telepathy, are called into play in building this fictitious personage out plausibly. On such a view of the control, the medium's *will to personate* runs the whole show; and if spirits be involved in it at all, they are passive beings, stray bits of whose memory she is able to seize and use for her purposes, without the spirit being any more aware of it than the sitter is aware of it when his own mind is similarly tapped.

This is one possible way of interpreting a certain type of psychical phenomenon. It uses psychological as well as "spiritual" factors, and quite obviously it throws open for us far more questions than it answers, questions about our subconscious constitution and its curious tendency to humbug, about the telepathic faculty, and about the possibility of an existent spirit-world.

What is "Pure Bosh?"

I do not instance this theory to defend it, but simply to show what complicated hypothesis one is inevitably led to consider, the moment one looks at the facts in their complexity and turns one's back on the naïve alternative of "revelation or imposture," which is as far as either spiritist thought or ordinary scientist thought goes. The phenomena are endlessly complex in their factors, and they are so little understood as yet that off-hand judgments, whether of "spirits" or of "bosh" are the one as silly as the other. When we complicate the subject still farther by considering what connection such things as rappings, apparitions, poltergeists, spirit-photographs, and materializations may have with it, the bosh end of the scale gets heavily loaded, it is true, but your genuine inquirer still is loath to give up. He lets the data collect, and bides his time. He believes that "bosh" is no more an ultimate element in Nature, or a really explanatory category in human life than "dirt" is in chemistry. Every kind of "bosh" has its own factors and laws; and patient study will bring them definitely to light.

The only way to rescue the "pure bosh" view of the matter is one which has sometimes appealed to my own fancy, but which I imagine few readers will seriously adopt. If, namely, one takes the theory of evolution radically, one ought to apply it not only to the rock-strata, the animals and the plants, but to the stars, to the chemical elements, and to the laws of nature. There must have been a far-off antiquity, one is then tempted to suppose, when things were really chaotic. Little by little, out of all the haphazard possibilities of that time, a few connected things and habits arose, and the rudiments of regular performance began. Every variation in the way of law and order added itself to this nucleus, which inevitably grew more considerable as history went on; while the aberrant and inconstant variations, not being similarly preserved, disappeared from being, wandered off as unrelated vagrants, or else remained so imperfectly connected with the part of the world that had grown regular as only to manifest their existence by occasional lawless intrusions, like those which "psychic" phenomena now make into our scientifically organized world. On such a view, these phenomena ought to remain "pure bosh" forever, that is, they ought to be forever intractable to intellectual methods, because they should not yet be organized enough in themselves to follow any laws. Wisps and shreds of the original chaos, they would

RICHARD HODGSON

Secretary and Treasurer of the American Branch of the Society for Psychical Research up to the time of his death in 1905. Many of Mr. Hodgson's associates in psychical research assert that since his death, intelligent and characteristic communications have been received from him through various mediums

be connected enough with the cosmos to affect its periphery every now and then, as by a momentary whiff or touch or gleam, but not enough ever to be followed up and hunted down and bagged. Their relation to the cosmos would be tangential solely.

Looked at dramatically, most occult phenomena make just this sort of impression. They are inwardly as incoherent as they are outwardly wayward and fitful. If they express anything, it is pure "bosh," pure discontinuity, accident, and disturbance, with no law apparent but to interrupt, and no purpose but to baffle. They seem like stray vestiges of that primordial irrationality, from which all our rationalities have been evolved.

To settle dogmatically into this bosh-view would save labor, but it would go against too many intellectual prepossessions to be adopted save as a last resort of despair. Your psychical researcher therefore bates no jot of hope, and has faith that when we get our data numerous enough, some sort of rational treatment of them will succeed.

The Effect on Myers and Hodgson

When I hear good people say (as they often say, not without show of reason), that dabbling in such phenomena reduces us to a sort of jelly, disintegrates the critical faculties, liquefies the character, and makes of one a *gobe-mouche* [credulous person] generally, I console myself by thinking of my friends Frederic Myers and Richard Hodgson. These men lived exclusively for psychical research, and it converted both to spiritism. Hodgson would have been a man among men anywhere; but I doubt whether under any other baptism he would have been that happy, sober and righteous form of energy which his face proclaimed him in his later years, when heart and head alike were wholly satisfied by his occupation. Myers's character also grew stronger in every particular for his devotion to the same inquiries. Brought up on literature and sentiment, something of a courtier, passionate, disdainful, and impatient naturally, he was made over again from the day when he took up psychical research seriously. He became learned in science, circumspect, democratic in sympathy, endlessly patient, and above all, happy. The fortitude of his last hours touched the heroic, so completely were the atrocious sufferings of his body cast into insignificance by his interest in the cause he lived for. When a man's pursuit gradually makes his face shine and grow handsome, you may be sure it is a worthy one. Both

Hodgson and Myers kept growing ever handsomer and stronger-looking.

Such personal examples will convert no one, and of course they ought not to. Nor do I seek at all in this article to convert anyone to my belief that psychical research is an important branch of science. To do that, I should have to quote evidence; and those for whom the volumes of SPR *Proceedings* already published count for nothing would remain in their dogmatic slumber, though one rose from the dead. No, not to convert readers, but simply to *put my own state of mind upon record publicly* is the purpose of my present writing. Someone said to me a short time ago that after my twenty-five years of dabbling in "Psychics," it would be rather shameful were I unable to state any definite conclusions whatever as a consequence. I had to agree; so I now proceed to take up the challenge and express such convictions as have been engendered in me by that length of experience, be the same true or false ones. I may be dooming myself to the pit in the eyes of better-judging posterity; I may be raising myself to honor; I am willing to take the risk, for what I shall write is my truth, as I now see it.

There is "Something in" These Phenomena

I began this article by confessing myself baffled. I *am* baffled, as to spirit-return, and as to many other special problems. I am also constantly baffled as to what to think of this or that particular story, for the sources of error in any one observation are seldom fully knowable. But weak sticks make strong faggots; and when the stories fall into consistent sorts that point each in a definite direction, one gets a sense of being in presence of genuinely natural types of phenomena. As to there being such real natural types of phenomena ignored by orthodox science, I am not baffled at all, for I am fully convinced of it. One cannot get demonstrative proof here. One has to follow one's personal sense, which, of course, is liable to err, of the dramatic probabilities of nature. Our critics here obey their sense of dramatic probability as much as we do. Take "raps" for ex- ample, and the whole business of objects moving without contact. "Nature," thinks the scientific man, is not so unutterably silly. The cabinet, the darkness, the tying, suggest a sort of human rat-hole life exclusively and "swindling" is for him the dramatically sufficient explanation. It probably is, in an indefinite majority of instances; yet it is to me dramatically improbable that the swindling should not have accreted round some originally genuine nucleus. If we look at human imposture as a historic phenomenon, we find it always imitative. One swindler imitates a previous swindler, but the first swindler of that kind imitated someone who was honest. You can no more create an absolutely new trick than you can create a new word without any previous basis—You don't know how to go about it. Try, reader, yourself, to invent an unprecedented kind of "physical phenomenon of spiritualism." When *I* try, I find myself mentally turning over the regular medium-stock, and thinking how I might improve some item. This being the dramatically probable human way, I think differently of the whole type, taken collectively, from the way in which I may think of the single instance. I find myself believing that there is "something in" these never-ending reports of physical phenomena, although I haven't yet the least positive notion of the something. It becomes to my mind simply a very worthy problem for investigation. Either I or the scientist is of course a fool, with our opposite views of probability here; and I only wish he might feel the liability, as cordially as I do, to pertain to both of us.

Professor James Goes on Record

I fear I look on Nature generally with more charitable eyes than his, though perhaps he would pause if he realized as I do, how vast the fraudulency is which in consistency he must attribute to her. Nature is brutal enough, Heaven knows; but no one yet has held her non-human side to be *dishonest*, and even in the human sphere deliberate deceit is far rarer than the "classic" intellect, with its few and rigid categories, was ready to acknowledge. There is a hazy penumbra in us all where lying and delusion meet, where passion rules beliefs as well as conduct, and where the term "scoundrel" does not clear up everything to the depths as it did for our forefathers. The first automatic writing I ever saw was forty years ago. I unhesitatingly thought of it as deceit, although it contained vague elements of supernormal knowledge. Since then I have come to see in automatic writing one example of a department of human activity as vast as it is enigmatic. Every sort of person is liable to it, or to something equivalent to it; and whoever encourages it in himself finds himself personating someone else, either signing what he writes by fictitious name, or spelling out, by ouija-board or table- tips, messages from the departed. Our subconscious region seems, as a rule, to be dominated either by a crazy "will to make-believe," or by some curious external force impelling us to personation. The first difference between the psychical researcher and the inexpert person is that the former realizes the commonness and typicality of the phenomenon here, while the latter, less informed, thinks it so rare as to be unworthy of attention. *I wish to go on record for the commonness.*

The next thing I wish to go on record for is *the presence*, in the midst of all the humbug, *of really supernormal knowledge*. By this I mean knowledge that cannot be traced to the ordinary sources of information—the senses namely, of the automatist. In really strong mediums this knowledge seems to be abundant, though it is usually spotty, capricious and unconnected. Really strong mediums are rarities; but when one starts with them and works downwards into less brilliant regions of the automatic life, one tends to interpret many slight but odd coincidences with truth as possibly rudimentary forms of this kind of knowledge.

What is one to think of this queer chapter in human nature? It is odd enough on any view. If all it means is a preposterous and inferior monkey-like tendency to forge messages, systematically embedded in the soul of all of us, it is weird; and weirder still that it should then own all this supernormal information. If on the other hand the supernormal information be the key to the phenomenon, it ought to be superior; and then how ought we to account for the "wicked partner," and for the undeniable mendacity and inferiority of so much of the performance? We are thrown, for our conclusions, upon our instinctive sense of the dramatic probabilities of nature. My own dramatic sense tends instinctively to picture the situation as an interaction between slumbering faculties in the automatist's mind and a cosmic environment of *other consciousness* of some sort which is able to work upon them. If there were in the universe a lot of diffuse soul-stuff, unable of itself to get into consistent personal form, or to take permanent possession of an organism, yet always craving to do so, it might get its head into the air, parasitically, so to speak, by profiting by weak spots in the armor of human minds, and slipping in and stirring up there the sleeping tendency to personate. It would induce habits in the subconscious region of the mind it used thus, and would seek above all things to prolong its social opportunities by making itself agreeable and plausible. It would drag stray scraps of truth with it from the wider environment, but would betray its mental inferiority by knowing little how to weave them into any important or significant story.

This, I say, is the dramatic view which my mind spontaneously takes, and it has the advantage of falling into line with ancient human traditions. The views of others are just as dramatic, *for the phenomenon is actuated by will of some sort anyhow*, and wills give rise to dramas. The spiritist view, as held by Messrs. Hyslop and Hodgson, sees a "will to communicate," struggling through inconceivable layers of obstruction in the conditions. I have heard Hodgson liken the difficulties to those of two persons who on earth should have only dead- drunk servants to use as their messengers. The scientist, for his part, sees a "will to deceive," watching its chance in all of us, and able (possibly?) to use "telepathy" in its service.

JAMES HERVEY HYSLOP
Professor of Logic and Ethics at Columbia University, an ardent psychologist who believes that there is a well-defined " will to communicate" evinced by the spirit world

Which kind of will, and how many kinds of will are most inherently probable? Who can say with certainty? The only certainty is that the phenomena are enormously complex, especially if one includes in them such intellectual flights of mediumship as Swedenborg's, and if one tries in any way to work the physical phenomena in. That is why I personally am as yet neither a convinced believer in parasitic demons, nor a spiritist, nor a scientist, but still remain a psychical researcher waiting for more facts before concluding.

Great Scientific Conquests of the Future

Out of my experience, such as it is (and it is limited enough) one fixed conclusion dogmatically emerges, and that is this, that we with our lives are like islands in the sea, or like trees in the forest. The maple and the pine may whisper to each other with their leaves, and Conanicut and Newport hear each other's fog-horns. But the trees also commingle their roots in the darkness underground, and the islands also hang together through the ocean's bottom. Just so there is a continuum of cosmic consciousness, against which our individuality builds but accidental fences, and into which our several minds plunge as into a mother-sea or reservoir. Our "normal" consciousness is circumscribed for adaptation to our external earthly environment, but the fence is weak in spots, and fitful influences from beyond leak in, showing the otherwise unverifiable common connection. Not only psychic research, but metaphysical philosophy, and speculative biology are led in their own ways to look with favor on some such "panpsychic" view of the universe as this. Assuming this common reservoir of consciousness to exist, this bank upon which we all draw, and in which so many of earth's memories must in some way be stored, or mediums would not get at them as they do, the question is, What is its own structure? What is its inner topography? This question, first squarely formulated by Myers, deserves to be called "Myers's problem" by scientific men hereafter. What are the conditions of individuation or insulation in this mother-sea? To what tracts, to what active systems functioning separately in it, do personalities correspond? Are individual "spirits" constituted there? How numerous, and of how many hierarchic orders may these then be? How permanent? How transient? And how confluent with one another may they become?

What again, are the relations between the cosmic consciousness and matter? Are there subtler forms of matter which upon occasion may enter into functional connection with the individuations in the psychic sea, and then, and then only, show themselves?—So that our ordinary human experience, on its material as well as on its mental side, would appear to be only an extract from the larger psycho-physical world?

Vast, indeed, and difficult is the inquirer's prospect here, and the most significant data for his purpose will probably be just these dingy little mediumistic facts which the Huxleyan minds of our time find so unworthy of their attention. But when was not the science of the future stirred to its conquering activities by the little rebellious exceptions to the science of the present? Hardly, as yet, has the surface of the facts called "psychic" begun to be scratched for scientific purposes. It is through following these facts, I am persuaded, that the greatest scientific conquests of the coming generation will be achieved. *Kühn ist das Mühen, herrlich der Lohn!* ["Bold is the adventure, Noble the reward!"; from Goethe's *Faust*].

PART IV

POSSESSION

21

MEDIUMSHIPS OR POSSESSIONS

*P**rinciples of Psychology* is one of James's key works, and is a complex, monumental tome. While little of it is devoted to psychical research per se, ideas about the soul, consciousness, and other related themes are scattered throughout.

In this excerpt from Chapter X, "The Consciousness of Self," he revisits automatic writing, though rather than focusing on telepathy as he did in "Notes on Automatic Writing" (Chapter 6, above), he frames the notion of mediumship as part of the continuum of possession phenomena. Although he concludes with a discussion on brain functioning during dissociated states such as trance and possession, his review of the "Watseka Wonder" case seems to lean towards a spiritualistic explanation.

James reused a long example of automatic writing (that of Sidney Dean) from "Notes on Automatic Writing," and it has been deleted here, where indicated.

In *"mediumships"* or *"possessions"* the invasion and the passing away of the secondary state are both relatively abrupt, and the duration of the state is usually short—i.e., from a few minutes to a few hours. Whenever the secondary state is well developed no memory for aught that happened during it remains after the primary consciousness comes back. The subject during the secondary consciousness speaks, writes, or acts as if animated by a foreign person, and often names this foreign person and gives his history. In old times the foreign "control" was usually a demon, and is so now in communities which favor that belief. With us he gives himself out at the worst for an Indian or other grotesquely speaking but harmless personage. Usually he purports to be the spirit of a dead person known or unknown to those present, and the subject is then what we call a "medium." Mediumistic possession in all its grades seems to form a perfectly natural special type of alternate personality, and the susceptibility to it in some form is by no means an uncommon gift, in persons who have no other obvious nervous anomaly. The phenomena are very intricate, and are only just beginning to be studied in a proper scientific way. The lowest phase of mediumship is automatic writing, and the lowest grade of that is where the Subject knows what words are coming, but feels impelled to write them as if from without. Then comes writing unconsciously, even whilst engaged in reading or talk. Inspirational speaking, playing on musical instruments, etc., also belong to the relatively lower phases of possession, in which the normal self is not excluded from conscious participation in the performance, though their initiative seems to come from elsewhere. In the highest phase the trance is complete, the voice, language, and everything are changed, and there is no after-memory whatever until the next trance comes. One curious thing about trance-utterances is their generic similarity in different individuals. The "control" here in America is either a grotesque, slangy, and flippant personage ("Indian" controls, calling the ladies "squaws," the men "braves," the house a "wigwam," etc., etc., are excessively common); or, if he ventures on higher intellectual flights, he abounds in a curiously vague optimistic philosophy-and-water, in which phrases about spirit, harmony, beauty, law, progression, development, etc., keep recurring. It seems exactly as if one author composed more than half of the trance-messages, no matter by whom they are uttered. Whether all sub-conscious selves are peculiarly susceptible to a certain stratum of the *Zeitgeist*, and get their inspiration from it, I know not; but this is obviously the case with the secondary selves which become "developed" in spiritualist circles. There the beginnings of the medium trance are indistinguishable from effects of hypnotic suggestion. The subject assumes the role of a medium simply because opinion expects it of him under the conditions which are present; and carries it out with a feebleness or a vivacity proportionate to his histrionic gifts. But the odd thing is that persons unexposed to spiritualist traditions will so often act in the same way when they become entranced, speak in the name of the departed, go through the motions of their several death-agonies, send messages about their happy home in the summer-land, and describe the ailments of those present. I have no theory to publish of these cases, several of which I have personally seen.

As an example of the automatic writing performances I will quote from an account of his own case kindly furnished me by Mr. Sidney Dean of Warren, R. I. ... [a long example copied verbatim from "Notes on Automatic Writing" has been deleted here; see Chapter 6, p. xx of the present volume].

I am myself persuaded by abundant acquaintance with the trances of one medium that the "control" may be altogether different from any *possible* waking self of the person. In the case I have in mind, it professes to be a certain departed French doctor; and is, I am convinced, acquainted with facts about the circumstances, and the living and dead relatives and acquaintances, of numberless sitters whom the medium never met before, and of whom she has never heard the names. I record my bare opinion here unsupported by the evidence, not, of course, in order to convert anyone to my view, but because I am persuaded that a serious study of these trance-phenomena is one of the greatest needs of psychology, and think that my personal confession may possibly draw a reader or two into a field which the *soi-disant* [self-styled] "scientist" usually refuses to explore.

Many persons have found evidence conclusive to their minds that in some cases the control is really the departed spirit whom it pretends to be. The phenomena shade off so gradually into cases where this is obviously absurd, that the presumption (quite apart from *a priori* "scientific" prejudice) is great against its being true. The case of Lurancy Vennum is perhaps as extreme a case of "possession" of the modern sort as one can find.[1] Lurancy was a young girl of fourteen, living with her parents at Watseka, Ill., who (after various distressing hysterical disorders and spontaneous trances, during which she was possessed by departed spirits of a more or less grotesque sort) finally declared herself to be animated by the spirit of Mary Roff (a neighbor's daughter, who had died in an insane asylum twelve years before) and insisted on being sent "home" to Mr. Roff's house. After a week of "homesickness"

---

[1] *The Watseka Wonder*, by E. W. Stevens. Chicago, Religio-Philosophical Publishing House, 1887.

and importunity on her part, her parents agreed, and the Roffs, who pitied her, and who were spiritualists into the bargain, took her in. Once there, she seems to have convinced the family that their dead Mary had exchanged habitations with Lurancy. Lurancy was said to be temporarily in heaven, and Mary's spirit now controlled her organism, and lived again in her former earthly home.

The girl, now in her new home, seemed perfectly happy and content, knowing every person and everything that Mary knew when in her original body, twelve to twenty-five years ago, recognizing and calling by name those who were friends and neighbors of the family from 1852 to 1865, when Mary died, calling attention to scores, yes, hundreds of incidents that transpired during her natural life. During all the period of her sojourn at Mr. Roff's she had no knowledge of, and did not recognize, any of Mr. Vennum's family, their friends or neighbors, yet Mr. and Mrs. Vennum and their children visited her and Mr. Roff's people, she being introduced to them as to any strangers. After frequent visits, and hearing them often and favorably spoken of, she learned to love them as acquaintances, and visited them with Mrs. Roff three times. From day to day she appeared natural, easy, affable, and industrious, attending diligently and faithfully to her household duties, assisting in the general work of the family as a faithful, prudent daughter might be supposed to do, singing, reading, or conversing as opportunity offered, upon all matters of private or general interest to the family.

The so-called Mary whilst at the Roffs' would sometimes "go back to heaven," and leave the body in a "quiet trance," i.e., without the original personality of Lurancy returning. After eight or nine weeks, however, the memory and manner of Lurancy would sometimes partially, but not entirely, return for a few minutes. Once Lurancy seems to have taken full possession for a short time. At last, after some fourteen weeks, conformably to the prophecy which "Mary" had made when she first assumed "control," she departed definitively and the Lurancy-consciousness came back for good. Mr. Roff writes:

> She wanted me to take her home, which I did. She called me Mr. Roff, and talked with me as a young girl would, not being acquainted. I asked her how things appeared to her—if they seemed natural. She said it seemed like a dream to her. She met her parents and brothers in a very affectionate manner, hugging and kissing each one in tears of gladness. She clasped her arms around her father's neck a long time,

fairly smothering him with kisses. I saw her father just now (eleven o'clock). He says she has been perfectly natural, and seems entirely well.

Lurancy's mother writes, a couple of months later, that she was

perfectly and entirely well and natural. For two or three weeks after her return home, she seemed a little strange to what she had been before she was taken sick last summer, but only, perhaps, the natural change that had taken place with the girl, and except it seemed to her as though she had been dreaming or sleeping, etc. Lurancy has been smarter, more intelligent, more industrious, more womanly, and more polite than before. We give the credit of her complete cure and restoration to her family, to Dr. E. W. Stevens, and Mr. and Mrs. Roff, by their obtaining her removal to Mr. Roff's, where her cure was perfected. We firmly believe that, had she remained at home, she would have died, or we would have been obliged to send her to the insane asylum; and if so, that she would have died there; and further, that I could not have lived but a short time with the care and trouble devolving on me. Several of the relatives of Lurancy, including ourselves, now believe she was cured by spirit power, and that Mary Roff controlled the girl.

Eight years later, Lurancy was reported to be married and a mother, and in good health. She had apparently outgrown the mediumistic phase of her existence.[2]

On the condition of the sensibility during these invasions, few observations have been made. I have found the hands of two automatic writers anesthetic during the act. In two others I have found this not to be the case. Automatic writing is usually preceded by shooting pains along the arm-nerves and irregular contractions of the arm-muscles. I have found one medium's tongue and lips apparently insensible to pin-pricks during her (speaking) trance.

---

[2] My friend Mr. R. Hodgson informs me that he visited Watseka in April 1889, and cross-examined the principal witnesses of this case. His confidence in the original narrative was strengthened by what he learned; and various unpublished facts were ascertained, which increased the plausibility of the spiritualistic interpretation of the phenomenon.

If we speculate on the brain-condition during all these different perversions of personality, we see that it must be supposed capable of successively changing all its modes of action, and abandoning the use for the time being of whole sets of well-organized association-paths. In no other way can we explain the loss of memory in passing from one alternating condition to another. And not only this, but we must admit that organized systems of paths can be thrown out of gear with others, so that the processes in one system give rise to one consciousness, and those of another system to another *simultaneously* existing consciousness. Thus only can we understand the facts of automatic writing, etc., whilst the patient is out of trance, and the false anesthesias and amnesias of the hysteric type. But just what sort of dissociation the phrase "thrown out of gear" may stand for, we cannot even conjecture; only I think we ought not to talk of the doubling of the self as if it consisted in the failure to combine on the part of certain systems of *ideas* which usually do so. It is better to talk of *objects* usually combined, and which are now divided between the two "selves," in the hysteric and automatic cases in question. Each of the selves is due to a system of cerebral paths acting by itself. If the brain acted normally, and the dissociated systems came together again, we should get a new affection of consciousness in the form of a third "Self" different from the other two, but knowing their objects together, as the result. ...

Some peculiarities in the lower automatic performances suggest that the systems thrown out of gear with each other are contained one in the right and the other in the left hemisphere. The subjects, e.g., often write backwards, or they transpose letters, or they write mirror-script. All these are symptoms of agraphic disease. The left hand, if left to its natural impulse, will in most people write mirror-script more easily than natural script. Mr. F. W. H. Myers has laid stress on these analogies.[3] He has also called attention to the usual inferior moral tone of ordinary planchette writing. On Hughlings Jackson's principles, the left hemisphere, being the more evolved organ, at ordinary times inhibits the activity of the right one; but Mr. Myers suggests that during the automatic performances the usual inhibition may be removed and the right hemisphere set free to act

---

[3] See his highly important series of articles on Automatic Writing, etc., in the *Proceedings of the Soc. for Psych. Research*, especially Article II (May 1885). Compare also Dr. Maudsley's instructive article in *Mind*, vol. xiv, p. 161, and Luys's essay, "Sur le Dédoublement," etc., in *l'Encephale* for 1889.

all by itself. This is very likely to some extent to be the case. But the crude explanation of "two" selves by "two" hemispheres is of course far from Mr. Myers's thought. The selves may be more than two, and the brain-systems severally used for each must be conceived as interpenetrating each other in very minute ways.

22

TWO REVIEWS OF *DEMON-POSSESSION AND ALLIED THEMES* BY REV. JOHN L. NEVIUS

William James's interest in demonic possession has gone largely unnoticed. In most of his writings on psychical research, it receives only passing reference alongside other phenomena such as "divinations, inspirations, demoniacal possessions, apparitions, trances, ecstasies, miraculous healings and productions of disease, and occult powers," as he wrote in "The Hidden Self" (Chapter 1).

His first writings on the subject of any length or depth were these two reviews of a book by John Livingstone Nevius, a US Protestant missionary to China. Nevius took a great interest in Chinese culture, language, and religion, and learned about local spirit possession beliefs from his language tutor. In the first review, far more space is taken up with James's own views on possession than with Nevius' book, and it is clear that he had already given the matter some serious thought.

* * *

1. From The Nation

Demon-Possession and Allied Themes; Being an Inductive Study of Phenomena of Our Own Times. By Rev. John L. Nevius, D.D., for forty years a missionary to the Chinese. Fleming H. Revell Co. 1894.

How the belief in demoniacal possession (which is one of the most articulately expressed doctrines of both Testaments, and which reigned for seventeen hundred years, hardly challenged, in all the churches) should have become the utterly dead letter which it now is in Christian countries, is an interesting historical question on which the present reviewer is unable to cast light. Its decay is far less intelligible than the decay of the belief in witchcraft, which Mr. Lecky has so vividly attributed to an unreasoned alteration of the intellectual fashions of the age, for most of the old witchcraft-accusations rested on direct demon testimony, and the phenomenon which announces itself as demon-possession has never ceased since men were men, and is probably as frequent at the present day in New York and Boston as it ever has been at any time and place in history. It follows at all times the local and temporal fashions and traditions, and, from causes which, once more, would form a highly interesting problem to unravel, it has with us assumed a benign and optimistic, instead of a diabolical and hurtful form, constituting what is familiarly known today as mediumship. It differs from all the classic types of insanity. Its attacks are periodic and brief, usually not lasting more than an hour or two, and the patient is entirely well between them, and retains no memory of them when they are over. During them, he speaks in an altered voice and manner, names himself differently, and describes his natural self in the third person as he would a stranger. The new impersonation offers every variety of completeness and energy, from the rudimentary form of unintelligible automatic scribbling, to the strongest convulsions with blasphemous outcries, or the most fluent "inspirational" speech. Imitation is a great determining factor, and suggestions from the bystanders are readily adopted and acted out. Exorcisms of various sorts often succeed in abolishing the condition, and the possessing spirit often makes treaties and compacts with the bystanders and carries them faithfully out. The condition may become epidemic, as in our own "developing circles," or in those Alpine villages whose "hystero-demonopathy" has recently been so well described by the French and Italian medical officials [Augustin] Constans, [Giuseppe] Chiap, and [Fernando] Franzolini; but more often it is sporadic and individual. At any rate it is a perfectly distinct and it may be a perfectly spontaneous "morbid entity" (as a Frenchman would say), or natural type of disease, and its essential characters seem to have been quite constant in every age and clime.

Of its causes, apart from suggestion and imitation, absolutely nothing definite is known, the psychical-researchers being the only persons who at present seem to believe that it offers a serious problem for investigation. The Charcot school has assimilated it to hysteria major, with which it unquestionably has generic affinities, but just why its specific peculiarities are what they are, this school leaves unexplained. The name hysteria, it must be remembered, is not an explanation of anything, but merely the title of a new set of problems. The tendency to prophesy, to profess to reveal remote facts, to make diagnoses and heal diseases, are among the commonest features of the demonopathic state.

Dr. Nevius is vouched for by the two editors of the book before us (he having died before its publication) as a singularly learned, versatile, and accurate man. His volume contains, in addition to a large amount of comparative natural history of the subject and a mass of bibliography, a number of interesting firsthand observations made in China. As in the Grecian oracles, in India, Japan, Polynesia, and elsewhere, the possessed person is in China prone to speak in the name of a god. This god often demands a shrine, worship, incense, food, and burnt-offerings from the household, and throws the patient into convulsions if these are withheld. Sometimes, again, a departed relative or other human being announces itself as the possessing spirit, but we seem not to hear in China of fox-demons as we hear of them in Japan. Dr. Nevius's book contains a great variety of cases, of which we have not space to extract a specimen. They are collected by missionaries or native Christian converts, and the remarkable thing about them is the almost invariable efficacy of Christian rites and invocations in setting the possessed person free. In China the name of Christ would seem to have even greater power to drive out demons than it had in Europe in the ages of faith.

One case related by the author has a curious analogy to one of the New Testament miracles. Two women of a Chinese village having been dispossessed by Christian services,

> an extraordinary commotion occurred among the fowls ... who after a while cowered up in a corner of the yard in a state of fright. The swine also belonging to the family ... were put into a singular state

of agitation, rushing about the enclosure, running over each other, and trying to scramble up the walls. The swine would not eat, and this state of disquiet continued until they were exhausted. These manifestations naturally excited a great deal of interest and remark, and were accounted for by the supposition that the demons had taken possession of the fowls and swine (p. 406).

It is but just to say that this particular account is at second hand, the witnesses being a Chinese family of converts. Such as it is, Dr. Nevius's book is one of the best contributions to the natural history of the subject, and a stepping-stone towards that not yet existing book which some day will treat this class of phenomena in a thoroughly objective and unprejudiced way, bringing it into comparison with all the other features of the "subliminal" life of which it is one modification.

2. From *Psychological Review*

Demon Possession and Allied Themes, Being an Inductive study of Phenomena of Our Own Times. John L. Nevius, D.D., with an introduction by Rev. F. F, Ellinwood, D.D. Fleming H. Revell Company, Chicago: New York: Toronto. Small 8°. Pp. x, 482. $1.50. [1894]

This interesting contribution to mental pathology would probably fifteen years ago have gained for its author a reputation for nothing but mendacity or childish credulity in scientific circles; but now, thanks to the "apperceiving mass" which recent investigations into trance-conditions have prepared, probably few readers of this journal will be seriously tempted to doubt its being a trustworthy report of facts. Dr. Nevius, for forty years a missionary in China, who died in 1893, is described by Drs. Ellinwood and Rankin as a man of rare learning, versatility and integrity. From the beginning of his sojourn in China his attention was attracted to the popular belief in demons and spirits. He found before long that the native converts very commonly believed in demoniacal possession and in the power of Christian rites and invocations to exorcise the spirit. In 1878 he met with his first case, that of a non-Christian native named Kwo who, having bought a picture of the goddess Wang, had been visited by a demon-counterfeit of the goddess in a dream who told him she had taken up her abode in his house. Various neurotic conditions and disorderly impulses had followed, ending in an attack of frenzy during which, the man being unconscious, the demon spoke through his lips, demanding incense, worship, etc. As usual, the demands were met by the family, and the pacified demon thereafter made periodical visitations, throwing the man into unconsciousness and speaking through his organism, healing the diseases of visitors, and giving practical advice. On Dr. Nevius assuring Kwo that conversion to Christianity would rid him of the encumbrance, he became baptized, the trance-state only recurring once afterwards and the demon bidding a formal farewell on that occasion. Fourteen years have passed without relapse. Kwo has had persecutions and trials but no return of his malady, and neither he nor his neighbors think of doubting that he was rescued from the dominion of an evil spirit through faith and trust in Christ.

This case can serve as a type. Dr. Nevius has personally observed several others, and collected a large amount of information on the subject from other missionaries and from native Christians. The possessed persons are unconscious during the attacks, which have often, though not always, a convulsive character. The possessing spirit usually names itself, often as a deity, sometimes as a departed human being, and demeans itself accordingly. Sometimes it makes a formal treaty to behave well, on condition of certain favors being granted it. Sometimes it is driven out by threats or needle-pricks, etc. Christian rites seem to have extraordinary exorcising efficacy. Epidemics of possession, like those recorded in Savoy by Constans and by Chiap Franzolini are not related by Dr. Nevius. The phenomena are among the most constant in history, and it is most extraordinary that "Science" should ever have become blind to them. The form which they take in our community is the benign one of mediumship. Dr. Nevius is a believer in the reality of the alleged demons, and in the objectivity of their driving out by the name of Christ, etc. Such questions cannot be fairly discussed, however, till the phenomena have been more adequately studied. Dr. Nevius gives a large amount of collateral material and biblio-graphical information; and we have to thank him and Dr. Rankin, the book's editor, for an extremely good contribution to a really important subject.

23

DEMONIACAL POSSESSION

Lecture Summary, Notes, and Correspondence

Part of the reason that there has been little attention to James's work on demonic possession is that his main contribution to the study of the subject has not been preserved: a talk that he delivered as part of the Lowell lecture series on abnormal psychology at Harvard University in 1897. Although he had planned on expanding the lectures into a book (the other subjects were "Dreams and Hypnotism," "Automatism," "Hysteria," "Multiple Personality," "Witchcraft," "Degeneration," and "Genius"), only his brief, fragmentary lecture notes survive.

As we have seen in the previous two chapters, James saw mediumship and possession phenomena as one and the same. Indeed, as he wrote in his lecture notes, "History shows that mediumship is identical with demon-possession. No one regards it as insanity." He further wrote, "When the pagan gods became demons, all possession was deemed diabolic," though such thinking has since been "Replaced by our optimistic mediumship." He concluded his notes by writing, "If there are devils – if there are supernatural powers it is through the cracked Self that they enter!"[1]

---

[1] **Lecture Notes in Eugene Taylor (ed.) (1983)** *William James on Exceptional Mental States: The 1896 Lowell Lectures Reconstructed by Eugene Taylor.* **New York:** Scribner, 93-94, 110.

While little more can be gleaned from the notes for this lecture, fortunately a fairly thorough summary of the talk as given at the New York Neurological Society was published at the time in the *Boston Medical and Surgical Journal*. The summary also includes a discussion with distinguished audience members afterwards. Written by the American neurologist Bernard Sachs, it is reprinted below (c). It is preceded first by (a) a letter on the subject that James wrote shortly before the lecture to Henry W. Rankin, a reverend, librarian, and the editor of the Nevius book. This is followed by (b) a selection from James's notes for his lecture on Multiple Personality which immediately preceded the Demoniacal Possession talk. In the notes he addresses psychical research more directly, and provides a segue to the demonical possession lecture.

There were also editorial commentaries in the spiritualist publications *Banner of Light: An Exponent of the Spiritual Philosophy of the Nineteenth Century* (d), and *Light: A Journal of Psychical, Occult, and Mystical Research* (e). Both are included below, following the lecture summary, as is a reply by James to the criticisms from the spiritualists (f). That James bothered to reply to them at all speaks volumes for his concern for his ideas to be properly understood. This is especially the case when we consider that these were hardly prestigious publications, especially for a scholar of James's stature. James rose to the occasion of responding to these seemingly willful misunderstandings that characterized the editors' objections to his lecture, their unscientific arguments based solely on personal beliefs, and their overall patronizing, combative tone.

It is also worth noting James's statement in his reply that "supernormal manifestations of intelligence are reported so frequently, and in my opinion certainly exist." It seems he was comfortable making such a clear, overt statement of belief in a spiritualist publication though less so in his psychological and philosophical works – or even in his SPR accounts.

a. Letter to Henry W. Rankin

One of my lectures in New York is at the Academy of Medicine before the Neurological Society, the subject being "Demoniacal Possession." I shall of course duly advertise the Nevius book. I am not as positive as you are in the belief that the obsessing agency is really demonic individuals. I am perfectly willing to adopt that theory if the facts lend themselves best to it; for who can trace limits to the hierarchies of personal existence in the world? But the lower stages of mere automatism shade off so continuously into the highest supernormal manifestations, through the intermediary ones of imitative hysteria and "suggestibility," that I feel as if no *general theory* as yet would cover all the facts. So that the most I shall plead for before the neurologists is the recognition of demon possession as a regular "morbid-entity" whose commonest homologue today is the "spirit-control" observed in test-mediumship, and which tends to become the more benignant and less alarming, the less pessimistically it is regarded. This last remark seems certainly to be true. Of course I shall not ignore the sporadic cases of old-fashioned malignant possession which still occur today. I am convinced that we stand with all these things at the threshold of a long inquiry, of which the end appears as yet to no one, least of all to myself. And I believe that the best theoretic work yet done in the subject is the beginning made by F. W. H. Myers in his papers in the SPR *Proceedings*. The first thing is to start the medical profession out of its idiotically *conceited ignorance* of all such matters – matters which have everywhere and at all times played a vital part in human history.

b. Lecture Notes for "Multiple Personality"

[I am] at the portal of psychical research, into which I said I would not enter. But I suppose that it would be over-cautious in me, and disappoint some of my hearers if I did not say here frankly what I think of the relations of the cases I have dwelt on to these supernormal cases. I put forth my impression merely as such, and with great diffidence; the only thing I am absolutely sure of, being the extreme complication of the facts.

Some minds would see a marvel in the simplest hypnosis — others would refuse to admit that there was anything new even if one rose from the dead. They would either deny the apparition, or say you could find a full explanation of it in Foster's *Physiology*. Of these minds one pursues idols of the tribe, another of the cave. Both may be right in respect to a portion of the facts. I myself have no question that the formula of dissociated personality will account for the phenomena I have brought before you. Hypnotism is sleep. Hysteria is obsession, not by demons, but by a fixed idea of the person that has dropped down—Janet's phrase suffices here. But to say that is one thing and to *deny any other range of phenomena is another*. Whether supernormal powers of cognition in certain persons may occur, is a matter to be decided by evidence. If they can occur, it may be that there must be a chink. The hypnotic condition is not in *itself* clairvoyant, but is *more favorable* to the cause of clairvoyance or thought-transference than the waking state. So alternate personality, the tendency for the self to break up, may, if there be spirit influences, yield them their opportunity.... And if there were real demons, they might possess only hysterics. Thus each side may see a portion of the truth.

c. "Demoniacal Possession" (Summary by Bernard Sachs)

Prof. Wm. James, of Harvard University, delivered an address on this subject. He said that our knowledge of altered personality had made rapid strides in recent years. We had the transient altered personality of epileptic insanity, and certain dream states that had been described under the name of "ambulatory automatism"—the subject going from home and returning after an interval of, perhaps, weeks, with the memory of what had happened during his wanderings utterly effaced. In one case that he had treated, hypnotic suggestion had brought back the memory of the wanderings. There was still another altered personality, that called "spirit control." This was connected with demoniacal possession. The obsolescence of public belief in the possession by demons was a very strange thing in Christian lands, when one considered that the sacred books of our religion were full of this belief. Every land and every age had exhibited the facts on which this belief was founded. The particular form of supernatural origin varied with the traditions and popular beliefs of each country. When the Pagan gods became demons, after the triumph of Christianity in Europe, all possession was looked upon as diabolic. It was now replaced by the thoroughly optimistic belief that changed personality is the spirit of a human being coming to bring messages of comfort from the sunny land. The unconsciousness, the speaker said, was usually ushered in by a more or less pronounced convulsion—the person's character became entirely changed in its attitude, voice and manifestations. After an hour or two, the manifestation passed off, leaving a complete amnesia behind of everything that had occurred. During the intervals of the attacks the person was entirely well. The condition was, therefore, entirely distinct from any form of insane delusion. Mr. Percival

Lowell had reported that in Tokyo, Japan, there were a number of persons who cultivated the power of passing into trances. In China there was a widespread belief that possession by gods and spirits could take place. Mr. Nevins, a missionary in China, had reported a number of cases of demoniacal possession. In Japan there was a curious superstition that the person afflicted was not affected by a demon but by a fox. In India instances of this kind were extremely common.

The speaker said that the witchcraft delusion had been explained in various ways, but to him witches were not neuropathic persons, but the accusers were. He had carefully examined the witchcraft trials, and had found that it started in some demon disease in the neighborhood. These "demon diseases" were very common in those days, being any functional neuropathic disease. If there were no obvious physical disorder, and the symptoms did not yield readily to the usual medical treatment, the case was considered to be one of demon disease. Professor James quoted from a book written in 1602, by a French magistrate, in which a detailed description was given of a girl possessed with five demons, and the manner in which they came out of her mouth and ran about the fire two or three times before disappearing. He said that these descriptions reminded one of the classical hysterical attack—the lump in the throat, the convulsive seizures, etc. The cases appeared to be examples of imitative hysteria, patterned after the case existing at that time. Differences in the different countries, of course, came from the differences in the psychological climate. Many interesting reports had been published of late years of epidemics of chorea, supposed to have resulted from imitation. These epidemics had been known to last for months or even years. An interesting case of demoniacal possession in France, in 1863, had been reported by Dr. Augustin Constance [sic, for Constans], in Savoy. A similar epidemic had been reported in Italy. The epidemic in France began with hysteria among certain children, and was propagated by example until at last a very large number of persons was attacked with all the symptoms of demoniacal possession. When Dr. Constance arrived upon the scene, a year after the breaking out of the epidemic, 110 persons were affected. He examined a number of these individuals, and found them to be suffering from hysterical attacks, brought on by suggestion. The patients were wisely sent away to other villages, and in that way he broke up the epidemic. Hysterodemonopathy is the name given to these symptoms.

No one could fail to recognize in these attacks the analogy to the performances of the numerous spiritualistic mediums of the present time. It would be strange, indeed, if a phenomenon which had played such a large part in history should have died out without leaving anything in its place. Medical men should learn from all this a certain lesson, i.e., that as our views had become optimistic, instead of pessimistic, the whole thing had become harmless. We live in a day when there is much alarmist writing in psychopathy about degeneration, and the alarming significance of all sorts of symptoms and signs, so that there is danger of drawing the line of health too narrowly.

Dr. C. A. Herter said that the idea of connecting the powers of modern spiritualistic mediums with the peculiar forms of demoniacal possession which occurred in former years, was a most interesting one. This fact had been brought out most interestingly and impressively in the address. He had been much interested in the gradual change from the damaging character to the comparatively beneficent character of these phenomena.

Mr. Martin said that it seemed to him rather remarkable that the suggestions which occurred to the possessed person related almost entirely to ethical matters, or religious subjects. A large portion of the recorded cases that he had met with referred to the possession by devils who were leading the person astray, or into immorality. He would like to ask if Professor James had observed the same thing.

Professor James replied that it was a law of the secondary consciousness that it took the religious form. He had no explanation to offer, however, of this law. It was a singular fact that involuntary writing was apt to take the spiritualistic form. This would occur in the case of persons who had no intellectual hospitality for that view, and who had not been exposed to spiritualistic influences. Spirits, religious truths and philosophical discourses were the staple of these communications.

Dr. Mary Putnam Jacobi said that as in so many cases of melancholia the grief was about having sinned against the Holy Ghost, even in persons who had had no religious or Calvinistic instruction, she would like to ask if Professor James considered it an example of the phenomena just spoken of. She would also like to ask his opinion of an essay that had been published, entitled, "Were the Salem Witches Entirely Guiltless?" According to this essay, although these witches were not possessed by devils, they were abandoning themselves to impulses coming from the lower structures of their natures—the result of ancestral influences.

Professor James replied that he did not think the delusions of melancholia had anything to do with the subject under discussion. The sin against the Holy Ghost was only an endeavor to explain the grief which was felt. Regarding the essay by Professor Barrett Wendell, to which allusion had been made, he would say that at the time of the witchcraft belief there were certainly persons attempting to do what they could by diabolical aid, but in all probability they formed a very small part of it. In Salem, the girls from whom the accusations emanated had been having hypnotic seances from a West Indian slave, who was herself practically insane. They passed then into such a condition that they were accused of witchcraft, and were tried under such circumstances as to impress them powerfully by suggestion. From what we know of imitative hysteria, the whole matter was entirely explicable on that basis, without any supposition of guilt upon the part of these children. It was a suggestive epidemic of a semi-hysterical nervous disorder.

Dr. C. L. Dana said that the speaker had made quite clear the relation of trance to demoniacal possession of old, but he would like to know how widespread was this condition now. He knew that about fifteen years ago spiritualism had been immensely prevalent in the Eastern states. If the condition had continued to exist and spread, there was certainly much more in the United States today than in civilized countries several hundred years ago.

Professor James replied that it would be difficult to answer this question statistically, as we had no trustworthy statistics. We knew, however, that at the present time there were many "faith healers."

d. "Prof. James's Discovery" (Editorial Commentary from Banner of Light)

In the wonderful times of electric discoveries, of Roentgen ray disclosures, and the other notable revelations of the forces of nature and their governing laws, it is no less wonderful that there should be disclosures, discoveries and revelations in regard to spirit, which is the parent of created nature, and furnishes all the forces, and establishes the law by which external nature is impelled and governed. We are now able to designate an entirely new discovery in the spirit realm, recently announced by Prof. James of Harvard University to the New York Neurological Society at the Academy of Medicine. The subject of his address was "Demoniacal Possession," and the gist of his talk was to—not show, but assert what satisfied him was the real meaning, if not the cause, of spirit control. He says it is nothing but "demoniac control." Well then, we should like to know what he considers demons, and whether he believes in good demons as well as bad ones—whether or no there are angel demons as well as devil demons. For certainly and notoriously there are good spirits and evil, and we profoundly commiserate Prof. James of Harvard University in not having found them in the course of his professed psychic researches.

Again, it is natural and reasonable to inquire how it is that evil spirits, called demons, have the power and the privilege to come to earth and communicate with mortals, but that good spirits have no such power, and are denied such a great privilege. Both classes must be spirits, rays from the same Universal Spirit, or they could not have existence at all. For all things are by Him and through Him, and without Him was not anything created. Prof. James seems to think he can jump this five-barred gate and make nothing of it. We will wait to see him do it. The fact is, these material scientists start in to "investigate" the spiritual realm, holding fast by the old leading-string of material discoveries. They do not seem capable of conceiving that the so-called natural world that is visible to the sense is the resultant of the spirit-force by which all outward things exist and are recognized. They seem to imagine that the external is first, sustaining and originating the internal.

But let that go. We will pause long enough to make an inquiry or two of Prof. James, in no sense subtle, mystic or involved. If he has indeed been an investigator, he has learned nothing unless he has learned that the spirits whom be calls demons have brought to mortal comfort and consolation; would his "demons" do this? They have restored again to its wholeness and perfection the love that short-sighted mortals thought to be cruelly sundered; is it the habit of "demons" to be engaged in such work as this? They come to warn and protect the mortals for whom they continue to care; are "demons" going about doing good in this way? They counsel the cultivation of sweet and pure thoughts, that mortals may develop Godward, and continually grow into the likeness of the divine; will he produce the particular class of "demons" who are addicted to this sort of deviltry, and love to teach perfection instead of the things that make perfection forever impossible?

The lecturing and posturing of such men on such a platform of assumption and theory without a bottom is really something ridiculous. In what are called practical affairs, it would not work at all. Prof. James himself would refuse to accept it. He and his class set up their vagrant theories, and then try to fit the facts to them. First they know all about it, and declare that they are nevertheless engaged in psychic research. Prof. James concluded his lecture by advising physicians to pay more attention to "mediumistic medical treatment," and tells them of cases "where mediums had succeeded in attaining good results in the treatment of patients suffering from certain forms of nervous disorder," and that "the physician could benefit by observing how the effects had been attained." That is right, but it is no physician's mechanism that does it. More psychic research is needed in the case.

e. Editorial Commentary from Light

The Banner of Light states that Professor James, of Harvard University, has given in to the theory that spirit mediumship is simply "demoniac control." We are sorry to hear it; but partly suspend our judgment, mainly because of the absence of a definition of "demoniac": and *The Banner of Light* itself says. ... [quote from last paragraph above (c) regarding physicians, "Professor James concluded. ..."].

That may indicate "demoniac control," but it certainly has very little suggestion of devil-control. For all we know, Professor James may have some beautiful Psychical Research definition of "demoniac" which might make us all in love with it—if we only knew.

But if Professor James has really gone over to the dismal people who think all spirit influence is evil, we are sorry for him. How can he go on believing in a wise and good God who allows the approach of subtle devils and shuts us out from the help of angels? *The Banner of Light* on this sad hypothesis, says very wisely. ... [long quotes from paragraph 2, above, "it is natural. ..."; and from paragraph 3, "If he has indeed been an investigator. ..."].

Professor James will probably do us the honor to read these remarks. Will he do us the very great service of vouchsafing an explanation to his London admirers and friends?

f. "Professor James on 'Demoniac Control'" (Reply to Light *and* Banner of Light*)*

That shrinking from pain which is instinctive in human beings may well make a lecturer avoid looking at any newspaper report of what he may have said when on the platform—in America, at least, where newspaper reports are less accurate than possibly they may be in England. Accordingly, the article in *Light* of March 6th, taking for its text an account of one of my Lowell Lectures reported (probably at second-hand) in the *Banner of Light* and courteously posted to me from your office, made me for the first time acquainted with any actual report of those lectures by the Press. The *Banner of Light* seems to have quoted me as saying that I believe mediumship to be simply demoniac control, and to have asked me to explain why it is, that if demons can control their victims for purposes of harm, good spirits may not do the like for purposes of good. You ask me to "vouchsafe an explanation" of my remarks, which I gladly do, since they have been so misunderstood.

The remarks in question were in a lecture on demoniacal possession. I stood up for it on historic grounds as a definite type of affliction, very widespread in place and time, and characterized by definite symptoms, the chief of which are these: The subject is attacked at intervals for short periods, a few hours at most, and between whiles is perfectly sane and well. During the attack the character, voice, and consciousness are changed, the subject assuming a new name and speaking of his natural self in the third person. The new name may in Christian countries be that of a demon, or spirit, elsewhere it may be that of a god; and the action and speech are frequently blasphemous or absurd. When the attack passes off the subject usually remembers nothing of it. He may manifest during it a tendency to foretell the future, or reveal facts at a distance, profess to understand foreign languages, sometimes speak them, and prescribe for diseases. The affection may be developed by the example of others similarly possessed. In all these respects it resembles the mediumship which is so common at the present day. If one is genuine, the other is; and they must be tested by the same rules. They are evidently phenomena of one type, the benignant turn which the type has taken of recent years being evidently "suggestive" and due in part to the optimistic character of our nineteenth century religion, just as the malignant turn of the older cases in Europe was suggested by the terrors of hell on which the popular religion laid such stress. Demonpossession and test-mediumship are, therefore, *homologous*, I said, and should be studied together. In their lowest phases they are simply phenomena of suggestion and imitation, with strong hysterical affinities. In their higher manifestations, of which supernormal manifestations of intelligence are reported so frequently, and in my opinion certainly exist, they form an object for the most careful "psychical research."

Into psychical research my lectures expressly abstained from entering. I contented myself with "rehabilitating" demoniac possession as a genuine phenomenon, instead of the "imposture" or "delusion" which at the present day it is popularly supposed to be. Of course I cited historical instances, ancient and modern, and left the whole question as to whence the "control" proceeds an open one, as, indeed, it is an entirely open one in my own mind. I certainly do not believe that "demons" control our contemporary test-mediums.

PART V

THE METAPHYSICS OF LIFE AFTER DEATH

24

MIND, SOUL, AND CONSCIOUSNESS

In these excerpts from *Principles of Psychology*, James critically investigates the concept of panpsychism: that everything is made up of consciousness. The discussions form a central part of the book, and it is impossible to do justice here to James's arguments and counter-arguments, which are both intricate and lengthy. Only some indicative excerpts can be reproduced here. Interested readers are directed to the full book which runs to over 700 pages.

One of the things that makes for challenging reading is that throughout the book, James *explores* ideas rather than succinctly putting forth a single favored theory. He spends much time and effort explaining one model only to critically dissect it before doing the same with an alternative model. By now readers will recognize this trait in James's other writings, reflected in his ambivalence about how to interpret the evidence from psychical research.

While his writings in *Principles of Psychology* have often been interpreted as a rejection of panpsychism, it might be more accurate to say that he was simply exploring the idea and its implications in all its permutations. Any conclusions he presents are provisional, as he makes clear, and only for the sake of argument. He adopts a similar stance in his discussion of competing theories, especially regarding the existence of a soul.

James defined the "mind-stuff" model as "the theory that our mental states are compounds," though he was not explicit about the distinction (if any) between "mind-stuff" and "mind-dust." It seems that the former was perhaps a more general term applying to consciousness overall, while the latter possibly referred to the "particles" that made up the "mind-stuff." For more on the theory, see note 3 in *Human Immortality: Two Supposed Objections to the Doctrine* (Chapter 24 of the present volume).

In the second part reprinted below, James explains some of his objections to the mind-stuff theory, arguing for the impossibility of separate elements combining of their own accord in order to form a discrete whole. The third section is James's fullest investigation on the idea of a soul, in which he again returns explicitly to psychical research.

From Chapter VI: The Mind-Stuff Theory

Evolution Psychology Demands a Mind-Dust

In a general theory of evolution the inorganic comes first, then the lowest forms of animal and vegetable life, then forms of life that possess mentality, and finally those like ourselves that possess it in a high degree. As long as we keep to the consideration of purely outward facts, even the most complicated facts of biology, our task as evolutionists is comparatively easy. We are dealing all the time with matter and its aggregations and separations; and although our treatment must perforce be hypothetical, this does not prevent it from being *continuous*. The point which as evolutionists we are bound to hold fast to is that all the new forms of being that make their appearance are really nothing more than results of the redistribution of the original and unchanging materials. The selfsame atoms which, chaotically dispersed, made the nebula, now, jammed and temporarily caught in peculiar positions, form our brains; and the "evolution" of the brains, if understood, would be simply the account of how the atoms came to be so caught and jammed. In this story no new *natures*, no factors not present at the beginning, are introduced at any later stage.

But with the dawn of consciousness an entirely new nature seems to slip in, something whereof the potency was *not* given in the mere outward atoms of the original chaos.

The enemies of evolution have been quick to pounce upon this undeniable discontinuity in the data of the world and many of them, from the failure of evolutionary explanations at this point, have inferred their general incapacity all along the line. Everyone admits the entire incommensurability of feeling as such with material motion as such. "A motion became a feeling!"— no phrase that our lips can frame is so devoid of apprehensible meaning. Accordingly, even the vaguest of evolutionary enthusiasts, when deliberately comparing material with mental facts, have been as forward as anyone else to emphasize the "chasm" between the inner and the outer worlds. ...

If evolution is to work smoothly, consciousness in some shape must have been present at the very origin of things. Accordingly we find that the more clear-sighted evolutionary philosophers are beginning to posit it there. Each atom of the nebula, they suppose, must have had an aboriginal atom of consciousness linked with it; and, just as the material atoms have formed bodies and brains by massing themselves together, so the mental atoms, by an analogous process of aggregation, have fused into those larger consciousnesses which we know in ourselves and suppose to exist in our fellow-animals. Some such doctrine of *atomistic hylozoism* as this is an indispensable part of a thoroughgoing philosophy of evolution. According to it there must be an infinite number of degrees of consciousness, following the degrees of complication and aggregation of the primordial mind-dust. To prove the separate existence of these degrees of consciousness by indirect evidence, since direct intuition of them is not to be had, becomes therefore the first duty of psychological evolutionism.

Self-Compounding of Mental Facts is Inadmissible

All the "combinations" which we actually know are effects, wrought by the units said to be "combined," upon some entity other than themselves. Without this feature of a medium or vehicle, the notion of combination [of mind-stuff particles] has no sense. ...

In other words, no possible number of entities (call them as you like, whether forces, material particles, or mental elements) can sum *themselves* together. Each remains, in the sum, what it always was; and the sum itself exists only *for a bystander* who happens to overlook the units and to apprehend the sum as such; or else it exists in the shape of some other *effect* on an entity external to the sum itself. Let it not be objected that H_2 and O combine of themselves into "water," and thenceforward exhibit new properties. They do not. The "water" is just the old atoms in the new position, H-O-H; the "new properties" are just their combined *effects*, when in this position, upon external media, such as our sense-organs and the various reagents on which water may exert its properties and be known. ...

Just so, in the parallelogram of forces, the "forces" themselves do not combine into the diagonal resultant; a *body* is needed on which they may impinge, to exhibit their resultant effect. No more do musical sounds combine *per se* into concords or discords. Concord and discord are names for their combined effects on that external medium, the *ear*.

Where the elemental units are supposed to be feelings, the case is in no wise altered. Take a hundred of them, shuffle them and pack them as close together as you can (whatever that may mean); still each remains the same feeling it always was, shut in its own skin, windowless, ignorant of what the other feelings are and mean. There would be a hundred-and-first feeling there, if, when a group or series of such feelings were set up, a consciousness *belonging to the group as such* should emerge. And this 101st feeling would be a totally new fact; the 100 original feelings might, by a curious physical law, be a signal for its *creation*, when they came together; but they would have no substantial identity with it, nor it with them, and one could never deduce the one from the others, or (in any intelligible sense) say that they *evolved* it. ...

This is what the spiritualists keep saying. ... The separate ideas exist, they say, but *affect* a third entity, the soul. *This* has the "compounded" idea, if you please so to call it; and the compounded idea is an altogether new psychic fact to which the separate ideas stand in the relation, not of constituents, but of occasions of production.

This argument of the spiritualists against the associationists has never been answered by the latter. It holds good against any talk about self-compounding amongst feelings, against any "blending," or "complication," or "mental chemistry," or "psychic synthesis," which supposes a resultant consciousness to float off from the constituents *per se*, in the absence of a supernumerary principle of consciousness which they may affect. The mind-stuff theory, in short, is unintelligible. Atoms of feeling cannot compose higher feelings, any more than atoms of matter can compose physical things! The "things," for a clear-headed atomistic evolutionist, are not. Nothing is but the everlasting atoms. When grouped in a certain way, *we* name them this "thing" or that; but the thing we name has no existence out of our mind. So of the states of mind which are supposed to be compound because they know many different things together. Since indubitably such states do exist, they must exist as single new facts, effects, possibly, as the spiritualists say, on the Soul (we will not decide that point here), but at any rate independent and integral, and not compounded of psychic atoms. ...

The Soul-Theory

...Many readers have certainly been saying to themselves for the last few pages: "Why on earth doesn't the poor man say *the Soul* and have done with it?" Other readers, of anti-spiritualistic training and prepossessions, advanced thinkers, or popular evolutionists, will perhaps be a little surprised to find this much-despised word now sprung upon them at the end of so physiological a train of thought. But the plain fact is that all the arguments for a "pontifical cell" or an "arch-monad" [the idea "Every brain-cell has its own individual consciousness, which no other cell knows anything about," p. 179] are also arguments for that well-known spiritual agent in which scholastic psychology and common-sense have always believed. And my only reason for beating the bushes so, and not bringing it in earlier as a possible solution of our difficulties, has been that by this procedure I might perhaps force some of these materialistic minds to feel the more strongly the logical respectability of the spiritualistic position. The fact is that one cannot afford to despise any of these great traditional objects of belief. Whether we realize it or not, there is always a great drift of reasons, positive and negative, towing us in their direction. If there be such entities as Souls in the universe, they may possibly be affected by the manifold occurrences that go on in the nervous centers. To the state of the entire brain at a given moment they may respond by inward modifications of their own. These changes of state may be pulses of consciousness, cognitive of objects few or many, simple or complex. The soul would be thus a medium upon which (to use our earlier phraseology) the manifold brain-processes *combine their effects*. Not needing to consider it as the "inner aspect" of any arch-molecule or braincell, we escape that physiological improbability; and as its pulses of consciousness are unitary and integral affairs from the outset, we escape the absurdity of supposing feelings which exist separately and then "fuse together" by themselves. The separateness is in the brain-world, on this theory, and the unity in the soul-world; and the only trouble that remains to haunt us is the metaphysical one of understanding how one sort of world or existent thing can affect or influence another at all. This trouble, however, since it also exists inside of both worlds, and involves neither physical improbability nor logical contradiction, is relatively small.

I confess, therefore, that to posit a soul influenced in some mysterious way by the brain-states and responding to them by conscious affections of its own, seems to me the line of least logical resistance, so far as we yet have attained.

If it does not strictly *explain* anything, it is at any rate less positively objectionable than either mind-stuff or a material-monad creed. *The bare phenomenon, however, the immediately known thing which on the mental side is in apposition with the entire brain-process is the state of consciousness and not the soul itself.* Many of the staunchest believers in the soul admit that we know it only as an inference from experiencing its states. In Chapter X, accordingly, we must return to its consideration again, and *ask ourselves whether, after all, the ascertainment of a blank unmediated correspondence, term for term, of the succession of states of consciousness with the succession of total brain-processes, be not the simplest psycho-physic formula, and the last word of a psychology which contents itself with verifiable laws, and seeks only to be clear, and, to avoid unsafe hypotheses.* Such a mere admission of the empirical parallelism will there appear the wisest course. By keeping to it, our psychology will remain positivistic and non-metaphysical; and although this is certainly only a provisional halting-place, and things must someday be more thoroughly thought out, we shall abide there in this book, and just as we have rejected mind-dust, we shall take no account of the soul. The spiritualistic reader may nevertheless believe in the soul if he will; whilst the positivistic one who wishes to give a tinge of mystery to the expression of his positivism can continue to say that nature in her unfathomable designs has mixed us of clay and flame, of brain and mind, that the two things hang indubitably together and determine each other's being, but how or why, no mortal may ever know.

From Chapter X: The Consciousness of Self

The Theory of the Soul

In Chapter VI we were led ourselves to the spiritualist theory of the "Soul," as a means of escape from the unintelligibilities of mind-stuff "integrating" with itself, and from the physiological improbability of a material monad, with thought attached to it, in the brain. But at the end of the chapter we said we should examine the "Soul" critically in a later place, to see whether it had any other advantages as a theory over the simple phenomenal notion of a stream of thought accompanying a stream of cerebral activity, by a law yet unexplained.

The theory of the Soul is the theory of popular philosophy and of scholasticism, which is only popular philosophy made systematic. It declares that the principle of individuality within us must be *substantial*, for psychic phenomena are activities, and there can be no activity without a concrete agent. This substantial agent cannot be the brain but must be something *immaterial*; for its activity, thought, is both immaterial, and takes cognizance of immaterial things, and of material things in general and intelligible, as well as in particular and sensible ways—all which powers are incompatible with the nature of matter, of which the brain is composed. Thought moreover is simple, whilst the activities of the brain are compounded of the elementary activities of each of its parts. Furthermore, thought is spontaneous or free, whilst all material activity is determined *ab extra* [from outside]; and the will can turn itself against all corporeal goods and appetites, which would be impossible were it a corporeal function. For these objective reasons the principle of psychic life must be both immaterial and simple as well as substantial, must be what is called *a Soul*. The same consequence follows from subjective reasons. Our consciousness of personal identity assures us of our essential simplicity: the owner of the various constituents of the self, as we have seen them, the hypothetical Arch-Ego whom we provisionally conceived as possible, is a real entity of whose existence self-consciousness makes us directly aware. No material agent could thus turn round and grasp *itself*—material activities always grasp something else than the agent. And if a brain *could* grasp itself and be self-conscious, it would be conscious of itself *as* a brain and not as something of an altogether different kind. The Soul then exists as a simple spiritual substance in which the various psychic faculties, operations, and affections inhere.

If we ask what a Substance is, the only answer is that it is a self-existent being, or one which needs no other subject in which to inhere. At bottom its only positive determination is Being, and this is something whose meaning we all realize even though we find it hard to explain. The Soul is moreover an *individual* being, and if we ask what that is, we are told to look in upon our Self, and we shall learn by direct intuition better than through any abstract reply. Our direct perception of our own inward being is in fact by many deemed to be the original prototype out of which our notion of simple active substance in general is fashioned. The *consequences* of the simplicity and substantiality of the Soul are its incorruptibility and natural *immortality*—nothing but God's direct *fiat* can annihilate it—and its *responsibility* at all times for whatever it may have ever done.

This substantialist view of the soul was essentially the view of Plato and of Aristotle. It received its completely formal elaboration in the middle ages. It was believed in by Hobbes, Descartes, Locke, Leibnitz, Wolf, Berkeley, and is now defended by the entire modern dualistic or spiritualistic or common-sense school. Kant held to it while denying its fruitfulness as a premise for deducing consequences verifiable here below. Kant's successors, the absolute idealists, profess to have discarded it—how that may be we shall inquire ere long. Let us make up our minds what to think of it ourselves.

It is at all events needless for expressing the actual subjective phenomena of consciousness as they appear. We have formulated them all without its aid, by the supposition of a stream of thoughts, each substantially different from the rest, but cognitive of the rest and "appropriative" of each other's content. At least, if I have not already succeeded in making this plausible to the reader, I am hopeless of convincing him by anything I could add now. The unity, the identity, the individuality, and the immateriality that appear in the psychic life are thus accounted for as phenomenal and temporal facts exclusively, and with no need of reference to any more simple or substantial agent than the present Thought or "section" of the stream. We have seen it to be single and unique in the sense of having no *separable* parts—perhaps that is the only kind of simplicity meant to be predicated of the soul. The present Thought also has being—at least all believers in the Soul believe so—and if there be no other Being in which it "inheres," it ought itself to be a "substance." If *this* kind of simplicity and substantiality were all that is predicated of the Soul, then it might appear that we had been talking of the soul all along, without knowing it, when we treated the present Thought as an agent, an owner, and the like. But the Thought is a perishing and not an immortal or incorruptible thing. Its successors may continuously succeed to it, resemble it, and appropriate it, but they *are* not it, whereas the Soul-Substance is supposed to be a fixed unchanging thing. By the Soul is always meant something *behind* the present Thought, another kind of substance, existing on a non-phenomenal plane.

When we brought in the Soul at the end of Chapter VI, as an entity which the various brain-processes were supposed to affect simultaneously, and which responded to their combined influence by single pulses of its thought, it was to escape integrated mind-stuff on the one hand, and an improbable cerebral monad on the other. But when (as now, after all we have been through since that earlier passage) we take the two formulations, first of a brain to whose processes pulses of thought *simply* correspond, and second, of one to whose processes pulses of thought *in a Soul* correspond, and compare them together, we see that at bottom the second formulation is only a more roundabout way than the first, of expressing the same bald fact. That bald fact is that *when the brain acts, a thought occurs*. The spiritualistic formulation says that the brain-processes knock the thought, so to speak, out of a Soul which stands there to receive their influence. The simpler formulation says that the thought simply *comes*. But what positive meaning has the Soul, when scrutinized, but the *ground of possibility* of the thought? And what is the "knocking" but the *determining of the possibility to actuality?* And what is this after all but giving a sort of concreted form to one's belief that the coming of the thought, when the brain-processes occur, has *some* sort of ground in the nature of things? If the world Soul be understood merely to express that claim, it is a good word to use. But if it be held to do more, to gratify the claim—for instance, to connect rationally the thought which comes, with the processes which occur, and to mediate intelligibly between their two disparate natures—then it is an illusory term. It is, in fact, with the word Soul as with the word Substance in general. To say that phenomena inhere in a Substance is at bottom only to record one's protest against the notion that the bare existence of the phenomena is the total truth. A phenomenon would not itself be, we insist, unless there were something *more* than the phenomenon. To the more we give the provisional name of Substance. So, in the present instance, we ought certainly to admit that there is more than the bare fact of coexistence of a passing thought with a passing brain-state. But we do not answer the question "What is that more?" when we say that it is a "Soul" which the brain-state affects. This kind of more *explains* nothing; and when we are once trying metaphysical explanations we are foolish not to go as far as we can. For my own part I confess that the moment I become metaphysical and try to define the more, I find the notion of some sort of an *anima mundi* [world soul] thinking in all of us to be a more promising hypothesis, in spite of all its difficulties, than that of a lot of absolutely individual souls. Meanwhile, as *psychologists*, we need not be metaphysical at all. The phenomena are enough, the passing Thought itself is the only *verifiable* thinker, and its empirical connection with the brain-process is the ultimate known law.

To the other arguments which would prove the need of a soul, we may also turn a deaf ear. The argument from free-will can convince only those who believe in free-will; and even they will have to admit that spontaneity is just as possible, to say the least, in a temporary spiritual agent like our "Thought" as in a permanent one like the supposed Soul. The same is true of the argument from the kinds of things cognized. Even if the brain could not cognize universals, immaterials, or its "Self," still the "Thought" which we have relied upon in our account is not the brain, closely as it seems connected with it; and after all, if the brain could cognize at all, one does not well see why it might not cognize one sort of thing as well as another. The great difficulty is in seeing how a thing can cognize *anything*. This difficulty is not in the least removed by giving to the thing that cognizes the name of Soul. The Spiritualists do not deduce any of the properties of the mental life from otherwise known properties of the soul. They simply find various characters ready-made in the mental life, and these they clap into the Soul, saying, "Lo! behold the source from whence they flow!" The merely verbal character of this "explanation" is obvious. The Soul invoked, far from making the phenomena more intelligible, can only be made intelligible itself by borrowing their form—it must be represented, if at all, as a transcendent stream of consciousness duplicating the one we know.

Altogether, the Soul is an outbirth of that sort of philosophizing whose great maxim, according to Dr. Hodgson, is: "Whatever you are *totally* ignorant of, assert to be the explanation of everything else."

Locke and Kant, whilst still believing in the soul, began the work of undermining the notion that we know anything about it. Most modern writers of the mitigated, spiritualistic, or dualistic philosophy—the Scotch school, as it is often called among us—are forward to proclaim this ignorance, and to attend exclusively to the verifiable phenomena of self-consciousness, as we have laid them down. Dr. Wayland, for example, begins his *Elements of Intellectual Philosophy* with the phrase "Of the essence of Mind we know nothing," and goes on:

All that we are able to affirm of it is that it is *something* which perceives, reflects, remembers, imagines, and wills; but what that something is which exerts these energies we know not. It is only as we are conscious of the action of these energies that we are conscious of the existence of mind. It is only by the exertion of its own powers that the mind becomes cognizant of their existence. The cognizance of its powers, however, gives us no knowledge of that essence of which they are predicated. In these respects our knowledge of mind is precisely analogous to our knowledge of matter.

This analogy of our two ignorances is a favorite remark in the Scotch school. It is but a step to lump them together into a single ignorance, that of the "Unknowable" to which any one fond of superfluities in philosophy may accord the hospitality of his belief, if it so please him, but which anyone else may as freely ignore and reject.

The Soul-theory is, then, a complete superfluity, so far as accounting for the actuary verified facts of conscious experience goes. So far, no one can be compelled to subscribe to it for definite scientific reasons. The case would rest here, and the reader be left free to make his choice, were it not for other demands of a more practical kind.

The first of these is *Immortality*, for which the simplicity and substantiality of the Soul seem to offer a solid guarantee. A "stream" of thought, for aught that we see to be contained in its essence, may come to a full stop at any moment; but a simple substance is incorruptible and will, by its own inertia, persist in Being so long as the Creator does not by a direct miracle snuff it out. Unquestionably this is the stronghold of the spiritualistic belief—as indeed the popular touchstone for all philosophies is the question, "What is their bearing on a future life?"

The Soul, however, when closely scrutinized, guarantees no immortality of a sort *we care for*. The enjoyment of the atom-like simplicity of their substance in *sœcula sœculorum* [though all the ages] would not to most people seem a consummation devoutly to be wished. The substance must give rise to a stream of consciousness continuous with the present stream, in order to arouse our hope, but of this the mere persistence of the substance *per se* offers no guarantee. Moreover, in the general advance of our moral ideas, there has come to be something ridiculous in the way our forefathers had of grounding their hopes of immortality on the simplicity of their substance. The demand for immortality is nowadays essentially teleological. We believe ourselves immortal because we believe ourselves *fit* for immortality. A "substance," ought surely to perish, we think, if not worthy to survive, and an insubstantial "stream" to prolong itself, provided it be worthy, if the nature of Things is organized in the rational way in which we trust it is. Substance or no substance, soul or "stream," what Lotze says of immortality is about all that human wisdom can say:

> We have no other principle for deciding it than this general idealistic belief: that every created thing will continue whose continuance belongs to the meaning of the world, and so long as it does so belong; whilst everyone will pass away whose reality is justified only in a transitory phase of the world's course. That this principle admits of no further application in human hands need hardly be said. *We* surely know not the merits which may give to one being a claim on eternity, nor the defects which would cut others off.[1]

A second alleged necessity for a soul-substance is our forensic responsibility before God. Locke caused an uproar when he said that the unity of *consciousness* made a man the same *person*, whether supported by the same *substance* or no, and that God would not, in the great day, make a person answer for what he remembered nothing of. It was supposed scandalous that our forgetfulness might thus deprive God of the chance of certain retributions, which otherwise would have enhanced his "glory." This is certainly a good speculative ground for retaining the Soul—at least for those who demand a plenitude of retribution. The mere stream of consciousness, with its lapses of memory, cannot possibly be as "responsible" as a soul which is at the judgment day all that it ever was. To modern readers, however, who are less insatiate for retribution than their grandfathers, this argument will hardly be as convincing as it seems once to have been.

One great use of the Soul has always been to account for, and at the same time to guarantee, the closed individuality of each personal consciousness. The thoughts of one soul must unite into oneself, it was supposed, and must be eternally insulated from those of every other soul. But we have already begun to see that, although unity is the rule of each man's consciousness, yet in some individuals, at least, thoughts may

---

[1] *Metaphysik*, §245*fin*. This writer, who in his early work, the *Medizinische Psychologie*, was (to my reading) a strong defender of the Soul-Substance theory, has written in §§ 243-5 of his *Metaphysik* the most beautiful criticism of this theory which exists.

split away from the others and form separate selves. As for insulation, it would be rash, in view of the phenomena of thought-transference, mesmeric influence and spirit-control, which are being alleged nowadays on better authority than ever before, to be too sure about that point either. The definitively closed nature of our personal consciousness is probably an average statistical resultant of many conditions, but not an elementary force or fact; so that, if one wishes to preserve the Soul, the less he draws his arguments from *that* quarter the better. So long as our self, on the whole, makes itself good and practically maintains itself as a closed individual, why, as Lotze says, is not that enough? And why is the *being*-an-individual in some inaccessible metaphysical way so much prouder an achievement?[2]

My final conclusion, then, about the substantial Soul is that it explains nothing and guarantees nothing. Its successive thoughts are the only intelligible and verifiable things about it, and definitely to ascertain the correlations of these with brain-processes is as much as psychology can empirically do. From the metaphysical point of view, it is true that one may claim that the correlations have a rational ground; and if the word Soul could be taken to mean merely some such vague problematic ground, it would be unobjectionable. But the trouble is that it professes to give the ground in positive terms of a very dubiously credible sort. I therefore feel entirely free to discard the word Soul from the rest of this book. If I ever use it, it will be in the vaguest and most popular way. The reader who finds any comfort in the idea of the Soul, is, however, perfectly free to continue to believe in it; for our reasonings have not established the non-existence of the Soul; they have only proved its superfluity for scientific purposes.

---

[2] On the empirical and transcendental conceptions of the self's unity, see Lotze, *Metaphysic*, §244.

25

REVIEW OF *HUMAN PERSONALITY AND ITS SURVIVAL OF BODILY DEATH* BY FREDERIC W. H. MYERS

Having initially refused to review Myers's landmark 2-volume work due to ill health, James ultimately agreed.[1] He was, however, dissatisfied with his effort, privately expressing regret that he had undertaken it at all. His assessment of Myers's book seems to have fluctuated somewhat, reflecting his overall ambivalence about survival and the evidence related to it. In a letter to the Swiss psychologist and psychical researcher Théodore Flournoy, James wrote:

> The fact is, such a book need not be criticized at all at present. It is obviously too soon for it to be either refuted or established by mere criticism. It is a hypothetical construction of genius which must be kept hanging up, as it were, for new observations to be referred to. As the years accumulate these in a more favorable or in a more unfavorable sense, it will tend to stand

---

[1] Postcard from William James to Oliver Lodge agreeing to review the book, 25 December, 1902. In William James (coll. 1986) *Essays in Psychical Research*. Frederick Burkhardt and Fredson Bowers (eds.) Cambridge, MA.: Harvard University Press, p. 487.

or to fall. I confess that reading the volumes has given me a higher opinion than ever of Myers's constructive gifts, but on the whole a lower opinion of the objective solidity of the system. So many of the facts which form its pillars are still dubious.[2]

During an interview with James at a psychology conference in Paris in 1905, he said of Myers:

> His hypothesis of the subliminal consciousness throws light on the problem of life, and on the sources of the ideal life. It lends itself to a wider generalization, and I have used it to explain the phenomena of religious experience, and to reduce them to some degree of systematic unity. Myers used it to establish survival of personality, but my own studies have not yet led me to pronounce definitely upon this question. This, however, does not affect my conception of human personality which is deeply rooted in the spiritual world – a region more profoundly spiritual than the subliminal consciousness, and from which come the most powerful moral impulses, the highest aspirations – a world which is a law to our outward one, and exerts a practical and decisive influence on our ordinary life.[3]

Human Personality and its Survival of Bodily Death. By Frederic W. H. Myers. 2 vols. 8vo. (Longmans, Green & Co., London, New York, and Bombay. 1903.)

Such large portions of the text of these bulky volumes, which are the legacy of Myers's literary life, have already appeared in these *Proceedings*, and their author's general conceptions are so familiar to my readers, that I feel free to omit from this notice all detailed account of the book's contents and composition. For aught I know such an account may be given by my fellow-reviewers. The contents are so intricate and the ideas so many that the great danger is that of not seeing the forest for the

---

[2] Letter from William James to Théodore Flournoy, 30 April, 1902. In ibid., p. 488.

[3] Interview with William James at 1905 Paris psychology conference, in ibid., p. 489. Originally published in *Light*, 5 August 1905, 369.

trees, and of not apprehending with distinctness the steps of Myers's reasoning. It seems to me wisest, therefore, to employ the opportunity accorded me in analyzing his argument into its essential features, following, as I do so, a logical rather than a textual order.

What would entitle Myers, if he were successful in what he attempted, to be regarded as the founder of a new science is that conception of the Subliminal Self, by which he colligated and coordinated a mass of phenomena which had never before been considered together, and thus made a sort of objective continuum of what, before him, had appeared so pure a disconnectedness that the ordinary scientific mind had either disdained to look at it, or pronounced it mostly fictitious. Two years ago I wrote in these *Proceedings* that Myers had endowed psychology with a new problem – *The exploration of the subliminal region* being destined to figure here after in that branch of learning as "Myers's problem." Reading these volumes, we gain a definite idea of how far he himself had pushed forward the topographical survey of that region.

Conservatives in anthropologic science will immediately say that Myers used the concept of the "subliminal" far too broadly, and that the only safe demarcation of the term is that of the neuropathologists. These observers for the most part now recognize a subliminal region frankly, but they recognize it only as a dissociated part of the normal personality. Experiences forgotten by the upper consciousness may here still lead a parasitic existence, and in an inferior, dreamlike way may interfere with normal processes. For these critics the subliminal is synonymous with the *forgotten* and forms a region of disintegration exclusively.

Most neurologists either ignore those other "evolutive," "superior," or "supernormal" phenomena, in which Myers's chief interest lay, or scout them wholesale as deceptions. The few who admit them are more likely to see in them another department of experience altogether than to treat them as having continuous connection with the ordinary phenomena of mental dissociation.

Those who simply ignore them (for whatever reason) may themselves be ignored here as belated students. However acutely aware one may be of the sources of fallacy in reports of the marvelous, I fail to see how the records quoted in these volumes, and in vastly greater profusion in Gurney's *Phantasms of the Living* and the other SPR publications, can rightfully be met by a wholesale and indiscriminating *non possumus* [statement of inability to act or engage]. Anyone with a healthy sense for evidence, a sense not methodically blunted by the sectarianism of

"Science," ought now, it seems to me, to feel that exalted sensibilities and memories, veridical phantasms, haunted houses, trances with supernormal faculty, and even experimental thought-transference, are natural kinds of phenomenon which ought, just like other natural events, to be followed up with scientific curiosity.

Hypnotic phenomena form the center of perspective for Myers's map of the subliminal region. In the first place, the system of faculty of a subject under hypnosis is quite different from his waking system of faculty. While portions of the usual waking system are inhibited, other portions are sometimes supernormally energized in hypnosis, producing not only hallucinations, but after-results in the way of sense-discrimination and control of organic function, to which the waking consciousness is unable to attain. We are thus led to the notion of two different currents of mental life, one deeper, and the other shallower, of which either is best appealed to while the other is in abeyance. That these currents may not only alternate but may co-exist with each other is proved by Gurney's, Binet's, and Janet's discovery of Subjects who, receiving suggestions during hypnosis and forgetting them when wakened, nevertheless then wrote them out automatically and unconsciously as soon as a pencil was placed in their hands.

Allying the curative phenomena of hypnosis with the great reparative powers of sleep, and its enhancements of faculty with the enhancements of faculty to which dreaming and natural somnambulism occasionally give rise, Myers postulates a region of sleeping consciousness present at all times in all of us, a region moreover which in certain respects has an advantage over the waking levels of the mind. This subliminal region is usually closed off from the ordinary waking consciousness, but under special conditions of appeal, which vary with the idiosyncrasy of the individual, it may break in with effects which reveal its presence to us. The popular word "suggestion" is only a name for a successful appeal to this subliminal consciousness.

The appeal, in hypnotic subjects, is made through the ordinary consciousness in the first instance; and into that consciousness the effects, when they are "post-hypnotic," return in the form of "automatisms," sensory or motor. In other words, hallucinations or unmotived impulses to act, which in some cases are upheavals from the subliminal into the supraliminal region, may be so in all cases. The two regions thus form environments for each other, with possibilities of interaction, though under ordinary conditions their intercourse is small.

So far Myers would seem to be on perfectly solid ground. There is a subliminal region of life which opens fitfully into the supraliminal region. The only doubt is as to whether it be general in human beings, or whether it be not limited to a few hypnotic and hysteric subjects.

The subliminal region being thus established as an actuality, the next question is as to its farther limits, where it exists. My subliminal, for instance, has my ordinary consciousness for one of its environments, but has it additional environments on the remoter side? Has it direct relations of intercourse, for example, with the consciousness, subliminal or supraliminal, of other men?

Some of the phenomena of hypnotism or mesmerism suggest that this is actually the case. I refer to the reports (several of them irreproachably recorded) of hypnotism at a distance, of obedience to unspoken orders, and of "community of sensation" between hypnotizer and subject, of which Sections 568 to 571 of Myers's Volume I give some account. Remote influences, to which the supraliminal region is closed, may thus occasionally pass into the subliminal region, showing that this latter communicates not only with the supraliminal mind of the subject himself, but with the mind of other persons, and possibly with a still wider world.

How wide this world may possibly be is suggested by all the various reports of thought-transference and clairvoyance in the hypnotic state. And if we now pass beyond conditions of artificial hypnosis, and take into account states of abstraction like those produced in some persons by crystal gazing and by automatic writing, and the "trances" of certain somnambulists and mediums, with the clairvoyant faculty reported to be found therein, we find ourselves obliged (if we credit the reports) to assume that the subliminal life has windows of outlook and doors of ingress which bring it (in some persons at least) into a commerce, of which the channels entirely escape our observation, with an indefinitely extended region of the world of truth.

The jump which Myers makes here is that of generalizing his conclusions. The "conservative" critic who does not deny the facts *in toto* would most probably call them pathological freaks of idiosyncrasy. He would protest against their being treated as revelations of the constitution of human nature at large. Myers, on the other hand, regards them as such revelations, and considers that the subjects show their "idiosyncrasy" rather in lying as open as they do to our observation, than in having the kind of human constitution which the observations disclose.

He is thus led to the general conception of a subliminal life belonging to human nature in general, and having its own indefinitely wide environment, distinct from that with which our bodily senses carry on their commerce. Set over against this subliminal life, and in strong contrast with it, we find the normal consciousness, dealing primarily through the senses with the material world, and in possession of faculties of attention, and in particular of memory, which are pitifully small in comparison with those which the subliminal consciousness wields. The normal consciousness is thus only a portion of our nature, adapted primarily to "terrene" conditions. Those more directly intuitive faculties which it lacks, and of which we get glimpses in individuals whose subliminal lies exceptionally open, can hardly be vestiges, degenerations of something which our ancestors once possessed. We should rather regard them as germs of something not yet evolved for methodical use in our natural environment, but possibly even now carrying on a set of active functions in their own wider "cosmic" environment.

The "supernormal" becomes thus for Myers synonymous with the "evolutive" as contrasted with the "dissolutive" with which the ordinary neurologist would prefer to connect it. The supernormal faculties of the subliminal take us into the cosmic environment; and for Myers this cosmic environment takes on more and more, as the volumes proceed, the character of a "spiritual world." From its intercourse with this spiritual world the subliminal self of each of us may draw strength, and communicate it to the supraliminal life. The "energizing of life" seems, in fact, to be one of its functions. The reparativeness of sleep, the curative effects of self-suggestion, the "uprushing" inspirations of genius, the regenerative influences of prayer and of religious self-surrender, the strength of belief which mystical experiences give, are all ascribed by Myers to the "dynamogeny" of the spiritual world, upon which we are enabled to make drafts of power by virtue of our connection with our subliminal. He dreams of a methodical evolution and extension, as our knowledge of the channels shall improve, of our resources in this direction.

Myers's theory, so far, is simple enough. It only postulates an indefinite inward extension of our being, cut off from common consciousness by a screen or diaphragm not absolutely impervious but liable to leakage and to occasional rupture. The "scientific" critic can only say it is a pity that so vast and vaguely defined a hypothesis should be reared upon a set of facts so few and so imperfectly ascertained.

The vagueness of the hypothesis at this point chiefly consists in the ill-defined relations of the subliminal with its "cosmic" environment. Is this latter the Absolute Soul of the World, with which all our subliminals may be supposed to be substantially continuous? Or are the various subliminals discontinuous? – and is their intercourse transacted across an isolating interval?

As the work proceeds, Myers tends more and more towards the latter conception: the "spiritual world" becomes a "world of spirits" which interact.

This follows naturally from the consideration, to which he next proceeds, of veridical phantasms and mediumistic messages. At first sight "ghosts," etc. (if admitted to be actual phenomena) would seem to require a physical rather than a mental hypothesis for their explanation; and mediumistic messages, if taken at their face value, suggest that the "controlling" spirit intrudes into the very organism of the medium rather than that it merely actuates the medium's subliminal mind. The plot thickens very much hereabouts, and obliges one to ask more definitely whether the environment of the subliminal be mental exclusively or whether it may not also be physical. Myers is shy of putting forth psychophysical hypotheses, but in his conceptions of "phantasmogenetic invasion" of space and of "telergy" and "telekinesis," we find that he is forced to abandon purely mental territory. Subliminal selves, affecting one another in their quality of purely psychic entities, are not the sole factors that need be considered in our explanations. Space and their physical relations to space are also required.

Let me indicate very briefly what are the essential points in Myers's handling of this new range of experiences.

In the first place, take the so-called "veridical phantasms of the living." Assuming them to be established by the evidence, the records show that the mind of the percipient must be at least one of the factors of their production. If they were purely physical or "astral" presences, why should they wear earthly clothes, and carry earthly accessories? and when the percipient is in the midst of companions, why should they so seldom appear to *them*?

Evidently the phantasm, whatever may be its remoter starting point, involves, as a mere immediate bit of experience, the psycho-physical process called "hallucination" on the part of the percipient himself.

Secondly, since there are well recorded cases where a living person, A, made his phantasm appear to B by simply willing that it should do so, and since in many of the other cases of phantasms of the living, the person who appeared probably *wished* to appear where he did appear, it seems fair to interpret these appearances generally as hallucinations produced by the action of one mind upon another, somewhat after the pattern of the hallucinations which a hypnotizer makes his subject experience so easily by suggesting that he shall have them, either during the hypnosis or after waking up. "Telepathy" is the name which Myers gave to the immediate influence of one subliminal upon another. The records seem to prove that telepathy either may or may not be a transfer of ready-made content from one mind to another. Sometimes the influencing mind appears to act only as a suggestive stimulus, and the results on the mind influenced show every variation from a vague emotional mood to an elaborated perception full of accessories, or to an automatically impulsive act.

Activity of the influencing mind at a distance from its body is at any rate proved, according to Myers, by these phantasms of the living and by other telepathic phenomena.

It is round this conception of action at a distance, to which Myers applies the term of "psychical invasion," that his theory now turns towards its ulterior developments.

The fact that a phantasm may appear to a whole collection of persons at once, or to an indifferent companion of the person, rather than to the person himself of whom the phantasm's original might reasonably be supposed to be thinking, suggests that our soul's invasive powers apply to outer space as well as to other minds. Myers cites examples of these, as of all other special types of case which his argument requires, and considers that the probability of this space invasion by the subliminal powers of the living is strengthened by two additional kinds of fact. First we have cases of apparent "bilocation" of mind and organism, as when a living person appears to view his own body from a remote position, or to see his own "double" as a phantasm; and second, we have an impressive array of cases which make for "travelling" clairvoyance, ("telæsthesia," as Myers calls it) whether in dream, in crystal gazing, or in the mesmeric trance. Myers indulges in no hypothesis whatever as to the *modus operandi* of this space-invasion by our subliminal. At any rate it seems to bring space in as a portion of the subliminal's environment. The subliminal has relations with space as well as with other minds.

So far the powers of living persons have been considered exclusively. But phantasms of the slowly or suddenly dying shade by continuity of time-relation into phantasms of the recently dead, and these in turn shade into phantasms of the long dead, i.e. into narratives of the haunted-house type, of which the mass recorded is decidedly imposing.

The order of theoretic construction, if we go back to the beginning, is thus somewhat as follows: From hyperesthesia in the hypnotic state we pass gradually into telepathy between the subject and the operator; from this to phantasmogenetic telepathy between living men at a distance from one another; from this to space-invasions, whether phantasmogenetic or clairvoyant, by the subliminal of living persons; and finally from this to similar invasions (phantasmogenetic, at any rate) by the dead. We thus reach the hypothesis of spirit survival. Primarily, we reach this only in the somewhat idiotic form of "ghosts," for up to this point we have been considering only what Myers calls automatisms of the *sensory* order.

But *motor* automatisms carry us a good deal further towards a "world of spirits." Sensory automatisms seem to be essentially fugacious. Rarely is their content elaborately developed or prolonged. It is quite otherwise with automatic writing and speech, for here the messages are consecutive, and bring explicit professions of origin and purpose along with them. This may obtain when the subject who offers them is awake as well as when he is entranced.

The whole topic of "spirit messages" is thus opened up to our reflection. Although Myers died before he could write out his review of the evidence for spirit messages in detail, he all along shows that he deemed it sufficient: some such messages, at any rate, he held to have been proved authentic. With this our "cosmic" environment, as he believed in it, comes into full view. Our subliminals surround one another and act upon one another, as well as upon space; and spirits of the departed (which may themselves be constituted as we are, and have something like a subliminal condition of their own) may also act upon us and upon space, and receive our action too. When the action is transient, it is probably merely an impact upon our subliminal, of which we need not necessarily suspect the source. When it is more protracted or "invasive," space gets affected, and we either see a ghost or feel a presence; and it is an open question, in such effects as these upon our consciousness, how far our subliminal mind exclusively receives the operation of the invader, and how far he may act directly on our physical nervous system. Prolonged "possession" or "control" of the organism seems to involve the profoundest sort of operation which is possible; and Myers is willing here to admit that the foreign spirit may directly actuate the medium's nervous system.

That spirits of departed men should actuate these living bodies of ours directly, shows a form of physical influence to which Myers gives the name of *telekinesis*, and of which still other instances would be the raps, the table-movings without contact, and the other "physical phenomena of mediumship," as they are commonly termed. Myers discusses these phenomena warily, using delicate methods of gradual approach (see especially the exquisitely ingenious "Scheme of Vital Faculty," which ought to have been prominently printed as the concluding chapter of the whole book, but which appears inconspicuously among the Appendices as Section 926 A, Vol. II, pp. 505-554). On the whole he seems well disposed to treat the evidence for physical phenomena as adequate.

And now his whole theory lies before us. It is a vast synthesis, but a coherent one, notwithstanding the vagueness of some of the terms that figure in it. No one of the dots by which his map is plotted out, no one of the "corners" required by his triangulation, is purely hypothetical. He offers empirical evidence for the concrete existence of every element which his scheme postulates and works with. In logical form the theory is thus a scientific construction of a very high order, against which one can urge only two general kinds of objection. One can say first that the stepping-stones themselves, the corners, are too frail, that the types of fact invoked need much additional corroboration; or one can say, even if the kinds of facts were admitted to be solid where they have been observed, that Myers has ascribed a universality and an extension to them for which he has no warrant, that he has drawn his rules from the exceptional cases, and made his spiritual universe too continuous.

Disregarding these criticisms for the moment, I am impelled to say a word about this matter of Myers's "scientific" ability. Reading him afresh in these two volumes, I find myself filled with an admiration which almost surprises me. The work, whatever weaknesses it may have, strikes me as at least a masterpiece of coordination and unification. The voluminous arsenal of "cases" of which the author's memory disposes might make the most erudite naturalist or historian envy him, and his delicate power of serially assorting his facts, so as to find always just the case he needs to fit into a gap in the scheme, is wholly admirable. He shows indeed a genius not unlike that of Charles Darwin for discovering shadings and transitions, and grading down discontinuities in his argument.

Three circumstances, probably, have worked against the general public recognition of Myers's scientific powers. These have been, first, the nature of the material he worked in; second, his literary fluency; and third, his emotional interest in immortality. The two latter characteristics, combining their effects, have given to certain passages in the present volumes a tone so lyrical that it may well make them distasteful to the ordinary scientific reader. For propagandist purposes the existence of these passages is, I think, to be regretted. Myers could well have afforded (having shown his undisputed lyrical power elsewhere) to be dryer in this argument, and by being so he would have doubtless turned certain possible disciples, now lost to him, into respectful listeners. But he so habitually saw the meanest subliminal phenomena in the light of that transterrene world with which they might remotely be connected, that they became glorified in his mind into experiences in themselves majestic. All his materials were objects of love to him, and the richly latinized and hellenized vocabulary in which he spoke of them shows how they affected his imagination.

From this point of view I think we need not regret a feature of these volumes which to some persons may have seemed pathetic. Myers, namely, was cut off by death before he could write his direct discussion of the evidence for spirit-return. But that discussion is a matter of dry-as-dust detail which may well be left to the pages of our *Proceedings* and *Journal*, and to workers who are not such universal geniuses. He has fully expressed in this book his general position on the subject; and being so lyrical a fountain in the direction of immortality, he could hardly have embarked on the evidence without alienating still more a class of students whose sympathy may on the whole be precious. Even though the capstone of the work, as he projected it, be lacking, still the essential Myers is in it, for it is as the organizer and coordinator, far more than as the critic of this or that particular set of observations, that posterity will best remember him.

As regards the truth of his theory, as contra-distinguished from its formal merits as a constructive effort, it is certainly too early for anyone to pass dogmatic judgment. Most readers, even those who admire the scheme as a whole, will doubtless shrink from yielding their credence to it unreservedly. It will seem like skating over ice too thin for any intellect less nimble than Myers's to place its feet on boldly. The types of case which he uses as stepping stones are some of them, at present, either in quality or quantity, decidedly weak supports for the weight which the theory would rest upon them, and it remains at least possible that future records may not remedy this frailty.

The reproach that he has over-generalized the exceptional is also one which, in the present state of our knowledge, cannot be decidedly rebutted. He may extend the subliminal too far when he supposes that all of us possess it, and that works of genius generally have their source in it. He may extend "phantasms" too far when he fills a whole cosmic environment with spirits able to engender them. As between the individual subliminal and the cosmic environment, he may also not have drawn the boundary correctly. There may well be more of the "dissolutive" subliminal and less of the "spirit" than he supposes, in some of his palmary phenomena. But however it may have to be contracted in one case, or extended in another, the subliminal region, as Myers conceived it, will remain a *vera causa* [true cause] in psychology, explanatory, either of the whole or of a part, of the great mass of occult occurrences so far as they are authentic. "Automatisms" are indeed what he first said they were, messages from the subliminal to the supraliminal regions.

The imperfection which I feel most acutely in Myers's survey of the subliminal life is its failure adequately to account for its being so impartially the home both of evolutive and of dissolutive phenomena. The parasitic ideas of psycho-neurosis, and the fictitious personations of planchette-writing and mediumship reside there side by side with the inspirations of genius, with the faculties of telepathy and telæsthesia, and with the susceptibility of genuine spirit-control. Myers felt the paradoxical character of such cohabitation, and, as usual, was ready with a suggestion for attenuating the difficulty. [He writes,]

> It may be expected that supernormal vital phenomena will manifest themselves as far as possible through the same channels as abnormal or morbid vital phenomena, when the same centers or the same synergies are used. ... If there be within us a secondary self aiming at manifestation by physiological means, it seems probable that its readiest path of externalization – its readiest outlet of visible action – may often lie along some track which has already been shown to be a line of low resistance by the disintegrating processes of disease, ... lie along some plane of cleavage which the morbid dissociations of our psychical synergies have already shown themselves disposed to follow (Vol. II, p. 84).

But this conception is deficient in clearness. Are there three zones of subliminal life, of which the innermost is *dissolutive*, the middle one *superior* (the zone of genius, telepathy, etc.), and the outermost *supreme* and receptive directly of the impact of the spirit world? And can the two latter zones reach the supraliminal consciousness only by passing through the interior and inferior zone, and consequently using its channels and mixing its morbid effects with their own? Or is the subliminal superior throughout when considered in itself, and are the curious parasitisms of hysteria and alternate personality, and the curious uncritical passivity to the absurdest suggestions which we observe in hypnosis to be explained by defective brain-action exclusively, without bringing in the subliminal mind? Is it the brain, in short, which vitiates and mixes results, or is it the interior zone of the subliminal mind? I make no attempt to solve the question.[4] It is practically as well as theoretically a vital one, for there can be no doubt whatever that the *great* obstacle to the reception of a *Weltanschauung* [worldview] like Myers's is that the superior phenomena which it believes in are so enveloped and smothered in the mass of their degenerative congeners and accompaniments that they beget a collective impression of disgust, and that only the strongest of mental stomachs can pick them over and seek the gold amongst the rubbish.

Meanwhile it must not be forgotten, if one finds Myers's map unsatisfactory, that no regular psychologist has ever tried his hand at the problem. Psychologists admit a subliminal life to exist in hypnosis and in hysteria, and they use a case like that of Janet's "Adrienne" to explain the manner in which "secondary personalities" may become organized. But the existence all about us of thousands and of tens of thousands of persons, not perceptibly hysteric or unhealthy, who are mediumistic to the degree at any rate of being automatic writers, and whose mediumism results in these grotesque impersonations, this, I say, is a phenomenon of human life which they do not even attempt to connect with any of the other facts of Nature. Add the fact that the mediumship often gives supernormal information, and it becomes evident that the phenomenon cannot consist of pure eccentricity and isolation. There is method in it; it must have a context of some sort and belong to a region where other things can be found also. It cries aloud for serious investigation. Myers's map is the only scientifically serious investigation that has yet been offered. It is to be hoped that those whom it dissatisfies may not merely reject it, but also make some effort to provide something better.

I cannot conclude without paying my tribute to the innumerable felicities of suggestion with which *Human Personality* abounds. Myers's urbanity of style, and his genius for analogy were never more profusely displayed, or in so many directions. Bold as his theory is, it is one of

---

[4] For Mr. Myers's treatment of the question, see especially Vol. I, pp. 72-75.

its merits that it should be so sober in the way of either physical or metaphysical hypothesis. What "spirits" are, or what their relations are to "space," he never tries to say, but uses the terms like a *Naturforscher* [naturalist], as mere designations for factors of phenomena. The book on the whole must be considered a worthy monument to his memory.

26

HUMAN IMMORTALITY:

Two Supposed Objections to the Doctrine

This essay, originally entitled *A Future Life*, was first published in its own slim volume in 1898, and was based on James's Ingersoll Lecture on the Immortality of Man at the Harvard Divinity School. James's notion of a possible afterlife involves a variation of the theory that the brain is a receiver of consciousness rather than its generator (though he calls it a "transmitter").

The essay reveals the otherwise unspoken theoretical framework behind James's psychical research, giving us a glimpse into how he conceptualized the possibility that Mrs. Piper's mediumship and other phenomena were evidence for life after death. This is demonstrated by the fact that he raises the evidence of psychical research as support for his ideas. Indeed, although James characteristically (and modestly) presents his theory as merely one option among many, the force with which he argues it suggests a degree of conviction. When the book was first reprinted, James felt it necessary to respond to critics who objected to his ideas on theological or materialist grounds, and that Preface is included below.

The essay includes extensive endnotes – nearly a third of the total word count. This is something of a contrast to James's other writings in which the use of notes was relatively spare, though here their depth and relevance to the overall arguments would seem to justify them (see especially note 3). James Hyslop rightly noted that they reveal "tendencies toward psychic research for a settlement of the problem" of immortality,[1] despite having been written over a decade before the *Report* on Mrs. Piper (Chapter 18). In a letter to the publisher, James specified that he wished for the endnotes in this piece to be published in the same size font as the body of the text, as they "have a substantive importance."[2] Those wishes have been respected here.

Preface to the Second Edition

So many critics have made one and the same objection to the doorway to immortality which my lecture claims to be left open by the "transmission-theory" of cerebral action, that I feel tempted, as the book is again going to press, to add a word of explanation.

If our finite personality here below, the objectors say, be due to the transmission through the brain of portions of a preexisting larger consciousness, all that can remain after the brain expires is the larger consciousness itself as such, with which we should thenceforth be perforce reconfounded, the only means of our existence infinite personal form having ceased.

But this, the critics continue, is the pantheistic idea of immortality, survival, namely, in the soul of the world; not the Christian idea of immortality, which means survival in strictly personal form.

In showing the possibility of a mental life after the brain's death, they conclude, the lecture has thus at the same time shown the impossibility of its identity with the personal life, which is the brain's function.

Now I am myself anything but a pantheist of the monistic pattern; yet for simplicity's sake I did in the lecture speak of the "mother-sea" in terms that must have sounded pantheistic, and suggested that I thought of it myself as a unit [...]. I even added that future lecturers

---

[1] James Hyslop (1914) "Belief in Personal Immortality. By E. S. P. Haynes" (Book Review). *Journal of the American Society for Psychical Research*, Vol. 8 No. 4, 176.

[2] Letter from William James to Houghton Mifflin, 31 May, 1898. In William James (coll. 1982) *Essays in Religion and Morality*. Frederick Burkhardt, Fredson Bowers, and Ignas K. Skrupskelis (eds.). Cambridge, MA: Harvard University Press, p. 230.

might prove the loss of some of our personal limitations after death not to be matter for absolute regret. The interpretation of my critics was therefore not unnatural; and I ought to have been more careful to guard against its being made.

In note 5 [p. 305] I partially guarded against it by saying that the "mother-sea" from which the finite mind is supposed to be strained by the brain, need not be conceived of in pantheistic terms exclusively. There might be, I said, many minds behind the scenes as well as one. The plain truth is that *one may conceive the mental world behind the veil in as individualistic a form as one pleases, without any detriment to the general scheme by which the brain is represented as a transmissive organ.*

If the extreme individualistic view were taken, one's finite mundane consciousness would be an extract from one's larger, truer personality, the latter having even now some sort of reality behind the scenes. And in transmitting it – to keep to our extremely mechanical metaphor, which confessedly throws no light on the actual *modus operandi* – one's brain would also leave effects upon the part remaining behind the veil; for when a thing is torn, both fragments feel the operation.

And just as (to use a very coarse figure) the stubs remain in a check-book whenever a check is used, to register the transaction, so these impressions on the transcendent self might constitute so many vouchers of the finite experiences of which the brain had been the mediator; and ultimately they might form that collection within the larger self of memories of our earthly passage, which is all that, since Locke's day, the continuance of our personal identity beyond the grave has by psychology been recognized to mean.

It is true that all this would seem to have affinities rather with preexistence and with possible reincarnations than with the Christian notion of immortality. But my concern in the lecture was not to discuss immortality in general. It was confined to showing it to be *not incompatible* with the brain-function theory of our present mundane consciousness. I hold that it is so compatible, and compatible moreover in fully individualized form. The reader would be in accord with everything that the text of my lecture intended to say, were he to assert that every memory and affection of his present life is to be preserved, and that he shall never *in sæcula sæculorum* [for all eternity] cease to be able to say to himself: "I am the same personal being who in old times upon the earth had those experiences."

Human Immortality

It is a matter unfortunately too often seen in history to call for much remark, that when a living want of mankind has got itself officially protected and organized in an institution, one of the things which the institution most surely tends to do is to stand in the way of the natural gratification of the want itself. We see this in laws and courts of justice; we see it in ecclesiasticisms, we see it in academies of the fine arts, in the medical and other professions, and we even see it in the universities themselves.

Too often do the place-holders of such institutions frustrate the spiritual purpose to which they were appointed to minister, by the technical light which soon becomes the only light in which they seem able to see the purpose, and the narrow way which is the only way in which they can work in its service.

I confess that I thought of this for a moment when the Corporation of our University invited me last spring to give this Ingersoll lecture. Immortality is one of the great spiritual needs of man. The churches have constituted themselves the official guardians of the need, with the result that some of them actually pretend to accord or to withhold it from the individual by their conventional sacraments – withhold it at least in the only shape in which it can be an object of desire. And now comes the Ingersoll lectureship. Its high-minded founder evidently thought that our University might serve the cause he had at heart more liberally than the churches do, because a university is a body so much less trammeled by traditions and by impossibilities in regard to choice of persons. And yet one of the first things which the university does is to appoint a man like him who stands before you, certainly not because he is known as an enthusiastic messenger of the future life, burning to publish the good tidings to his fellow-men, but apparently because he is a university official.

Thinking in this way, I felt at first as if I ought to decline the appointment. The whole subject of immortal life has its prime roots in personal feeling. I have to confess that my own personal feeling about immortality has never been of the keenest order, and that, among the problems that give my mind solicitude, this one does not take the very foremost place. Yet there are individuals with a real passion for the matter, men and women for whom a life hereafter is a pungent craving, and the thought of it an obsession; and in whom keenness of interest has bred an insight into the relations of the subject that no one less penetrated with the mystery of it can attain. Some of these people are known to me. They are not official personages; they do not speak as the scribes, but as having direct authority. And surely, if anywhere a prophet clad in goatskins, and not a uniformed official, should be called to give inspiration, assurance, and instruction, it would seem to be here, on such a theme. Office, at any rate, ought not to displace spiritual calling.

And yet, in spite of these reflections, which I could not avoid making, I am here tonight, all uninspired and official as I am. I am sure that prophets clad in goatskins, or, to speak less figuratively, laymen inspired with emotional messages on the subject, will often enough be invited by our Corporation to give the Ingersoll lecture hereafter. Meanwhile, all negative and deadening as the remarks of a mere professional psychologist like myself may be in comparison with the vital lessons they will give, I am sure, upon mature reflection, that those who have the responsibility of administering the Ingersoll foundation are in duty bound to let the most various kinds of official personages take their turn as well. The subject is really an enormous subject. At the back of Mr. Alger's *Critical History of the Doctrine of a Future Life*, there is a bibliography of more than five thousand titles of books in which it is treated. Our Corporation cannot think only of the single lecture: it must think of the whole series of lectures *in futuro*. Single lectures, however emotionally inspired and inspiring they may be, will not be enough. The lectures must remedy each other, so that out of the series there shall emerge a collective literature worthy of the importance of the theme. This unquestionably was what the founder had in mind. He wished the subject to be turned over in all possible aspects, so that at last results might ponderate harmoniously in the true direction. Seen in this long perspective, the Ingersoll foundation calls for nothing so much as for minute division of labor. Orators must take their turn, and prophets; but narrow specialists as well. Theologians of every creed, metaphysicians, anthropologists, and psychologists must alternate with biologists and physicists and psychical researchers – even with mathematicians. If any one of them presents a grain of truth, seen from his point of view, that will remain and accrete with truths brought by the others, his will have been a good appointment.

In the hour that lies before us, then, I shall seek to justify my appointment by offering what seem to me two such grains of truth, two points well fitted, if I am not mistaken, to combine with anything that other lecturers may bring.

These points are both of them in the nature of replies to objections, to difficulties which our modern culture finds in the old notion of a life hereafter – difficulties that I am sure rob the notion of much of its old power to draw belief, in the scientifically cultivated circles to which this audience belong.

The first of these difficulties is relative to the absolute dependence of our spiritual life, as we know it here, upon the brain. One hears not only physiologists, but numbers of laymen who read the popular science books and magazines, saying all about us, How can we believe in life hereafter when Science has once for all attained to proving, beyond possibility of escape, that our inner life is a function of that famous material, the so-called "gray matter" of our cerebral convolutions? How can the function possibly persist after its organ has undergone decay?

Thus physiological psychology is what is supposed to bar the way to the old faith. And it is now as a physiological psychologist that I ask you to look at the question with me a little more closely.

It is indeed true that physiological science has come to the conclusion cited; and we must confess that in so doing she has only carried out a little farther the common belief of mankind. Everyone knows that arrests of brain development occasion imbecility, that blows on the head abolish memory or consciousness, and that brain-stimulants and poisons change the quality of our ideas. The anatomists, physiologists, and pathologists have only shown this generally admitted fact of a dependence to be detailed and minute. What the laboratories and hospitals have lately been teaching us is not only that thought in general is one of the brain's functions, but that the various special forms of thinking are functions of special portions of the brain. When we are thinking of things seen, it is our occipital convolutions that are active; when of things heard, it is a certain portion of our temporal lobes; when of things to be spoken, it is one of our frontal convolutions. Professor Flechsig of Leipzig (who perhaps more than anyone may claim to have made the subject his own) considers that in other special convolutions those processes of association go on, which permit the more abstract processes of thought, to take place. I could easily show you these regions if I had here a picture of the brain.[1] Moreover, the diminished or exaggerated associations of what this author calls the *Körperfühlsphäre* [somatosensory cortex] with the other regions, accounts, according to him, for the complexion of our emotional life, and eventually decides whether one shall be a callous brute or criminal, an unbalanced sentimentalist, or a character accessible to feeling, and yet well poised. Such special opinions may have to be corrected; yet so firmly established do the main positions worked out by the anatomists, physiologists, and pathologists of the brain appear, that the youth of our medical schools are everywhere taught unhesitatingly to believe them. The assurance that observation will go on to establish them ever more and more minutely is the inspirer of all contemporary research. And almost any of our young psychologists will tell you that only a few belated scholastics, or possibly some crack-brained theosophist or psychical researcher, can be found holding back, and still talking as if mental phenomena might exist as independent variables in the world.

For the purposes of my argument, now, I wish to adopt this general doctrine as if it were established absolutely, with no possibility of restriction. During this hour I wish you also to accept it as a postulate, whether you think it incontrovertibly established or not; so I beg you to agree with me today in subscribing to the great psycho-physiological formula: *Thought is a function of the brain.*

The question is, then, Does this doctrine logically compel us to disbelieve in immortality? Ought it to force every truly consistent thinker to sacrifice his hopes of a hereafter to what he takes to be his duty of accepting all the consequences of a scientific truth?

Most persons imbued with what one may call the puritanism of science would feel themselves bound to answer this question with a yes. If any medically or psychologically bred young scientists feel otherwise, it is probably in consequence of that incoherency of mind of which the majority of mankind happily enjoy the privilege. At one hour scientists, at another they are Christians or common men, with the will to live burning hot in their breasts; and, holding thus the two ends of the chain, they are careless of the intermediate connection. But the more radical and uncompromising disciple of science makes the sacrifice, and, sorrowfully or not, according to his temperament, submits to giving up his hopes of heaven.[2]

This, then, is the objection to immortality; and the next thing in order for me is to try to make plain to you why I believe that it has in strict logic no deterrent power. I must show you that the fatal consequence is not coercive, as is commonly imagined; and that, even though our soul's life (as here below it is revealed to us) may be in literal strictness the function of a brain that perishes, yet it is not at all impossible, but on the contrary quite possible, that the life may still continue when the brain itself is dead.

The supposed impossibility of its continuing comes from too superficial a look at the admitted fact of functional dependence. The moment we inquire more closely into the notion of functional dependence, and ask ourselves, for example, how many kinds of functional dependence there may be, we immediately perceive that there is one kind at least that does not exclude a life hereafter at all. The fatal conclusion of the physiologist flows from his assuming offhand another kind of functional dependence, and treating it as the only imaginable kind.[3]

When the physiologist who thinks that his science cuts off all hope of immortality pronounces the phrase, "Thought is a function of the brain," he thinks of the matter just as he thinks when he says, "Steam is a function of the tea-kettle," "Light is a function of the electric circuit," "Power is a function of the moving waterfall." In these latter cases the several material objects have the function of inwardly creating or engendering their effects, and their function must be called *productive* function. Just so, he thinks, it must be with the brain. Engendering consciousness in its interior, much as it engenders cholesterin and creatin and carbonic acid, its relation to our soul's life must also be called productive function. Of course, if such production be the function, then when the organ perishes, since the production can no longer continue, the soul must surely die. Such a conclusion as this is indeed inevitable from that particular conception of the facts.[4]

But in the world of physical nature productive function of this sort is not the only kind of function with which we are familiar. We have also releasing or permissive function; and we have transmissive function.

The trigger of a crossbow has a releasing function: it removes the obstacle that holds the string, and lets the bow fly back to its natural shape. So when the hammer falls upon a detonating compound. By knocking out the inner molecular obstructions, it lets the constituent gases resume their normal bulk, and so permits the explosion to take place.

In the case of a colored glass, a prism, or a refracting lens, we have transmissive function. The energy of light, no matter how produced, is by the glass sifted and limited in color, and by the lens or prism determined to a certain path and shape. Similarly, the keys of an organ have only a transmissive function. They open successively the various pipes and let the wind in the air-chest escape in various ways. The voices of the various pipes are constituted by the columns of air trembling as they emerge. But the air is not engendered in the organ. The organ proper, as distinguished from its air-chest, is only an apparatus for letting portions of it loose upon the world in these peculiarly limited shapes.

My thesis now is this: that, when we think of the law that thought is a function of the brain, we are not required to think of productive function only; *we are entitled also to consider permissive or transmissive function.* And this the ordinary psycho-physiologist leaves out of his account.

Suppose, for example, that the whole universe of material things – the furniture of earth and choir of heaven – should turn out to be a mere surface-veil of phenomena, hiding and keeping back the world of genuine realities. Such a supposition is foreign neither to common sense nor to philosophy. Common sense believes in realities behind the veil even too superstitiously; and idealistic philosophy declares the whole world of natural experience, as we get it, to be but a time-mask, shattering or refracting the one infinite Thought which is the sole reality into those millions of finite streams of consciousness known to us as our private selves.

> *Life, like a dome of many-colored glass,*
> *Stains the white radiance of eternity.*
> [from "Adonais" by Percy Bysshe Shelley]

Suppose, now, that this were really so, and suppose, moreover, that the dome, opaque enough at all times to the full super-solar blaze, could at certain times and places grow less so, and let certain beams pierce through into this sublunary world. These beams would be so many finite rays, so to speak, of consciousness, and they would vary in quantity and quality as the opacity varied in degree. Only at particular times and places would it seem that, as a matter of fact, the veil of nature can grow thin and rupturable enough for such effects to occur. But in those places gleams, however finite and unsatisfying, of the absolute life of the universe, are from time to time vouchsafed. Glows of feeling, glimpses of insight, and streams of knowledge and perception float into our finite world.

Admit now that *our brains* are such thin and half-transparent places in the veil. What will happen? Why, as the white radiance comes through the dome, with all sorts of staining and distortion imprinted on it by the glass, or as the air now comes through my glottis determined and limited in its force and quality of its vibrations by the peculiarities of those vocal chords which form its gate of egress and shape it into my personal voice, even so the genuine matter of reality, the life of souls as it is in its fullness, will break through our several brains into this world in all sorts of restricted forms, and with all the imperfections and queernesses that characterize our finite individualities here below.

According to the state in which the brain finds itself, the barrier of its obstructiveness may also be supposed to rise or fall. It sinks so low, when the brain is in full activity, that a comparative flood of spiritual energy pours over. At other times, only such occasional waves of thought as heavy sleep permits get by. And when finally a brain stops acting altogether, or decays, that special stream of consciousness which it subserved will vanish entirely from this natural world. But the sphere of being that supplied the consciousness would still be intact; and in that more real world with which, even whilst here, it was continuous, the consciousness might, in ways unknown to us, continue still.

You see that, on all these suppositions, our soul's life, as we here know it, would none the less in literal strictness be the function of the brain. The brain would be the independent variable, the mind would vary dependently on it. But such dependence on the brain for this natural life would in no wise make immortal life impossible – it might be quite compatible with supernatural life behind the veil hereafter.

As I said, then, the fatal consequence is not coercive, the conclusion which materialism draws being due solely to its one-sided way of taking the word "function." And, whether we care or not for immortality in itself, we ought, as mere critics doing police duty among the vagaries of mankind, to insist on the illogicality of a denial based on the flat ignoring of a palpable alternative. How much more ought we to insist, as lovers of truth, when the denial is that of such a vital hope of mankind!

In strict logic, then, the fangs of cerebralistic materialism are drawn. My words ought consequently already to exert a releasing function on your hopes. You *may* believe henceforward, whether you care to profit by the permission or not. But, as this is a very abstract argument, I think it will help its effect to say a word or two about the more concrete conditions of the case.

All abstract hypotheses sound unreal; and the abstract notion that our brains are colored lenses in the wall of nature, admitting light from the super-solar source, but at the same time tingeing and restricting it, has a thoroughly fantastic sound. What is it, you may ask, but a foolish metaphor? And how can such a function be imagined? Isn't the common materialistic notion vastly simpler? Is not consciousness really more comparable to a sort of steam, or perfume, or electricity, or nerve-glow, generated on the spot in its own peculiar vessel? Is it not more rigorously scientific to treat the brain's function as function of production?

The immediate reply is, that, if we are talking of science positively understood, function can mean nothing more than bare concomitant variation. When the brain-activities change in one way, consciousness changes in another; when the currents pour through the occipital lobes, consciousness *sees* things; when through the lower frontal region, consciousness *says* things to itself; when they stop, she goes to sleep, etc. In strict science, we can only write down the bare fact of concomitance; and all talk about either production or transmission, as the mode of taking place, is pure superadded hypothesis, and metaphysical hypothesis at that, for we can frame no more notion of the details on the one alternative than on the other. Ask for any indication of the exact process either of transmission or of production, and Science confesses her imagination to be bankrupt. She has, so far, not the least glimmer of a conjecture or suggestion – not even a bad verbal metaphor or pun to offer. *Ignoramus, ignorabimus* ["we do not know and will not know"], is what most physiologists, in the words of one of their number, will say here. The production of such a thing as consciousness in the brain, they will reply with the late Berlin professor of physiology, is the absolute world-enigma – something so paradoxical and abnormal as to be a stumbling block to Nature, and almost a self-contradiction. Into the mode of production of steam in a tea-kettle we have conjectural insight, for the terms that change are physically homogeneous one with another, and we can easily imagine the case to consist of nothing but alterations of molecular motion. But in the production of consciousness by the brain, the terms are heterogeneous natures altogether; and as far as our understanding goes, it is as great a miracle as if we said, Thought is "spontaneously generated," or "created out of nothing."

The theory of production is therefore not a jot more simple or credible in itself than any other conceivable theory. It is only a little more popular. All that one need do, therefore, if the ordinary materialist should challenge one to explain how the brain *can* be an organ for limiting and determining to a certain form a consciousness elsewhere produced, is to retort with a *tu quoque*, asking him in turn to explain how it can be an organ for producing consciousness out of whole cloth. For polemic purposes, the two theories are thus exactly on a par.

But if we consider the theory of transmission in a wider way, we see that it has certain positive superiorities, quite apart from its connection with the immortality question.

Just how the process of transmission may be carried on, is indeed unimaginable; but the outer relations, so to speak, of the process, encourage our belief. Consciousness in this process does not have to be generated *de novo* [beginning anew] in a vast number of places. It exists already, behind the scenes, coeval with the world. The transmission-theory not only avoids in this way multiplying miracles, but it puts itself in touch with general idealistic philosophy better than the production-theory does. It should always be reckoned a good thing when science and philosophy thus meet.[5]

It puts itself also in touch with the conception of a "threshold" – a word with which, since Fechner wrote his book called *Psychophysik*, the so-called "new Psychology" has rung. Fechner imagines as the condition of consciousness a certain kind of psycho-physical movement, as he terms it. Before consciousness can come, a certain degree of activity in the movement must be reached. This requisite degree is called the "threshold"; but the height of the threshold varies under different circumstances: it may rise or fall. When it falls, as in states of great lucidity, we grow conscious of things of which we should be unconscious at other times; when it rises, as in drowsiness, consciousness sinks in amount. This rising and lowering of a psycho-physical threshold exactly conforms to our notion of a permanent obstruction to the transmission of consciousness, which obstruction may, in our brains, grow alternately greater or less.[6]

The transmission-theory also puts itself in touch with a whole class of experiences that are with difficulty explained by the production-theory. I refer to those obscure and exceptional phenomena reported at all times throughout human history, which the "psychical researchers," with Mr. Frederic Myers at their head, are doing so much to rehabilitate;[7] such phenomena, namely, as religious conversions, providential leadings in answer to prayer, instantaneous healings, premonitions, apparitions at time of death, clairvoyant visions or impressions, and the whole range of mediumistic capacities, to say nothing of still more exceptional and incomprehensible things. If all our human thought be a function of the brain, then of course, if any of these things are facts – and to my own mind some of them are facts – we may not suppose that they can occur without preliminary brain-action. But the ordinary production-theory of consciousness is knit up with a peculiar notion of how brain-action *can* occur – that notion being that all brain-action, without exception, is due to a prior action, immediate or remote, of the bodily sense-organs *on* the brain. Such action makes the brain produce sensations and mental images, and out of the sensations and images the higher forms of thought and knowledge in their turn are framed. As transmissionists, we also must admit this to be the condition of all our usual thought. Sense-action is what lowers the brain-barrier. My voice and aspect, for instance, strike upon your ears and eyes; your brain thereupon becomes more pervious, and an awareness on your part of what I say and who I am slips into this world from the world behind the veil. But, in the mysterious phenomena to which I allude, it is often hard to see where the sense-organs can come in. A medium, for example, will show knowledge of his sitter's private affairs which it seems impossible he should have acquired through sight or hearing, or inference therefrom. Or you will have an apparition of someone who is now dying hundreds of miles away. On the production-theory one does not see from what sensations such odd bits of knowledge are produced. On the transmission-theory, they don't have to be "produced" – they exist ready-made in the transcendental world, and all that is needed is an abnormal lowering of the brain-threshold to let them through. In cases of conversion, in providential leadings, sudden mental healings, etc., it seems to the subjects themselves of the experience as if a power from without, quite different from the ordinary action of the senses or of the sense-led mind, came into their life, as if the latter suddenly opened into that greater life in which it has its source. The word "influx," used in Swedenborgian circles, well describes this impression of new insight, or new willingness, sweeping over us like a tide. All such experiences, quite paradoxical and meaningless on the production-theory, fall very naturally into place on the other theory. We need only suppose the continuity of our consciousness with a mother-sea, to allow for exceptional waves occasionally pouring over the dam. Of course the causes of these odd lowerings of the brain's threshold still remain a mystery on any terms.

Add, then, this advantage to the transmission-theory – an advantage which I am well aware that some of you will not rate very high – and also add the advantage of not conflicting with a life hereafter, and I hope you will agree with me that it has many points of superiority to the more familiar theory. It is a theory which, in the history of opinion on such matters, has never been wholly left out of account, though never developed at any great length. In the great orthodox philosophic tradition, the body is treated as an essential condition to the soul's life in this world of sense; but after death, it is said, the soul is set free, and becomes a purely intellectual and non-appetitive being. Kant expresses this idea in terms that come singularly close to those of our transmission-theory. The death of the body, he says, may indeed be the end of the sensational use of our mind, but only the beginning of the intellectual use. "The body," he continues, "would thus be, not the cause of our thinking, but merely a condition restrictive thereof, and, although essential to our sensuous and animal consciousness, it may be regarded as an impeder of our pure spiritual life."[8] And in a recent book of great suggestiveness and power, less well-known as yet than it deserves – I mean *Riddles of the Sphinx*, by Mr. F. C. S. Schiller of Oxford, late of Cornell University – the transmission-theory is defended at some length.[9]

But still, you will ask, in what positive way does this theory help us to realize our immortality in imagination? What we all wish to keep is just these individual restrictions, these selfsame tendencies and peculiarities that define us to ourselves and others, and constitute our identity, so called. Our finitenesses and limitations seem to be our personal essence; and when the finiting organ drops away, and our several spirits revert to their original source and resume their unrestricted condition, will they then be anything like those sweet streams of feeling which we know, and which even now our brains are sifting out from the great reservoir for our enjoyment here below? Such questions are truly living questions, and surely they must be seriously discussed by future lecturers upon this Ingersoll foundation. I hope, for my part, that more than one such lecturer will penetratingly discuss the conditions of our immortality, and tell us how much we may lose, and how much we may possibly gain, if its finiting outlines should be changed? If all determination is negation, as the philosophers say, it might well prove that the loss of some of the particular determinations which the brain imposes would not appear a matter for such absolute regret.

But into these higher and more transcendental matters I refuse to enter upon this occasion; and I proceed, during the remainder of the hour, to treat of my second point. Fragmentary and negative it is, as my first one has been. Yet, between them, they do give to our belief in immortality a freer wing.

My second point is relative to the incredible and intolerable number of beings which, with our modern imagination, we must believe to be immortal, if immortality be true. I cannot but suspect that this, too, is a stumbling-block to many of my present audience. And it is a stumbling-block which I should thoroughly like to clear away.

It is, I fancy, a stumbling-block of altogether modern origin, due to the strain upon the quantitative imagination which recent scientific theories, and the moral feelings consequent upon them, have brought in their train.

For our ancestors the world was a small, and – compared with our modern sense of it – a comparatively snug affair. Six thousand years at most it had lasted. In its history a few particular human heroes, kings, ecclesiarchs, and saints stood forth very prominent, overshadowing the imagination with their claims and merits, so that not only they, but all who were associated familiarly with them, shone with a glamour which even the Almighty, it was supposed, must recognize and respect. These prominent personages and their associates were the nucleus of the immortal group; the minor heroes and saints of minor sects came next, and people without distinction formed a sort of background and filling in. The whole scene of eternity (so far, at least, as Heaven and not the nether place was concerned in it) never struck to the believer's fancy as an overwhelmingly large or inconveniently crowded stage. One might call this an aristocratic view of immortality; the immortals – I speak of Heaven exclusively, for an immortality of torment need not now concern us – were always an elite, a select and manageable number.

But, with our own generation, an entirely new quantitative imagination has swept over our western world. The theory of evolution now requires us to suppose a far vaster scale of times, spaces, and numbers than our forefathers ever dreamed the cosmic process to involve. Human history grows continuously out of animal history, and goes back possibly even to the tertiary epoch. From this there has emerged insensibly a democratic view, instead of the old aristocratic view, of immortality. For our minds, though in one sense they may have grown a little cynical, in another they have been made sympathetic by the evolutionary perspective. Bone of our bone and flesh of our flesh are these half-brutish prehistoric brothers. Girdled about with the immense darkness of this mysterious universe even as we are, they were born and died, suffered and struggled. Given over to fearful crime and passion, plunged in the blackest ignorance, preyed upon by hideous and grotesque delusions, yet steadfastly serving the profoundest of ideals in their fixed faith that existence in any form is better than non-existence, they ever rescued triumphantly from the jaws of ever-imminent destruction the torch of life, which, thanks to them, now lights the world for us.

How small indeed seem individual distinctions when we look back on these overwhelming numbers of human beings panting and straining under the pressure of that vital want! And how inessential in the eyes of God must be the small surplus of the individual's merit, swamped as it is in the vast ocean of the common merit of mankind, dumbly and undauntedly doing the fundamental duty and living the heroic life! We grow humble and reverent as we contemplate the prodigious spectacle. Not our differences and distinctions – we feel – no, but our common animal essence of patience under suffering and enduring effort must be what redeems us in the Deity's sight. An immense compassion and kinship fill the heart. An immortality from which these inconceivable billions of fellow-strivers should be excluded becomes an irrational idea for us. That our superiority in personal refinement or in religious creed should constitute a difference between ourselves and our messmates at life's banquet, fit to entail such a consequential difference of destiny as eternal life for us, and for them torment hereafter, or death with the beasts that perish, is a notion too absurd to be considered serious. Nay, more, the very beasts themselves – the wild ones at any rate – are leading the heroic life at all times. And a modern mind, expanded as some minds are by cosmic emotion, by the great evolutionist vision of universal continuity, hesitates to draw the line even at man. If any creature lives forever, why not all? – why not the patient brutes? So that a faith in immortality, if we are to indulge it, demands of us nowadays a scale of representation so stupendous that our imagination faints before it, and our personal feelings refuse to rise up and face the task. The supposition we are swept along to is too vast, and, rather than face the conclusion, we abandon the premise from which it starts. We give up our own immortality sooner than believe that all the hosts of Hottentots and Australians that have been, and shall ever be, should share it with us in *secula seculorum*. Life is a good thing on a reasonably copious scale; but the very heavens themselves, and the cosmic times and spaces, would stand aghast, we think, at the notion of preserving eternally such an ever-swelling plethora and glut of it.

Having myself, as a recipient of modern scientific culture, gone through a subjective experience like this, I feel sure that it must also have been the experience of many, perhaps of most, of you who listen to my words. But I have also come to see that it harbors a tremendous fallacy; and, since the noting of the fallacy has set my own mind free again, I have felt that one service I might render to my listeners tonight would be to point out where it lies.

It is the most obvious fallacy in the world, and the only wonder is that all the world should not see through it. It is the result of nothing but an invincible blindness from which we suffer, an insensibility to the inner significance of alien lives, and a conceit that would project our own incapacity into the vast cosmos, and measure the wants of the Absolute by our own puny needs. Our Christian ancestors dealt with the problem more easily than we do. We, indeed, lack sympathy; but they had a positive antipathy for these alien human creatures, and they naively supposed the Deity to have the antipathy, too. Being, as they were, "heathen," our forefathers felt a certain sort of joy in thinking that their Creator made them as so much mere fuel for the fires of hell. Our culture has humanized us beyond that point, but we cannot yet conceive them as our comrades in the fields of heaven We have, as the phrase goes, *no use for them*, and it oppresses us to think of their survival. Take, for instance, all the Chinamen. Which of you here, my friends, sees any fitness in their eternal perpetuation unreduced in numbers? Surely not one of you. At most, you might deem it well to keep a few chosen specimens alive to represent an interesting and peculiar variety of humanity; but as for the rest, what comes in such surpassing numbers, and what you can only imagine in this abstract summary collective manner, must be something of which the units, you are sure, can have no individual preciousness. God himself, you think, can have no use for them. An immortality of every separate specimen must be to him and to the universe as indigestible a load to carry as it is to you. So, engulfing the whole subject in a sort of mental giddiness and nausea, you drift along, first doubting that the mass can be immortal, then losing all assurance in the immortality of your own particular person, precious as you all the while feel and realize the latter to be. This, I am sure, is the attitude of mind of some of you before me.

But is not such an attitude due to the veriest lack and dearth of your imagination? You take these swarms of alien kinsmen as they are *for you*: an external picture painted on your retina, representing a crowd oppressive by its vastness and confusion. As they are for you, so you think they positively and absolutely are. *I* feel no call for them, you say; therefore there *is* no call for them. But all the while, beyond this externality which is your way of realizing them, they realize themselves with the acutest internality, with the most violent thrills of life. 'Tis you who are dead, stone-dead and blind and senseless, in your way of looking on. You open your eyes upon a scene of which you miss the whole significance. Each of these grotesque or even repulsive aliens is animated by an inner joy of living as hot or hotter than that which you feel beating in your private breast. The sun rises and beauty beams to light his path. To miss the inner joy of him, as Stevenson says, is to miss the whole of him.[10] Not a being of the countless throng is there whose continued life is not called for, and called for intensely, by the consciousness that animates the being's form. That *you* neither realize nor understand nor call for it, that you have no use for it, is an absolutely irrelevant circumstance. That you have a saturation-point of interest tells us nothing of the interests that absolutely are. The Universe, with every living entity which her resources create, creates at the same time a call for that entity, and an appetite for its continuance – creates it, if nowhere else, at least within the heart of the entity itself. It is absurd to suppose, simply because our private power of sympathetic vibration with other lives gives out so soon, that in the heart of infinite being itself there can be such a thing as plethora, or glut, or supersaturation. It is not as if there were a bounded room where the minds in possession had to move up or make place and crowd together to accommodate new occupants. Each new mind brings its own edition of the universe of space along with it, its own room to inhabit; and these spaces never crowd each other – the space of my imagination, for example, in no way interferes with yours. The amount of possible consciousness seems to be governed by no law analogous to that of the so-called conservation of energy in the material world. When one man wakes up, or one is born, another does not have to go to sleep, or die, in order to keep the consciousness of the universe a constant quantity. Professor Wundt, in fact, in his *System of Philosophy*, has formulated a law of the universe which he calls the law of increase of spiritual energy, and which he expressly opposes to the law of conservation of energy in physical things.[11] There seems no formal limit to the positive increase of being in spiritual respects; and since spiritual being, whenever it comes, affirms itself, expands and craves continuance, we may justly and literally say, regardless of the defects of our own private sympathy, that the supply of individual life in the universe can never possibly, however immeasurable it may become, exceed the demand. The demand for that supply is there the moment the supply itself comes into being, for the beings supplied demand their own continuance.

I speak, you see, from the point of view of all the other individual beings, realizing and enjoying inwardly their own existence. If we are pantheists, we can stop there. We need, then, only say that through them, as through so many diversified channels of expression, the eternal

Spirit of the Universe affirms and realizes its own infinite life. But if we are theists, we can go farther without altering the result. God, we can then say, has so inexhaustible a capacity for love that his call and need is for a literally endless accumulation of created lives. He can never faint or grow weary, as we should, under the increasing supply. His scale is infinite in all things. His sympathy can never know satiety or glut.

I hope now that you agree with me that the tiresomeness of an over peopled Heaven is a purely subjective and illusory notion, a sign of human incapacity, a remnant of the old narrow-hearted aristocratic creed. "Revere the Maker, lift thine eye up to his style and manners of the sky," and you will believe that this is indeed a democratic universe, in which your paltry exclusions play no regulative part. Was your taste consulted in the peopling of this globe? How, then, should it be consulted as to the peopling of the vast City of God? Let us put our hand over our mouth, like Job, and be thankful that in our personal littleness we ourselves are here at all. The Deity that suffers us, we may be sure, can suffer many another queer and wondrous and only half-delightful thing.

For my own part, then, so far as logic goes, I am willing that every leaf that ever grew in this world's forests and rustled in the breeze should become immortal. It is purely a question of fact: are the leaves so, or not? Abstract quantity, and the abstract needlessness in our eyes of so much reduplication of things so much alike, have no connection with the subject. For bigness and number and generic similarity are only manners of our finite way of thinking; and, considered in itself and apart from our imagination, one scale of dimensions and of numbers for the Universe is no more miraculous or inconceivable than another, the moment you grant to a universe the liberty to be at all, in place of the Non-entity that might conceivably have reigned.

The heart of being can have no exclusions akin to those which our poor little hearts set up. The inner significance of other lives exceeds all our powers of sympathy and insight. If we feel a significance in our own life which would lead us spontaneously to claim its perpetuity, let us be at least tolerant of like claims made by other lives, however numerous, however unideal they may seem to us to be. Let us at any rate not decide adversely on our own claim, whose grounds we feel directly, because we cannot decide favorably on the alien claims, whose grounds we cannot feel at all. That would be letting blindness lay down the law to sight.

Notes

[1] The gaps between the centers first recognized as motor and sensory – gaps which form in man two thirds of the surface of the hemispheres – are thus positively interpreted by Flechsig as intellectual centers strictly so called. (Compare his *Gehirn und Seele*, 2te Ausgabe, 1896, p. 23.) They have, he considers, a common type of microscopic structure; and the fibers connected with them are a month later in gaining their medullary sheath than are the fibers connected with the other centers. When disordered, they are the starting-point of the insanities, properly so called. Already Wernicke had defined insanity as disease of the organ of association, without so definitely pretending to circumscribe the latter – compare his *Grundriss der Psychiatrie*, 1894, p. 7. Flechsig goes so far as to say that he finds a difference of symptoms in general paralytics according as their frontal or their more posterior association-centers are diseased. Where it is the frontal centers, the patient's consciousness of self is more deranged than is his perception of purely objective relations. Where the posterior associative regions suffer, it is rather the patient's system of objective ideas that undergoes disintegration (*loc. cit.* pp. 89-91). In rodents Flechsig thinks there is a complete absence of association-centers – the sensory centers touch each other. In carnivora and the lower monkeys the latter centers, still exceed the association-centers in volume. Only in the katarhinal apes do we begin to find anything like the human type (p. 84).

In his little pamphlet, *Die Grenzen geistiger Gesundizeit und Krankheit*, Leipzig, 1896, Flechsig ascribes the moral insensibility which is found in certain criminals to a diminution of internal pain-feeling due to degeneration of the "Körperfühlsphäre," that extensive anterior region first so named by Munk, in which he lays the seat of all the emotions and of the consciousness of self (*Gehirn und Seele*, pp. 62-68; *die Grenzen*, etc., pp. 31-39, 48). I give these references to Flechsig for concreteness' sake, not because his views are irreversibly made out.

[2] So widespread is this conclusion in positivistic circles, so abundantly is it expressed in conversation, and so frequently implied in things that are written, that I confess that my surprise was great when I came to look into books for a passage explicitly denying immortality on physiological grounds, which I might quote to make my text more concrete. I was unable to find anything blunt and distinct enough to serve. I looked through all the books that would naturally suggest themselves, with

no effect; and I vainly asked various psychological colleagues. And yet I should almost have been ready to take oath that I had read several such passages of the most categoric sort within the last decade. Very likely this is a false impression, and it may be with this opinion as with many others. The atmosphere is full of them; many a writer's pages logically presuppose and involve them; yet, if you wish to refer a student to an express and radical statement that he may employ as a text to comment on, you find almost nothing that will do. In the present case there are plenty of passages in which, in a general way, mind is said to be conterminous with brain-function, but hardly one in which the author thereupon explicitly denies the possibility of immortality. The best one I have found is perhaps this: "Not only consciousness, but every stirring of life, depends on functions that go out like a flame when nourishment is cut off. ... The phenomena of consciousness correspond, element for element, to the operations of special parts of the brain. ... The destruction of any piece of the apparatus involves the loss of some one or other of the vital operations; and the consequence is that, as far as life extends, we have before us only an organic function, not a *Ding-an-sich*, or an expression of that imaginary entity the Soul. This fundamental proposition ... carries with it the denial of the immortality of the soul, since, where no soul exists, its mortality or immortality cannot be raised as a question. ... The function fills its time – the flame illuminates and therein gives out its whole being. That is all; and verily that is enough. ... Sensation has its definite organic conditions, and, as these decay with the natural decay of life, it is quite impossible for a mind accustomed to deal with realities to suppose any capacity of sensation as surviving when the machinery of our natural existence has stopped" (*E. Duhring: der Werth des Lehens*, 3d edition, pp. 48, 168).

[3] The philosophically instructed reader will notice that I have all along been placing myself at the ordinary dualistic point of view of natural science and of common sense. From this point of view mental facts like feelings are made of one kind of stuff or substance, physical facts of another. An absolute phenomenism, not believing such a dualism to be ultimate, may possibly end by solving some of the problems that are insoluble when propounded in dualistic terms. Meanwhile, since the physiological objection to immortality has arisen on the ordinary dualistic plane of thought, and since absolute phenomenism has as yet said nothing articulate enough to count about the matter, it is proper that my reply to the objection should be expressed in dualistic terms

– leaving me free, of course, on any later occasion to make an attempt, if I wish, to transcend them and use different categories.

Now, on the dualistic assumption, one cannot see more than two really different sorts of dependence of our mind on our brain: Either

(1) The brain brings into being the very stuff of consciousness of which our mind consists; or else

(2) Consciousness preexists as an entity, and the various brains give to it its various special forms.

If supposition 2 be the true one, and the stuff of mind preexists, there are, again, only two ways of conceiving that our brain confers upon it the specifically human form. It may exist

(a) In disseminated particles; and then our brains are organs of concentration, organs for combining and massing these into resultant minds of personal form. Or it may exist

(b) In vaster unities (absolute "world-soul," or something less); and then our brains are organs for separating it into parts and giving them finite form.

There are thus three possible theories of the brain's function, and no more. We may name them, severally:

1. The theory of production;
2*a*. The theory of combination;
2*b*. The theory of separation.

In the text of the lecture, theory number 2*b* (specified more particularly as the transmission-theory) is defended against theory number 1. Theory 2*a*, otherwise known as the mind-dust or mind-stuff theory, is left entirely unnoticed for lack of time. I also leave it uncriticized in these Notes, having already considered it, as fully as the so-far published forms of it may seem to call for, in my work, *The Principles of Psychology*, New York, Holt & Co., 1892 chapter VI. I may say here, however, that Professor W. K. Clifford, one of the ablest champions of the combination-theory, and originator of the useful term "mind-stuff," considers that theory incompatible with individual immortality, and in his review of Stewart's and Tait's book, *The Unseen Universe*, thus expresses his conviction:

"The laws connecting consciousness with changes in the brain are very definite and precise, and their necessary consequences are not to be evaded. ... Consciousness is a complex thing made up of elements, a stream of feelings. The action of the brain is also a complex thing made up of elements, a stream of nerve-messages. For every feeling in consciousness there is at the same time a nerve message in the brain. ... Consciousness is not a simple thing, but a complex; it is the combination of feelings into a stream. It exists at the same time with the combination of nerve-messages into a stream. If individual feeling always goes with individual nerve-message, if combination or stream of feelings always goes with stream of nerve-messages, does it not follow that, when the stream of nerve-messages is broken up, the stream of feelings will be broken up also, will no longer form a consciousness? Does it not follow that, when the messages themselves are broken up, the individual feelings will be resolved into still simpler elements? The force of this evidence is not to be weakened by any number of spiritual bodies. Inexorable facts connect our consciousness with this body that we know; and that not merely as a whole, but the parts of it are connected severally with parts of our brain-action. If there is any similar connection with a spiritual body, it only follows that the spiritual body must die at the same time with the natural one" (*Lectures and Essays*, vol. I, p. 247-49. Compare also passages of similar purport in vol. II pp. 65-70).

[4] The theory of production, or materialistic theory, seldom ventures to formulate itself very distinctly. Perhaps the following passage from Cabanis is as explicit as anything one can find:

"To acquire a just idea of the operations from which thought results, we must consider the brain as a particular organ specially destined to produce it; just as the stomach and intestines are destined to operate digestion, the liver to filter bile, the parotid and maxillary glands to prepare the salivary juices. The impressions, arriving in the brain, force it to enter into activity; just as the alimentary materials, falling into the stomach, excite it to a more abundant secretion of gastric juice, and to the movements which result in their own solution. The function proper to the first organ is that of receiving (*percevoir*) each particular impression, of attaching signs to it, of combining the different impressions, of comparing them with each other, of drawing from them judgments and resolves; just as the function of the other organ is to act upon the nutritive substances whose presence excites it, to dissolve them, and to assimilate their juices to our nature.

"Do you say that the organic movements by which the brain exercises these functions are unknown? I reply that the action by which the nerves of the stomach determine the different operations which constitute digestion, and the manner in which they confer so active a solvent power upon the gastric juice, are equally hidden from our scrutiny. We see the food-materials fall into this viscus with their own proper qualities; we see them emerge with new qualities, and we infer that the stomach is really the author of this alteration. Similarly we see the impressions reaching the brain by the intermediation of the nerves; they then are isolated and without coherence. The viscus enters into action; it acts upon them, and soon it emits (*renvoie*) them metamorphosed into ideas, to which the language of physiognomy or gesture, or the signs of speech and writing, give an outward expression. We conclude, then, with an equal certitude, that the brain digests, as it were, the impressions; that it performs organically the secretion of thought" (*Rapports du Physique et du Moral*, 8th edition, 1844, p. 137).

It is to the ambiguity of the word "impression" that such an account owes whatever plausibility it may seem to have. More recent forms of the production-theory have shown a tendency to liken thought to a "force" which the brain exerts, or to a "state" into which it passes. Herbert Spencer, for instance, writes:

"The law of metamorphosis, which holds among the physical forces, holds equally between them and the mental forces. ... How this metamorphosis takes place; how a force existing as motion, heat, or light can become a mode of consciousness; how it is possible for aerial vibrations to generate the sensation we call sound, or for the forces liberated by chemical changes in the brain to give rise to emotion – these are mysteries which it is impossible to fathom. But they are not profounder mysteries than the transformations of the physical forces into each other" (*First Principles*, 2nd Edition, p. 217).

So Büchner says: "Thinking must be regarded as a special mode of general natural motion, which is as characteristic of the substance of the central nervous elements as the motion of contraction is of the nerve-substance, or the motion of light is of the universal-ether. ... That thinking is and must be a mode of motion is not merely a postulate of logic, but a proposition which has of late been demonstrated experimentally. ... Various ingenious experiments have proved that the swiftest thought that we are able to evolve occupies at least the eighth or tenth part of a second" (*Force and Matter*, New York, 1891, p. 241).

Heat and light, being modes of motion, "phosphorescence" and "incandescence" are phenomena to which consciousness has been likened by the production-theory: "As one sees a metallic rod, placed in a glowing furnace, gradually heat itself, and – as the undulations of the caloric grow more and more frequent – pass successively from the shades of bright red to dark red (*sic*), to white, and develop, as its temperature rises, heat and light – so the living sensitive cells, in presence of the incitations that solicit them, exalt themselves progressively as to their most interior sensibility, enter into a phase of erethism, and at a certain number of vibrations, set free (*dégagent*) pain as a physiological expression of this same sensibility superheated to a red-white." (J. Luys: *le Cerveau*, p. 91).

In a similar vein Mr. Percival Lowell writes: "When we have, as we say, an idea, what happens inside of us is probably something like this: the neural current of molecular change passes up the nerves, and through the ganglia reaches at last the cortical cells. ... When it reaches the cortical cells, it finds a set of molecules which are not so accustomed to this special change. The current encounters resistance, and in overcoming this resistance it causes the cells to glow. This white-heating of the cells we call consciousness. Consciousness, in short, is probably nerve-glow" (*Occult Japan*, Boston, 1895, p. 311).

[5] The transmission-theory connects itself very naturally with that whole tendency of thought known as transcendentalism. Emerson, for example, writes: "We lie in the lap of immense intelligence, which makes us receivers of its truth and organs of its activity. When we discern justice, when we discern truth, we do nothing of ourselves; but allow a passage to its beams" (*Self-Reliance*, p. 56). But it is not necessary to identify the consciousness postulated in the lecture, as preexisting behind the scenes, with the Absolute Mind of transcendental Idealism, although, indeed, the notion of it might lead in that direction. The absolute Mind of transcendental Idealism is one integral Unit, one single World-mind. For the purposes of my lecture, however, there might be many minds behind the scenes as well as one. All that the transmission-theory absolutely requires is that they should transcend our minds – which thus come from something mental that pre-exists, and is larger than themselves.

[6] Fechner's conception of a "psycho-physical threshold" as connected with his "wave-scheme" is little known to English readers. I accordingly subjoin it, in his own words, abridged:

"The psychically one is connected with a physically many; the physically many contract psychically into a one, a simple, or at least a more simple. Otherwise expressed: the psychically unified and simple are resultants of physical multiplicity; the physically manifold gives unified or simple results. ...

"The facts which are grouped together under these expressions, and which give them their meaning, are as follows:... With our two hemispheres we think singly; with the identical parts of our two retinæ we see singly. ... The simplest sensation of light or sound in us is connected with processes which, since they are started and kept up by outer oscillations, must themselves be somehow of an oscillatory nature, although we are wholly unaware of the separate phases and oscillations. ...

"It is certain, then, that some unified or simple psychic resultants depend on physical multiplicity. But, on the other hand, it is equally certain that the multiplicities of the physical world do not always combine into a simple psychical resultant – no, not even when they are compounded in a single bodily system. Whether they may not nevertheless combine into a unified resultant is a matter for opinion, since one is always free to ask whether the entire world, as such, may not have some unified psychic resultant. But of any such resultant we at least have no consciousness. ...

"For brevity's sake, let us distinguish *psycho-physical continuity* and *discontinuity* from each other. Continuity, let us say, takes place so far as a physical manifold gives a unified or simple psychic resultant; discontinuity, so far as it gives a distinguishable multiplicity of such resultants. Inasmuch, however, as, within the unity of a more general consciousness or phenomenon of consciousness, there still maybe a multiplicity distinguished, the continuity of a more general consciousness does not exclude the discontinuity of particular phenomena.

"One of the most important problems and tasks of Psycho-physics now is this: to determine the conditions (*Gesichtspunkte*) under which the cases of continuity and of discontinuity occur.

"Whence comes it that different organisms have separate consciousnesses, although their bodies are just as much connected by general Nature as the parts of a single organism are with each other, and these latter give a single conscious resultant? Of course we can say that the connection is more intimate between the parts of an organism than between the organisms of Nature. But what do we mean by a more intimate connection? Can an absolute difference of result depend on anything so relative? And does not Nature as a whole show as strict a connection as any organism does – yea, one even more indissoluble? And the same questions come up within each organism. How comes it that, with different nerve-fibers of touch and sight, we distinguish different space-points, but with one fiber distinguish nothing, although the different fibers are connected in the brain just as much as the parts are in the single fiber? We may again call the latter connection the more *intimate*, but then the same sort of question will arise again.

"Unquestionably the problem which here lies before Psycho-physics cannot be *sharply* answered; but we may establish a general point of view for its treatment, consistently with what we laid down in a former chapter on the relations of more general with more particular phenomena of consciousness."

([The earlier passage is here inserted]): "The essential principle is this: That human psycho-physical activity must exceed a certain intensity for any waking consciousness at all to occur, and that during the waking state any particular specification of the said activity (whether spontaneous or due to stimulation), which is capable of occasioning a particular specification of consciousness, must exceed in its turn a certain further degree of intensity for the consciousness actually to arise. ...

"This state of things (in itself a mere fact needing no picture) may be made clearer by an image or scheme, and also more concisely spoken of. Imagine the whole psycho-physical activity of man to be a wave, and the degree of this activity to be symbolized by the height of the wave above a horizontal basal line or surface, to which every psychophysically active point contributes an ordinate. ... The whole form and evolution of the consciousness will then depend on the rising and falling of this wave; the intensity of the consciousness at any time on the wave's height at that time; and the height must always *somewhere* exceed a certain limit, which we will call a *threshold*, if waking consciousness is to exist at all.

"Let us call this wave the *total wave*, and the threshold in question the *principal threshold*."

([Since our various states of consciousness recur, some in long, some in short periods]), "we may represent such a long period as that of the slowly fluctuating condition of our general wakefulness and the general direction of our attention as a wave that slowly changes the place of its summit. If we call this the *under-wave*, then the movements of shorter period, on which the more special conscious states depend, can be symbolized by wavelets superposed upon the under-wave, and we can call these *over-waves*. They will cause all sorts of modifications of the under-wave's surface, and the total wave will be the resultant of both sets of waves.

"The greater, now, the strength of the movements of short period, the amplitude of the oscillations of the psycho-physical activity, the higher will the crests of the wavelets that represent them rise above, and the lower will their valleys sink below the surface of the underwave that bears them. And these heights and depressions must exceed a certain limit of quantity which we may call the *upper threshold*, before the special mental state which is correlated with them can appear in consciousness" (pp. 454-456).

"So far now as we symbolize any system of psycho-physical activity, to which a generally unified or principal consciousness corresponds, by the image of a total wave rising with its crest above a certain "threshold," we have a means of schematizing in a single diagram the physical solidarity of all these psycho-physical systems throughout Nature, together with their pyscho-physical discontinuity. For we need only draw all the waves so that they run into each other below the threshold, whilst above it they appear distinct, as in the figure below.

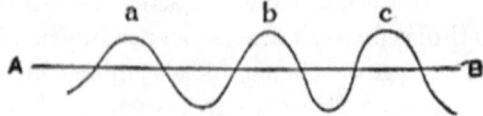

"In this figure *a, b, c* stand for three organisms, or rather for the total waves of psycho-physical activity of three organisms, whilst *A B* represents the threshold. In each wave the part that rises above the threshold is an integrated thing, and is connected with a single consciousness. Whatever lies below the threshold, being unconscious, separates the conscious crests, although it is still the means of physical connection.

"In general terms: wherever a psycho-physical total wave is continuous with itself above the threshold, there we find the unity or identity of a consciousness, inasmuch as the connection of the psychical phenomena which correspond to the parts of the wave also appears in consciousness. Whenever, on the contrary, total waves are disconnected, or connected only underneath the threshold, the corresponding consciousness is broken, and no connection between its several parts appears. More briefly: consciousness is continuous or discontinuous, unified or discrete, according as the psycho-physical total waves that it are themselves continuous or discontinuous above the threshold. ...

"If, in the diagram, we should raise the entire line of waves so that not only the crests but the valleys appeared above the threshold, then these latter would appear only as depressions in one great continuous wave above the threshold, and the discontinuity of the consciousness would be converted into continuity. We of course cannot bring this about. We might also squeeze the wave together so that the valleys should be pressed up, and the crests above the threshold flow into a line; then the discretely-feeling organisms would have become a singly-feeling organism. This, again, Man cannot voluntarily bring about, but it is brought about in Man's nature. His two halves, the right one and the left one, are thus united; and the number of segments of radiates and articulates show that more than two parts can be thus psychophysically conjoined. One need only cut them asunder, i. e. interpolate another part of nature between them under the threshold, and they break into two separately conscious beings. ..." (*Elemente der Psychophysik*, 1860, vol. II, pp. 526-530).

One sees easily how, on Fechner's wave-scheme, a world-soul may be expressed. All psycho-physical activity being continuous "below the threshold," the consciousness might also become continuous if the threshold sank low enough to uncover all the waves. The threshold throughout nature in general is, however, very high, so the consciousness that gets over it is of the discontinuous form.

[7] See the long series of articles by Mr. Myers in the *Proceedings of the Society for Psychical Research*, beginning in the third volume with automatic writing, and ending in the latest volumes with the higher manifestations of knowledge by mediums. Mr. Myers's theory of the whole range of phenomena is, that our normal consciousness is in continuous connection with a greater consciousness of which we do not know the extent, and to which he gives, in its relation to the particular person, the not very felicitous name – though no better one has been proposed – of his or her "subliminal" self.

[8] See *Kritik der reinen Vernunft*, second edition, P. 809.

[9] I subjoin a few extracts from Mr. Schiller's work: "Matter is an admirably calculated machinery for regulating, limiting, and restraining the consciousness which it encases. ... If the material encasement be coarse and simple, as in the lower organisms, it permits only a little intelligence to permeate through it; if it is delicate and complex, it leaves more pores and exits, as it were, for the manifestations of consciousness. ... On this analogy, then, we may say that the lower

animals are still entranced in the lower stage of brute *lethargy*, while we have passed into the higher phase of *somnambulism*, which already permits us strange glimpses of a lucidity that divines the realities of a transcendent world. And this gives the final answer to Materialism: it consists in showing in detail…that Materialism is a hysteron proteron, a putting of the cart before the horse, which may be rectified by just inverting the connection between Matter and Consciousness. Matter is not that which *produces* Consciousness, but that which *limits* it, and confines its intensity within certain limits: material organization does not construct consciousness out of arrangements of atoms, but contracts its manifestation within the sphere which it permits. This explanation… admits the connection of Matter and Consciousness, but contends that the course of interpretation must proceed in the contrary direction. Thus it will fit the facts alleged in favor of Materialism equally well, besides enabling us to understand facts which Materialism rejected as "supernatural." It explains the lower by the higher, Matter by Spirit, instead of *vice versa*, and thereby attains to an explanation which is ultimately tenable, instead of one which is ultimately absurd. And it is an explanation the possibility of which no evidence in favor of Materialism can possibly affect. For if, e. g., a man loses consciousness as soon as his brain is injured, it is clearly as good an explanation to say the injury to the brain destroyed the mechanism by which the manifestation of the consciousness was rendered possible, as to say that it destroyed the seat of consciousness. On the other hand, there are facts which the former theory suits far better. If, e.g., as sometimes happens, the man, after a time, more or less, recovers the faculties of which the injury to his brain had deprived him, and that not in consequence of a renewal of the injured part, but in consequence of the inhibited functions being performed by the vicarious action of other parts, the easiest explanation certainly is that, after a time, consciousness constitutes the remaining parts into a mechanism capable of acting as a substitute for the lost parts. And again, if the body is a mechanism for inhibiting consciousness, for preventing the full powers of the Ego from being prematurely actualized, it will be necessary to invert also our ordinary ideas on the subject of memory, and to account for forgetfulness instead of for memory. It will be during life that we drink the bitter cup of Lethe, it will be with our brain that we are enabled to forget. And this will serve to explain not only the extraordinary memories of the drowning and the dying generally, but also the curious hints which experimental psychology occasionally affords us that nothing is ever forgotten wholly and beyond recall" (*Riddles of the Sphinx*, London, Swan Sonnenschein, 1891, p. 293 ff).

Mr. Schiller's conception is much more complex in its relations than the simple "theory of transmission" postulated in my lecture, and to do justice to it the reader should consult the original work.

[10] I beg the reader to peruse R. L. Stevenson's magnificent little essay entitled "The Lantern Bearers," reprinted in the collection entitled *Across the Plains*. The truth is that we are doomed, by the fact that we are practical beings with very limited tasks to attend to, and special ideals to look after, to be absolutely blind and insensible to the inner feelings, and to the whole inner significance of lives that are different from our own. Our opinion of the worth of such lives is absolutely wide of the mark, and unfit to be counted at all.

[11] W. Wundt: *System der Philosophie*, Leipzig, Engelmann, 1889, p. 315.

27

POSTSCRIPT

The Postscript to *The Varieties of Religious Experience* has an interesting backstory, as related by James Hyslop in the *American Journal of Psychical Research*.

Dr. Hodgson saw the proofs of the lectures before they were printed and finding that Professor James, after mentioning four incidents in the experience of Dr. Hodgson, had altered them to eviscerate them of their real meaning, in the chapter on "The Unseen Reality," told him that he had omitted all reference to the real subject of the volume and Professor James admitted that he had done so, and then set about writing the Postscript in which his sympathy with spiritistic theories was expressed, tho he did not definitely indorse them. It was purely an afterthought and no part of the original purpose and he showed that he had not even caught the connection between his subject and the problem of psychic research until Dr. Hodgson showed him the fact.[1]

Hyslop's notion that James saw no connection between his more philosophical writings and psychical research is belied by much of the contents of the present volume. It is much more likely that James

---

[1] James Hyslop (1919) "The Philosophy of William James. By Th. Flournoy." (Book Review). *Journal of the American Society for Psychical Research*, Vol. 13 No. 11, 562-563. See also, James Hyslop (1914) "Belief in Personal Immortality. By E. S. P. Haynes" (Book Review). *Journal of the American Society for Psychical Research*, Vol. 8 No. 4, 175-77.

omitted such discussion out of a concern for his book to be taken seriously as a "respectable" one in contrast to how psychical research was perceived. In any case, while James did attempt to clarify his thoughts on the survival question in the Postscript, he somewhat downplayed just *how* impressed he was with the evidence from psychical research.

In writing my concluding lecture I had to aim so much at simplification that I fear that my general philosophic position received so scant a statement as hardly to be intelligible to some of my readers. I therefore add this epilogue, which must also be so brief as possibly to remedy but little the defect. In a later work I may be enabled to state my position more amply and consequently more clearly.

Originality cannot be expected in a field like this, where all the attitudes and tempers that are possible have been exhibited in literature long ago, and where any new writer can immediately be classed under a familiar head. If one should make a division of all thinkers into naturalists and supernaturalists, I should undoubtedly have to go, along with most philosophers, into the supernaturalist branch. But there is a crasser and a more refined supernaturalism, and it is to the refined division that most philosophers at the present day belong. If not regular transcendental idealists, they at least obey the Kantian direction enough to bar out ideal entities from interfering causally in the course of phenomenal events. Refined supernaturalism is universalistic supernaturalism; for the "crasser" variety "piecemeal" supernaturalism would perhaps be the better name. It went with that older theology which to-day is supposed to reign only among uneducated people, or to be found among the few belated professors of the dualisms which Kant is thought to have displaced. It admits miracles and providential leadings, and finds no intellectual difficulty in mixing the ideal and the real worlds together by interpolating influences from the ideal region among the forces that causally determine the real world's details. In this the refined supernaturalists think that it muddles disparate dimensions of existence. For them the world of the ideal has no efficient causality, and never bursts into the world of phenomena at particular points. The ideal world, for them, is not a world of facts, but only of the meaning of facts; it is a point of view for judging facts. It appertains to a different "-ology," and inhabits a different dimension of being altogether from that in which existential propositions obtain. It cannot get down upon the flat level of experience and interpolate itself piecemeal between distinct portions of nature, as those who believe, for example, in divine aid coming in response to prayer, are bound to think it must.

Notwithstanding my own inability to accept either popular Christianity or scholastic theism, I suppose that my belief that in communion with the Ideal new force comes into the world, and new departures are made here below, subjects me to being classed among the supernaturalists of the piecemeal or crasser type. Universalistic supernaturalism surrenders, it seems to me, too easily to naturalism. It takes the facts of physical science at their face-value, and leaves the laws of life just as naturalism finds them, with no hope of remedy, in case their fruits are bad. It confines itself to sentiments about life as a whole, sentiments which may be admiring and adoring, but which need not be so, as the existence of systematic pessimism proves. In this universalistic way of taking the ideal world, the essence of practical religion seems to me to evaporate. Both instinctively and for logical reasons, I find it hard to believe that principles can exist which make no difference in facts.[2] But all facts are particular facts, and the whole interest of the question of God's existence seems to me to lie in the consequences for particulars which that existence may be expected to entail. That no concrete particular of experience should alter its complexion in consequence of a God being there seems to me an incredible proposition, and yet it is the thesis to which (implicitly at any rate) refined supernaturalism seems to cling. It is only with experience *en bloc*, it says, that the Absolute maintains relations. It condescends to no transactions of detail.

---

[2] Transcendental idealism, of course, insists that its ideal world makes *this* difference, that facts *exist*. We owe it to the Absolute that we have a world of fact at all. "A world" of fact!—that exactly is the trouble. An entire world is the smallest unit with which the Absolute can work, whereas to our finite minds work for the better ought to be done within this world, setting in at single points. Our difficulties and our ideals are all piecemeal affairs, but the Absolute can do no piecework for us; so that all the interests which our poor souls compass raise their heads too late. We should have spoken earlier, prayed for another world absolutely, before this world was born. It is strange, I have heard a friend say, to see this blind corner into which Christian thought has worked itself at last, with its God who can raise no particular weight whatever, who can help us with no private burden, and who is on the side of our enemies as much as he is on our own. Odd evolution from the God of David's psalms!

I am ignorant of Buddhism and speak under correction, and merely in order the better to describe my general point of view; but as I apprehend the Buddhistic doctrine of Karma, I agree in principle with that. All supernaturalists admit that facts are under the judgment of higher law; but for Buddhism as I interpret it, and for religion generally so far as it remains unweakened by transcendentalistic metaphysics, the word "judgment" here means no such bare academic verdict or platonic appreciation as it means in Vedantic or modern absolutist systems; it carries, on the contrary, *execution* with it, is *in rebus* as well as *post rem*, and operates "causally" as partial factor in the total fact. The universe becomes a gnosticism[3] pure and simple on any other terms. But this view that judgment and execution go together is that of the crasser supernaturalist way of thinking, so the present volume must on the whole be classed with the other expressions of that creed.

I state the matter thus bluntly, because the current of thought in academic circles runs against me, and I feel like a man who must set his back against an open door quickly if he does not wish to see it closed and locked. In spite of its being so shocking to the reigning intellectual tastes, I believe that a candid consideration of piecemeal supernaturalism and a complete discussion of all its metaphysical bearings will show it to be the hypothesis by which the largest number of legitimate requirements are met. That of course would be a program for other books than this; what I now say sufficiently indicates to the philosophic reader the place where I belong.

If asked just where the differences in fact which are due to God's existence come in, I should have to say that in general I have no hypothesis to offer beyond what the phenomenon of "prayerful communion," especially when certain kinds of incursion from the subconscious region take part in it, immediately suggests. The appearance is that in this phenomenon something ideal, which in one sense is part of ourselves and in another sense is not ourselves, actually exerts an influence, raises our center of personal energy, and produces regenerative effects unattainable in other ways. If, then, there be a wider world of being than that of our every-day consciousness, if in it there be forces whose effects on us are intermittent, if one facilitating condition of the effects be the openness of the "subliminal" door, we have the elements of a theory to which the phenomena of religious life lend

---

[3] See my *Will to Believe and other Essays in Popular Philosophy*, 1897, p. 165.

plausibility. I am so impressed by the importance of these phenomena that I adopt the hypothesis which they so naturally suggest. At these places at least, I say, it would seem as though transmundane energies, God, if you will, produced immediate effects within the natural world to which the rest of our experience belongs.

The difference in natural "fact" which most of us would assign as the first difference which the existence of a God ought to make would, I imagine, be personal immortality. Religion, in fact, for the great majority of our own race *means* immortality, and nothing else. God is the producer of immortality; and whoever has doubts of immortality is written down as an atheist without farther trial. I have said nothing in my lectures about immortality or the belief therein, for to me it seems a secondary point. If our ideals are only cared for in "eternity," I do not see why we might not be willing to resign their care to other hands than ours. Yet I sympathize with the urgent impulse to be present ourselves, and in the conflict of impulses, both of them so vague yet both of them noble, I know not how to decide. It seems to me that it is eminently a case for facts to testify. Facts, I think, are yet lacking to prove "spirit-return," though I have the highest respect for the patient labors of Messrs. Myers, Hodgson, and Hyslop, and am somewhat impressed by their favorable conclusions. I consequently leave the matter open, with this brief word to save the reader from a possible perplexity as to why immortality got no mention in the body of this book.

The ideal power with which we feel ourselves in connection, the "God" of ordinary men, is, both by ordinary men and by philosophers, endowed with certain of those metaphysical attributes which in the lecture on philosophy I treated with such disrespect. He is assumed as a matter of course to be "one and only" and to be "infinite"; and the notion of many finite gods is one which hardly anyone thinks it worthwhile to consider, and still less to uphold. Nevertheless, in the interests of intellectual clearness, I feel bound to say that religious experience, as we have studied it, cannot be cited as unequivocally supporting the infinitist belief. The only thing that it unequivocally testifies to is that we can experience union with *something* larger than ourselves and in that union find our greatest peace. Philosophy, with its passion for unity, and mysticism with its monoideistic bent, both "pass to the limit" and identify the something with a unique God who is the all-inclusive soul of the world. Popular opinion, respectful to their authority, follows the example which they set.

Meanwhile the practical needs and experiences of religion seem to me sufficiently met by the belief that beyond each man and in a fashion continuous with him there exists a larger power which is friendly to him and to his ideals. All that the facts require is that the power should be both other and larger than our conscious selves. Anything larger will do, if only it be large enough to trust for the next step. It need not be infinite, it need not be solitary. It might conceivably even be only a larger and more godlike self, of which the present self would then be but the mutilated expression, and the universe might conceivably be a collection of such selves, of different degrees of inclusiveness, with no absolute unity realized in it at all.[4] Thus would a sort of polytheism return upon us—a polytheism which I do not on this occasion defend, for my only aim at present is to keep the testimony of religious experience clearly within its proper bounds.

Upholders of the monistic view will say to such a polytheism (which, by the way, has always been the real religion of common people, and is so still to-day) that unless there be one all-inclusive God, our guarantee of security is left imperfect. In the Absolute, and in the Absolute only, *all* is saved. If there be different gods, each caring for his part, some portion of some of us might not be covered with divine protection, and our religious consolation would thus fail to be complete. It goes back to what was said on pages 131-133, about the possibility of there being portions of the universe that may irretrievably be lost. Common sense is less sweeping in its demands than philosophy or mysticism have been wont to be, and can suffer the notion of this world being partly saved and partly lost. The ordinary moralistic state of mind makes the salvation of the world conditional upon the success with which each unit does its part. Partial and conditional salvation is in fact a most familiar notion when taken in the abstract, the only difficulty being to determine the details. Some men are even disinterested enough to be willing to be in the unsaved remnant as far as their persons go, if only they can be persuaded that their cause will prevail—all of us are willing, whenever our activity-excitement rises sufficiently high. I think, in fact, that a final philosophy of religion will have to consider the pluralistic hypothesis more seriously than it has hitherto been willing to consider it. For practical life at any rate, the *chance* of salvation is enough. No fact in human nature is more characteristic than its willingness to

---

[4] Such a notion is suggested in my Ingersoll Lecture on *Human Immortality*, Boston and London, 1899 [see above, chapter 26 of this volume].

live on a chance. The existence of the chance makes the difference, as Edmund Gurney says, between a life of which the keynote is resignation and a life of which the keynote is hope.[5] But all these statements are unsatisfactory from their brevity, and I can only say that I hope to return to the same questions in another book.

---

[5] *Tertium Quid*, 1887, p. 99. See also pp. 148, 149.

APPENDICES

APPENDIX A

EXPERIMENTS SINCE THE DEATH OF PROFESSOR JAMES (EXCERPTS)

James H. Hyslop

In 1911, the year following the death of William James, James Hyslop undertook experiments with the mediums "Mrs. Smead" (Willis M. Cleveland) and "Mrs. Chenoweth" (Minnie Meserve Soule) "to see if communication with Professor William James could be established." Hyslop's report takes up the entire 1912 volume of the *Proceedings of the American Society for Psychical Research* plus a number of sections in the *Journal*.[1] Taken together, they total over a thousand pages, making this an astonishing undertaking on Hyslop's part. This is especially the case when we consider the general dearth of evidential value the project yielded. Notwithstanding a few cross-correspondences between the two mediums, and the odd verified statement of a fact allegedly unknown by the medium, taken as a whole these are hardly persuasive cases.

---

[1] Hyslop, J.H. (1912a) "Prospectus of Experiments Since the Death of Professor James." *Journal of the American Society for Psychical Research* vol. VI No. 5, 269-90 (quote on p. 269); Hyslop, J.H. (1912b) "Summary of Experiments Since the Death of Professor James, I. Professor William James." *Journal of the American Society for Psychical Research* vol. VI No. 5, 291-326.

Nor do the scripts contain much in the way of philosophical or psychological value, as one might expect to emanate from the spirit of William James. Indeed, the living James himself might have seen much of it as "bosh" or "twaddle." Hyslop didn't think they were very good, either, though seeing traits he felt he recognized as being James-like in the communications, and thinking fraud unlikely, he had a generally favorable opinion of the material. In any case, among the many hundreds of pages purporting to be communications from William James, a few paragraphs deal with the metaphysical and philosophical topics that so interested him when alive. The most interesting feature is perhaps the description of his out-of-body transition to the afterlife after his death

From Experiment with Mrs. Smead

I want to describe to you this experience as best I can. When I left the earth it was as if I were suffocating at first, then I realized I was going to leave. I was soon out of my body. It was so quickly done I did not have time to suffer but they would not let me stay there at first but after I had been out a very short time they let me return to see that I was surely living but not of the earth. I then asked Hodgson what we must do. He said go and make yourself known. I tried to do this on both sides of the earth....

Then I waited for this opportunity and I came here expecting to go through all kinds of experiences losing myself. I thought to try one of my own ways I have so stated to you. It is very difficult but it can be done by this method. One word at a time and all other friends here on my side away in the distance so that I will not get their ideas mixed with mine. They thought to help but I said I would prefer it alone. It exhausts us but by stopping we can get new light-energy and can continue for a greater time as you know there must be one of greater power that supplies the light energy and by his keeping near it remains for a period as he does not try to talk. Can remain but the earth souls are so desirous of talking it causes confusion and hence your difficulty of getting what is said from here.

From Experiment with Mrs. Chenoweth

I seem to be able to reason while I am at work and that pleases me. So much of the work recorded in the past lacked that function. It always stood between me and my theories of what ought to be and I often said: This seems more like snatches of broken recollections detached and left as solitary or wandering brain. You may recall what I am trying to tell you: fugitive phantasms. Unreal. Unattached floating in ethereal waves caught, retained, expressed as if attached by subliminal states not able to distinguish between the attached and unattached. The embodied or fugitive phantasms. This I forced to consider when I would most gladly throw it away as inadequate....

So few understand the reality of this life I now live and cannot know it if they do not desire to know. They do not try to have a genuine reason for what they think they know and are as much surprised as if they were atheists when they enter here. This life should be as real as the one I left in so short a time. Atoms and souls are not Equal, nor is the soul made up of them. Atoms will only apply to the Material universe, not the ethereal one.... You see we have to deal here without material substances. Atoms do not count for anything when we learn here. And do you think the ether composed of them could affect the spiritual world? It is just a Hypothesis not a reality. You could see we would need to feel or have feelings if we were composed of atoms here. Can you touch your own thoughts? Then thinking is not composed of atoms.

We are able by learning to think there to remember our thoughts and that is why we appear to have our earthly bodies. They are real to us as yours to you, but not composed of atoms. It is more a mental reality. Ether, when coming in contact with the Earth atmosphere, can by our thinking be made visible. What produces light to make a Spirit seen on earth? It is a light given the individual Spirit from the Father of all Lights. The substance not yet revealed to us. But by coming into relationship with the Ether and Earth, atmosphere can be visible to Earth friends. That Light we are not yet given the power of understanding. A new knowledge for us to have revealed to us. We have not only begun our work when there. Mysteries are here yet to be solved. It is right that it should be so, else we would be too well satisfied with our existence to be willing to help others, so we must continue work here. You know a self-satisfied soul would be worthless. God or The Father of all Lights is wise not to let us know all.

APPENDIX B

FROM WILLIAM JAMES? (EXCERPTS)

E. F. Friend

Edwin William Friend (1886 – 1915) was a Harvard professor of Classics and Indic philology. In 1913, he became assistant to James Hyslop and was appointed editor of the *Journal of the American Society for Psychical Research*. He was quickly suspended from the role, however, after publishing accounts of séances with his wife Marjorie rather than the more rigorous research articles Hyslop had sent him.

Marjorie practiced automatic writing, specializing in the souls of deceased psychical researchers and others relevant to the field. This included ostensible communications from Frederic Myers, Richard Hodgson, and William James (as well as Mrs. Piper's "Imperator" control). Friend published some of Marjorie's scripts in the *JASPR* in 1915, in an article entitled "A Series of Recent 'Non-Evidential' Scripts."[1]

After his dispute with Hyslop, Friend embarked on a sea voyage to England, hoping to secure support for a proposed Organization of the Massachusetts Society for Psychical Research. Unfortunately, the ship he took was the *Lusitania*, which was torpedoed by a German submarine, killing most of its passengers – including Friend. Just prior

---

[1] Friend, E. F. (1915) "A Series of Recent Non-Evidential Scripts." *Journal of the American Society for Psychical* Research vol. IX, 108-13.

to sailing, however, he had submitted an article to *The Unpopular Review*, focusing specifically on Marjorie's William James scripts.[2] *The Unpopular Review* was a conservative-leaning journal concerning economic, social, and philosophical issues of the time, which somewhat unusually for a publication of its kind featured a number of articles on psychical research. The editor was the famous publisher Henry Holt, himself an ASPR council member and author of *The Cosmic Relations and Immortality*.[3]

While there is nothing evidential about the Friend sittings (as he himself acknowledged), if genuine, they could constitute James's final words on subjects related to psychical research. At minimum, they reveal how James's literary "afterlife" was interpreted at the intersection of spiritualism and psychical research. It is interesting to compare them in both style and content to scripts of Mrs. Smead and Mrs. Chenoweth above.

The article is, in any case, a curious and fascinating piece, written by a well-educated though neglected figure in the field. Together with his *JASPR* article, Friend's analyses and discussions of the purported James material in light of his life and works are lengthy and highly detailed. Only relevant representative excerpts of the purported spirit-James's own words are reprinted here.

World upon world and life after life is the tremendous scheme of things. Children see in the world a light which dims with experience. Why? Because experience in your world is turned away from Life. "Seek and ye shall find" has been said; but it must be a new seeking after a new thing, before you will find.

In the messages which follow we [James, Myers, and Hodgson] intend to give you instructions as to the pragmatic value of the future life.

*　*　*

---

[2] For biographical details about Friend, see Arthur S. Beger (1988) *Lives and Letters in American Parapsychology: A Biographical History*. Jefferson, N.C.: McFarland, 57; Kalafus, J. (n.d.) "Professor Edwin William Friend." *The Lusitania Resource*, https://www.rmslusitania.info/people/saloon/edwin-friend/ (Retrieved 20 September, 2023); and Holt's editorial comments in the article in question, Edwin F. Friend (1915) "From William James?" *Unpopular Review* IV, 172, 201-20.

[3] Henry Holt (1919) *The Cosmic Relations and Immortality*, 2 vols. Boston: Houghton Mifflin.

When a spirit unhampered by material mechanism calls to his being a thought, it calls to him the whole meaning of the subject in its true universal relation. And when he wishes to express this back into material surroundings, he must separate each idea on the subject and pass them through one by one. It is truly like the spectroscope. Each light has its particular differentiation I mean by that, each element....

[Here, W.F. Friend asks] *If we were to call our mechanism, which in our life separates ideas, the cinematographic mechanism of thought, should you assent?*

Yes. Ours is a process of synthetic perception. You see, we live by our perceptions, whereas you have of necessity to separate your perceptions into conceptions for practical use. It is no simple conception, but a conception which has been modified by innumerable, indiscernible, sub-conscious perceptions in a human mind...

When the cinematograph is wrecked by the shipwreck of the material body, how do you come by this direct perception of the ideal world? Isn't it a matter of years to organize it?

It *is* and the individual drops in and takes his place whenever he is ready...whenever he is at the point of understanding to see it. There are some people who are years, as you say, in coming to after leaving their beloved material home.

Will our evolution here bring us to anything like your sort of perception?

In time there will be very much more which can be spoken of directly. Your growth is continuously toward the better, I should say *fuller* perception of things as they are. It will take ages though.... The nearest thing in your experience is that feeling which comes to you when, with a friend whom you understand, you walk out into the night and talk and commonly feel the pulse of all Life behind the darkness.

* * *

Do not forget that this act of communicating with you is a very much more intricate task than it seems to you there. No matter what complications you imagine when talking over the difficulties, it is quite certain that you do not even dream of the true intricacy of it. It will take years for us to explain all of this, and, though our attempts thus far to bring some specific truths to your minds have been successful and even more successful than we had hoped it is quite impossible to start in on a discourse regarding the difficulties of communication before we have given you some idea of the interrelationship of Body and Mind.

If you think over what was said yesterday, you will remember we intimated the whole mechanical structure to be a phantasmagoric structure. Understand? In its direct interpretation this sentence brings to you the seed and kernel of the whole idea. It is *in reality* existent, and yet a structure of untutored minds searching for the light! The scheme is vast. Law pervades it in its most minute details.... The first perception of the great synthesis is order and law in the world about you. *This* is real, everlasting, and a part of the great whole. Life's first task is, you see, to make a primer for herself to see if she can read. She has taken the form of a mechanically perfect universe in order that she may read her own law with eyes of her own creation. Is this clear?

It is difficult to see how an unconscious impulse can create the mechanical universe, so perfect and intricate in every detail.

Because it is your appreciation of actual purified truth of developed effort and unending loving sacrifice which makes you see it as perfect. If this is incomprehensible now, do not lay it aside, but please think about it with all the insight you possess....

We will take the example of the brute. This is the first stage of consciousness which has perception of its own surrounding in relation to the whole, in any degree whatsoever. The life of a dog, for example, is a *real* part of the whole developmental scheme. His eyes are eyes which recognize; his nose one which tells him the good and the bad in the world; and his ears proclaim to him the life of stirring other creatures over which he feels his advantage! This is consciousness in babyhood. If you would march in thorough accord on your earth, then brutes and humans would learn one from the other. The more developed the consciousness, the more deeply is the unending purity of the laws about you revealed....

Brutes recognize the superior virtue in man, and, in consequence, bestow upon him an affection so deep and pure that few understand its capacity. Do you remember what was said yesterday about the true meaning of love? It is the recognition in one conscious being of the same deep all-pervading power which lies in his own heart, in that of another.

Now can you see any plan in the appearance of brutes in your world? Do you not see that this lower type is the necessary outcome of development? You are stages further on; your perception is vast in comparison to that of the dog. But do you not see that he too is an onward process? that in his recognition of your superiority, and his devotion, he is finding his first lessons? Is this sane?

* * *

The state of mind which leads one to suppose the conscious life to be most vivid is that one which in reality is reaching forward into the conscious state which lies ordinarily beyond the threshold, and translating it back through the medium of words to the usual plane comprehendable to men....

Conscious memory and conscious super-perception are parts of a whole. In the lives of most men there is but time for the former, and there is little or no real super-conscious perception.... Now, memory is a persistent constituent part of each personality, and even is there persistent memory of the events which concern the lives of individuals other than oneself. I mean to say, my memory is not limited to perception, reflex perception, we will say, of my own state alone, but I have also memory of states and states of consciousness of others, too.... *I* have memory, meaning to tell you that persistent reflex perception persists not only for my own acts and thoughts but also it persists in me for the acts and thoughts of other individuals whose lives have been close to mine.

* * *

It seems to me, as I regard the past and all its contingent beliefs and desires, that I was then living in a vast factory. It was all a great tight machinery of thought.... It was a producer of lives, this machine, but of such puppet lives as it makes me shudder to remember. It was a creator of desires and purposes, but of what a sort, of what a sort! It is a picture of tense, cramped, stunted thought that greets me as I consider from whence I came, and I desire now with my whole soul to draw such a picture of its unnatural purposes and vain striving as to make you pause....

The great wrong in modern life on earth is a desperate struggle for a four-cornered contentment. It leads even the wise to a huge misshapen discontent which consumes millions and millions of lives. Teach those who come your way that it is not a formal peace which is worth having in life; it is the deep consciousness of power to create and progress, to create *new* in life, and to live for wide, free, unsullied things, which never fail and never can decay.

SOURCES

1. "The Hidden Self." (1890) *Scribner's Magazine*, 7, 361–73.
2. "What Psychical Research Has Accomplished." (1892) *Forum*, 13, 727–742.
3. "Address of the President Before the Society for Psychical Research." (1896) *Proceedings of the Society for Psychical Research* 12 (June), 2-10.
4. "Psychical Research." (1896) *Psychological Review*, 3, 649–52.
5. "Sense of Presence." (1902) *Varieties of Religious Experience*. London: Longmans Green, 58-63.
6. "Lang's *Cock-Lane and Common Sense*, Du Prel's *Die Entdeckung der Seele*." (1894) *The Psychological Review* Vol. I, 630-632.
7. "Telepathy." (1895) In C.K. Adams (ed.) *Johnson's Universal Cyclopedia* vo. 8. New York: Appleton, 45-47.
8. "Notes on Automatic Writing." (1889) *Proceedings of the American Society for Psychical Research*, 1, 548–564.
9. "Report of the Committee on Hypnotism." (1886) *Proceedings of the American Society for Psychical Research*, 1, 95-102.
10. "The Consciousness of Lost Limbs." (1887) *Proceedings of the American Society for Psychical Research*, 1, 249-258. Quotes in editorial introduction, p. 257.
11. "Review of *Telepathic Dreams Experimentally Induced* by G. B. Ermacora." (1896) *Psychological Review* vol. III, 99-100

12. "Review of *Phantasms of the Living*." (1887) *Science*, 9, 18–20.
13. "A Suggestion about Mysticism" (1910) *Journal of Philosophy, Psychology, and Scientific Methods*, 1910, 7, 85-92.
14. "Report of the Committee on Mediumistic Phenomena." (1886) *Proceedings of the American Society for Psychical Research*, 1, 102–106.
15. "A Record of Observations of Certain Phenomena of Trance" (1890) Part III. *Proceedings of the Society for Psychical Research*, 6, 651–659.
16. "Review of *A Further Record of Observations of Certain Phenomena of Trance* by R. Hodgson." (1898) *Psychological Review*, 5, 420–424.
17. "Mrs. Piper, 'the Medium.'" (1889) *Science* 7, 640–41; Letter from James to Cattell, 8 May 1898. In James, W. (coll. 1986) *Essays in Psychical Research*. Burkhardt, Frederick and Fredson Bowers (eds.) Cambridge, MA.: Harvard University Press, 485.
18. "Report on Mrs. Piper's Hodgson-Control." (1909) *Proceedings of the Society for Psychical Research*, 1909, 23, 1-121. Excerpts p. 2-6, p. 17-18, 28-29, 32-36, 115-120.
19. "Physical Phenomena at a Private Circle." (1909) *Journal of the American Society for Psychical Research*, 3, 109–113.
20. "The Confidences of a 'Psychical Researcher.'" (1909) *American Magazine*, 68, 580–589. Also as "Final Impressions of a Psychical Researcher," In W. James (coll. 1917) *Memories and Studies*. H. James (ed.). London: Longmans Green, 171-206.
21. "Mediumships or Possessions" (1890) *Principles of Psychology*. New York: Henry Holt (2 vols.), 393-400.
22a. "Review of *Demon-Possession and Allied Themes* by Rev. John L. Nevius." (1895) *The Nation*, Vol. 61, No. 1573, Aug. 22, 139-40.
22b. "Review of *Demon-Possession and Allied Themes*." (1895) *Psychological Review*, Vol. 2 No. 5, 529-31.
23a. "Letter to Henry W. Rankin." (1897) In Henry James (1920, ed.) *The Letters of William James* Vol. 2. Boston: Atlantic Monthly, 56-57.
23b. "At the portal of psychical research." In Perry, R.B. (1935) *The Thought and Character of William James*, Vol. II. Boston: Little Brown, 169.

23c. "Demoniacal Possession (Summary by Bernard Sachs)" (1897) *Boston Medical and Surgical Journal* (March 4, Vol. 136 No. 9, 1897, 210-12).

23d. "Prof. James's Discovery (Editorial Commentary)." (1897) *Banner of Light* Vol. 80, No. 18, Feb. 13, p. 4.

23e. "Editorial Commentary." (1897) *Light: A Journal of Psychical, Occult, and Mystical Research*, No. 843, Vol. XVII, March 6, p. 109.

23f. "Professor James on 'Demoniac Control'" (1897) *Light: A Journal of Psychical, Occult, and Mystical Research*, No. 851 —Vol. XVII, May 1, 1897, p. 211.

24. "Mind, Soul, and Consciousness" (1890) Selections from *Principles of Psychology*. New York: Henry Holt (2 vols.), 146, 149-150, 158-162, 180-182, 342-350.

25. "Review of *Human Personality and Its Survival of Bodily Death*." (1903) *Proceedings of the Society for Psychical Research*, 18, 22–33.

26. *Human Immortality: Two Supposed Objections to the Doctrine.* (1899, 2nd ed.) Boston and New York: Houghton Mifflin.

27. "Postscript." (1902) *Varieties of Religious Experience*. London: Longmans Green, 520-27.

Appendix A

Hyslop, J.H. (1912c) "A Record of Experiments" (excerpts). *Proceedings of the American Society for Psychical Research* VI, 113-14, 171-72, 895-98.

Appendix B

Friend, E.F. (1915) "From William James?" *Unpopular Review* IV, 178, 184-85, 193-94, 195-96, 198.

FURTHER READING

1. Primary Sources

Burkhardt, Frederick and Fredson Bowers (eds.) (1986) *Essays in Psychical Research.* Cambridge, MA.: Harvard University Press (the sixteenth volume of *The Works of William James*, a 19-volume series published 1975–1988).

Murphy, Gardner & Robert O. Ballou (eds.) (1960) *William James on Psychical Research.* New York: Viking.

Taylor, Eugene (ed.) (1983) *William James on Exceptional Mental States: The 1896 Lowell Lectures Reconstructed by Eugene Taylor.* New York: Scribner.

2. Secondary Sources

Alvarado, Carlos S. and Stanley Krippner (2010) "Nineteenth Century Pioneers in the Study of Dissociation: William James and Psychical Research." *Journal of Consciousness Studies* 17(11–12), 19–43.

Barnard, G. William (1997) *Exploring Unseen Worlds: William James and the Philosophy of Mysticism.* Albany: State University of New York Press.

Blum, Deborah (2006) *Ghost Hunters: William James and the Search for Scientific Proof of Life after Death.* New York: Penguin.

Ford, Marcus (1998) "William James's Psychical Research and its Philosophical Implications." *Transactions of the Charles S. Peirce Society* 34(3), 605–626.

Gardner, Martin (1992) "Communicating with the Dead: William James and Mrs. Piper." Part 1. *Free Inquiry* 12 (Spring), 20–27; Part 2. *Free Inquiry* 12 (Summer), 38–48.

Gitre Edward J. K. (2006) "William James on Divine Intimacy: Psychical Research, Cosmological Realism and a Circumscribed Re-Reading of *The Varieties of Religious Experience*." *History of the Human Sciences* 19(2), 1–21.

Knapp, Krister Dylan (2017) *William James, Psychical Research and the Challenge of Modernity*. Chapel Hill: University of North Carolina Press.

Leja, Michael (2001) "William James and Automatic Drawing." *Intellectual History Newsletter* 23, 11–23.

Perry, R.B. (1935) *The Thought and Character of William James*, 2 vols. Boston: Little Brown. See especially Vol. 2, Chapter LXI "Psychical Research," 155-72.

Schmeidler, Gertrude R. (1992) "William James: Pioneering Ancestor of Modern Parapsychology." In M. E. Donnelly (ed.) *Reinterpreting the Legacy of William James*. Washington D.C.: American Psychological Association, 339–52.

Sech Jr., Alexandre, Saulo de Freitas Araujo, and Alexander Moreira-Almeida (2012) "William James and Psychical Research: Towards a Radical Science of Mind." *History of Psychiatry* 24 (1), 62-78.

Sommer, Andreas (2012) "Psychical Research and the Origins of American Psychology: Hugo Münsterberg, William James and Eusapia Palladino." *History of the Human Sciences* 25: 23–44.

—(2020) "James and Psychical Research in Context." In *The Oxford Handbook of William James*, edited by Alexander Klein. Oxford: Oxford University Press. DOI: 10.1093/oxfordhb/9780199395699.013.37 (Epub ahead of print).

Taylor, Eugene (1996) *William James on Consciousness Beyond the Margin*. Princeton, NJ: Princeton University Press.

INDEX

A

Africa, 77
afterlife, 25, 281, 322, 326
Alger, William Rounseville, 285
alien hand syndrome, 42-46, 108-112, 114
American Magazine, 205
American Society for Psychical Research, 13, 54, 127, 131, 155, 164, 199, 282, 313, 321, 325, 326
"Amherst Mystery" (poltergeist case), 75
amnesia, 37, 39, 230, 242
anatomy, 12
anesthesia, 33-35, 38, 44, 45, 48, 49, 108, 140, 229, 230
anthropology, 71, 93-94, 269, 285
aphasia, 115
apparitions, 31, 52–53, 57–58, 63, 72, 77, 83–85, 94, 105, 138, 213–214, 233, 292
 (*see also*, crisis apparitions)
Arnold, John N., 118–119
automatic writing, 25, 30, 41, 43, 46, 57, 60, 66, 91, 95, 107, 109, 111, 113, 115, 117, 119–121, 123, 125, 127, 133, 158, 175, 191, 218, 225–227, 229–230, 271, 275, 309, 325
automatism, 25, 46, 60, 75, 97, 157, 183, 213, 239, 241–242, 270, 275, 278

B

Bacon, Francis, 19, 122
Balfour, Arthur, 52, 55–56
Banner of Light, 12, 240, 245, 247–248
baptism, 216, 237
Barrett, William, 52, 54, 56, 102, 206, 245
Barrows, Ira, 111
Bernheim, Hippolyte, 41, 43
Berry, Helen, 155–156
Bible, 234, 235
bilocation, 274
Binet, Alfred, 33, 41–43, 57, 270
blasphemy, 234, 248
Blavatsky, Helena, 58–59
blindness, 33–34, 43–44, 48–49, 91–92, 112, 297, 299
Boston Medical and Surgical Journal, 240

337

Bottazzi, Filippo, 16
Bourne, Ansel, 10
Bourru, Henri, 37
brain, 16, 48, 95, 118, 157, 196, 225, 230–231, 254–255, 257–259, 261–262, 265, 279, 281–283, 286–294, 301–304, 307, 310, 323
Büchner, Ludwig, 304
Buddhism, 316
Burot, P., 37

C

Cabanis, Pierre, 303
card guessing, 44, 71, 103, 120-21, 127, 158
Carpenter, William Benjamin, 12, 15, 114
Carrington, Hereward, 207
Cattell, James McKeen, 81–83, 177–180
channeling, 9
Chiap, Giuseppe, 234, 237
children, childhood, 37, 38, 39, 49, 103, 134, 150, 228, 243, 245, 326
China, 75, 116, 233–236, 243
Christianity, 16, 237, 242, 315
clairvoyance, clairvoyants, 59, 61, 72, 95, 100, 103, 119, 127, 206, 242, 271, 274
Clifford, William Kingdon, 2
Constans, Augustin, 234, 237, 243
controls (in mediumship), 58, 59, 115–16, 156–158, 163-65, 166, 172, 175, 181-97, 202, 205, 211, 214, 226-29, 241, 242, 245, 247-49, 265, 273, 275, 278, 325,
conversion (religious), 11, 18–19, 172, 237, 292, 293
Cook, Florence, 207
Coon, Deborah J., 14

cosmic consciousness, 220–221
cosmic reservoir, 162, 184, 193–194, 221
crisis apparitions, 6, 57-58, 72, 83-85, 104-05, 292-93
Crookes, William, 207
crystal gazing, 59, 167, 271, 274
Curie, Marie, 5, 14, 16
Curie, Pierre, 14, 16

D

Dana, C. L., 245
Darwin, Charles, 9, 11, 31, 63, 78, 209, 276
Davey, S.J., 10, 58, 74
Dean, Sidney, 116, 225, 227
delirium, 45, 46, 48, 111, 112
delusion, 12, 48, 66, 209, 218, 242–244, 248, 295
dementia, 148, 149
Descartes, René, 78, 260
disease, 31, 33, 36, 43, 48, 65, 139, 230, 233, 235, 237, 243, 248, 278, 300
dissociation, 10, 111, 225, 230, 241, 269, 278
dissociative identity disorder, see multiple personality disorder
divining rod, 56
dream telepathy, 96, 133–135, 147–150, 274
dreams, 10, 63, 90, 96, 133–135, 146–150, 183, 190, 195, 197, 214, 228-28, 236, 239, 242, 270, 272, 274
du Prel, Carl, 93–96
dualism, 260, 262, 301–303, 314

E

ecstatic states, 31, 60, 233
Ellinwood, Frank Field, 236

Elvira (spirit control), 134
emotions, 38, 76, 90, 95, 96, 144, 145, 147, 203, 211, 274, 285, 286, 296, 300, 304
England, 6–7, 9, 12, 52, 54, 59, 70, 84, 199, 247, 325
epilepsy, 32, 38, 66, 111, 242
Ermacora, Giovanni Battista, 133–134
ether (anaesthetic), 150–151, 168, 196, 304, 323
Europe, 16, 19, 54, 140, 167, 235, 242, 248
evil, 89, 96, 148, 237, 246–247
evolution, 10–11, 161, 215, 254–255, 272, 295, 307, 315, 327
exorcism, 234, 236
experiential source hypothesis, 87ff, 94–95, 240–42, 272, 317
extended consciousness, 25, 97, 143

F

fairies, 94
false memories, 83, 139
Fechner, Gustav, 144, 147, 195, 292, 305, 309
Fillmore, C. W., 111
Flechsig, Paul, 286, 300
Flournoy, Théodore, 91, 267–268, 313
folklore, 83, 93, 94
Forum, The, 51
France, 16, 32, 122, 165, 243
Franzolini, Fernando, 234, 237
fraud, 7, 11–12, 14, 21, 76, 82, 94, 155, 173, 175–177, 189–190, 207, 209, 211–212, 322

G

Galileo, 19, 31

ghosts, 61–63, 74–75, 83, 140, 206, 209, 273, 275
Gibbens, Eliza, 162
God, 1, 17, 19, 31, 79, 82, 87–88, 90, 235, 239, 242–243, 247–248, 260, 264, 296–297, 299, 315–318, 323
Greece, ancient, 87, 88ff
Gurney, Edmund, 5–6, 10, 41, 45–46, 50, 52–53, 55–58, 61–62, 73, 91, 102, 111, 137–141, 206, 213, 269–270, 319
Guthrie, Malcolm, 55–56, 101–102

H

Hall, Frederick, 150
Hall, G. Stanley, 12, 13-15
hallucination, 6, 10–12, 45–49, 57–60, 62–67, 72, 83–84, 88–92, 104–105, 111, 138–141, 270, 273–274
haunted houses, 52, 61, 75, 270
healings (miraculous), 31, 233, 235, 237, 245, 292, 293
heaven, 228, 287, 289, 295, 297, 299 (see also, afterlife; Summerland)
Helmholtz, Hermann von, 61, 62
Herter, Christian Archibald, 244
hoaxes, 139
Hodgson, Richard, 10–11, 54–55, 58, 74, 99, 108–109, 161–162, 165, 168, 171–175, 177–178, 181–187, 189, 191–197, 205, 207, 216–217, 220, 229, 262, 313, 317, 322, 325–326
Holy Ghost, 244
Home, D. D., 207
Hutton, R. H., 52
Huxley, Thomas Henry, 1–4, 11–12, 15–17, 19, 21, 61–62, 162, 211–212
hypnosis, hypnotic suggestion, 8, 30, 32, 33, 35, 38–40, 43–45, 47–49,

52, 56-57, 60, 63, 66, 71, 94, 100,
  103-05, 108, 111, 114, 124, 127–29,
  157–58, 161, 190, 213, 226, 239,
  214–42, 245, 270–71, 274–75, 279
hypnotizability, 49, 155, 157
Hyslop, James, 13, 182, 191, 197, 220,
  282, 313, 317, 321–322, 325
hysteria, 33, 49–50, 140, 235, 239,
  241, 243, 245, 279
hystero-demonopathy, 234, 243
hystero-epilepsy, 32, 38, 66, 111

I

imagination, 31, 49–50, 77, 104, 190,
  195, 277, 291, 294–299
immortality, 25, 254, 260, 263–264,
  276–277, 281–285, 287–297,
  299–303, 305, 307, 309, 311, 313,
  317–318, 326
India, 235, 243
insanity, 12, 48, 77, 234, 239, 242, 300

J

Jacobi, Mary Putnam, 244
Janet, Jules, 36, 43, 44
Janet, Pierre, 33–38, 40, 41, 43–50,
  57, 65–67, 104, 108, 242, 270, 279
Japan, 116, 235, 243, 305
Jastrow, Joseph, 12–15
Jesus, 235, 237
Johnson's Universal Cyclopedia, 99
*Journal of the American Society for
  Psychical Research*, 199, 282, 313,
  321, 325, 326
*Journal of the Society for Psychical
  Research*, 21, 77, 90, 91, 282, 381

K

Kant, Immanuel, 88, 260, 262, 294, 314
karma, 316

L

Lang, Andrew, 72, 87, 93–96
Langley, Samuel P., 52, 54
Lecky, W. E. H., 139, 234
Léonie (Léontine, Léonore), 33, 36,
  38-42, 46-47, 104
Light (spiritualist journal), 240, 247,
  268
Locke, John, 41, 260, 262, 264, 283
Lodge, Oliver, 7, 52, 55, 161, 171, 267
logic, 4–5, 73–74, 82–83, 105, 119,
  178–180, 188–189, 287, 290, 299,
  304
Lombroso, Cesare, 207
Lotze, Hermann, 264–265
Lowell, Percival, 239, 243, 248, 305
Lucie, 33–38, 41, 44–46

M

magnetism, 31–32, 35, 39, 40, 100,
  112, 128, 129
Marcella, 66
Maria, Signora, 133-34
Marillier, Léon, 6, 55
Martin, H. Newell, 15, 210, 244
materialism, 1–2, 15–16, 19, 22, 29,
  47, 78, 171, 257, 281, 290, 291, 303,
  310
materialization (mediumistic), 12,
  155, 159, 207, 214
medicine (science), 18, 19, 20, 22,
  32, 34, 49, 139, 149, 241, 243, 244,
  284, 287
melancholy, 66, 244
memory, 10, 35–38, 48, 56–57, 59–
  60, 64, 66, 75, 83, 90, 94, 104, 110,
  113, 126, 139, 144–145, 149–150,
  157, 162, 165, 173–175, 184–185,
  187–188, 191, 193–195, 205, 210,
  214, 221, 225–226, 228, 230, 234,

242, 264, 270, 272, 276, 280, 283, 286, 310, 329
Mesmer, Franz, 10, 31
mesmerism, 5, 100, 157, 265, 271, 274
metempsychosis, 117
mind-dust, mind-stuff 175, 254-56, 258-59, 261, 302
mirror-writing, 115, 119, 122, 230
Mitchell, J. K., 128
Mitchell, S. Weir, 128, 178
monism 95, 282, 318
Morselli, Enrico, 16–17, 207
mortality, 301
Moses, Stainton, 52, 72, 74, 207
multiple personality disorder, 10, 11, 13, 30, 34ff, 239, 240-42, 279
Münsterberg, Hugo, 14, 15
Myers, Frederic W. H., 6–9, 22, 50, 52, 55–56, 59–63, 69, 72, 74–75, 94–96, 108, 115, 137, 139–41, 161–62, 195, 206, 213, 214–17, 221, 230–31, 241, 267–80, 292, 309, 317, 325, 326,
mystical experience, 17, 143, 146, 272
mysticism, 90, 94, 96, 143–145, 147, 149–151, 317–318

N

naturalism, 1–2, 9, 15–17, 19, 22, 315
nature, 1, 3, 14, 32, 61–63, 73–74, 76–77, 82, 96, 185, 196–197, 203, 206, 213, 215, 217–219, 245, 258, 288–291, 306, 308–309, 315
Nevius, John Livingstone, 75, 233–237, 240
Newton, Isaac, 19, 78
Nova Scotia, 75

O

Ochorowicz, Julian, 104–105

Ouija board (*see also*, planchette), 214, 218
out-of-body experience, 228, 274, 322

P

Paladino, Eusapia (alt. Palladino), 74, 203, 207
panpsychism, 221, 253
pathologization, 12, 19, 21, 271
pathology, 12, 18, 20, 139, 236
Pease, Edward R., 56
Perrier, Alfred, 40
Perry, Thomas Sergeant, 30, 69, 143, 181
Phantasms of the Living, 6, 55, 57, 91, 137–139, 141, 269, 273–274
phantom limb syndrome, 30, 131-32
Phinuit (spirit control), 163-167, 172, 197
photographs, photography, 40, 134, 164, 214
physical phenomenon (in mediumship) 196-97, 199–203, 207, 211, 218, 220, 275-76
physiology, 31–32, 114, 210, 241, 291
Piper, Leonora, 7–11, 13–14, 21, 30, 59, 72–73, 100, 104, 143, 155, 161–162, 164–169, 171–175, 177–179, 181–193, 195, 197, 211, 281–282, 325
Pitres, Albert, 43
planchette, 45–46, 57, 108–109, 111, 114–115, 120–123, 194, 214, 230, 278
Podmore, Frank, 6, 55, 59, 105, 137, 139, 207
poltergeist, 214
Polynesia, 235
positivism, 16, 258, 300

possession (demonic, spirit), 61, 75, 115, 191, 195, 219, 225–231, 233–37, 239–49, 275, 298,
premonition, 95–96, 292
Principles of Psychology, 7–8, 30, 87, 137, 225, 253, 302
Proceedings of the American Society for Psychical Research 131, 155, 164, 321
Proceedings of the Society for Psychical Research, 6–7, 9–10, 16, 52, 53, 55, 56, 58, 59, 60, 62, 65, 69, 70, 74, 75, 77, 101, 102, 103, 104, 105, 108, 111, 127, 133, 161, 162, 171, 177, 179, 181, 187, 230, 241, 268, 269, 277, 309
psychic phenomena, 11–12, 17, 51, 143, 171, 259
psychical research, 5–7, 9–10, 12–13, 15–17, 19–23, 25–27, 29–30, 33, 51–55, 57, 59, 61, 63, 65, 67, 69–70, 74, 76–77, 81–83, 85, 87, 90, 93–96, 99, 101–105, 107, 127, 131–133, 137–138, 143, 155, 161, 164, 171–172, 177, 179–181, 199, 205–206, 216–217, 225, 233, 240–241, 247–248, 253–254, 267, 281–282, 309, 313–314, 321, 325–326
Psychological Review, 81, 99, 171, 236
psychology, 5–9, 12–15, 17, 19–20, 22, 27, 29–32, 57–58, 73, 81, 87–88, 111, 131, 137, 158, 175, 180, 190, 225, 227, 239, 253–254, 257–258, 265, 268–269, 278, 283, 286, 292, 302, 310
psychometry, 196

R

Rankin, Henry W., 236–237, 240
rappings (spirit), 214
Rayleigh, Lord John William Strutt, 5
Rector (spirit control), 183, 194, 211
reincarnation, 117, 283
religion, 2, 9, 16, 19, 87–88, 143, 233, 242, 248, 282, 315–318
Report on the Census of Hallucinations, 6, 72, 83
Richet, Charles, 6, 16, 52, 55, 103, 104
Roff, Mary, 227–229
romanticism, 76–77, 175, 212, 213

S

Sachs, Bernard, 240, 242
Salem, 75, 244–245
Savage, Rev. Minot J., 155, 164
Schiaparelli, Giovanni, 207
Schiller, F. C. S., 175, 294, 309, 311
Science (journal), 69, 177
Scribner's Magazine, 239
senses, 8, 39, 73, 88–89, 92, 95, 219, 272, 293
Sidgwick, Eleanor, 5–6, 11, 52, 55, 56, 58, 59, 103, 214
Sidgwick, Henry, 5–6, 11, 52, 72, 83–84, 103, 182, 206–207
skepticism, 7, 11, 15, 17, 56, 69, 72, 81, 94, 161, 166, 199
sleep, 7, 10, 38–40, 47, 49, 64, 91, 100, 104, 109, 112–114, 134, 147–149, 241, 270, 272, 290–291, 298
Smith, George Albert, 56, 103, 109, 114
Smith, William L. 101, 108, 119
Society for Psychical Research, 5–15, 16, 21, 26, 51–55, 59, 61–62, 69–70, 77, 81, 83, 90, 91, 93, 94, 101–105, 127, 131, 133, 155, 161, 164, 171–172, 177, 179, 181, 199, 206, 207, 209, 211, 217, 240, 282, 309, 313, 321, 325

INDEX

somnambulism, 38–39, 48, 95, 134, 270, 310

soul, 3–4, 25, 94–96, 100, 162, 180, 219, 225, 253–265, 273–274, 282, 287–288, 290, 294, 301–302, 309, 315, 317, 322–323, 325, 329

Spencer, Herbert, 16, 304

spirit-world (*see also*, heaven, Summerland), 214, 278

spirits, 1, 9, 14, 19, 118, 157, 163–165, 175, 181, 184–185, 187, 189–191, 193–196, 206, 211, 214, 221, 227, 236, 243–244, 246, 248, 273, 275, 278, 280, 294

spiritual body, 303

spiritualism, spiritualists, 5, 8, 11, 13-17, 90, 159, 207, 211–212, 218, 226–27, 228, 240, 245, 256–57, 316

Stevens, E. Winchester, 227, 229

Stevenson, R. L., 298, 311

Stewart, Balfour, 52, 56, 302

subconscious, 5, 8, 41, 43, 47, 59, 64–65, 91, 145, 189, 191, 214, 218–219, 316

subliminal, 8, 60, 63–64, 67, 75, 95–96, 134, 144–145, 172, 174–175, 185–186, 190, 193, 236, 268–275, 277–279, 309, 316, 323

suggestibility, 46, 241

suicidality, 67, 212

Summerland (*see also*, spirit world), 115, 214, 227

supernaturalism, 1–2, 16, 22, 207, 314–316

survival hypothesis, 8-9, 16, 25, 143, 267-280, 282, 314ff

Swedenborg, Emanuel, 220, 293

T

table-turning, 199-202, 218, 276

telekinesis, 273, 276

telepathy, 5, 8, 10–11, 25, 55-56, 61-62, 71, 73, 83, 95, 97, 99–101, 103–105, 107, 119, 124, 126–127, 133, 140, 141, 143, 158, 162, 166l, 167, 173–174, 184, 189–190, 209, 214, 220, 225, 242, 265, 270, 271, 274–275, 278

telesthesia, 274, 278

Tertium Quid, 55, 319

Theosophy, 61-63, 287

thought-transference, see telepathy

Times (newspaper) 59

touch, sense of, 36-37, 38, 43, 58, 306

trance, 7–8, 10, 12–13, 29, 31, 33, 35–40, 43–48, 50, 57, 59–60, 62–63, 65, 73, 94–95, 105, 108, 111, 114–115, 128–129, 133, 140, 155–159, 161, 163–169, 171–175, 177–178, 182–186, 188, 194–196, 214, 225–230, 233, 237, 243, 245, 270–271, 274

transcendental idealism, 305, 315

transmission-theory of consciousness, 282, 292–294, 302, 305

trauma, 10, 131

U

United States of America, 65, 245

V

Vedanta, 316

Vennum, Lurancy, 227–228

veridical cases, 6-8, 10–12, 57-58, 62–63, 72, 83–85, 104-05, 138–41, 151, 184, 188, 192, 195, 197, 213, 270, 273

visions, 11–12, 59, 292

W

Wallace, Alfred Russel, 11–12, 52
Wang-mu (Chinese deity), 236
Ward, James, 143
"Watseka Wonder", 225, 227
Wayland, Francis, 262
Wedgwood, Hensleigh, 52
Wendell, Barrett, 245
Wesley, John, 75
West Indies, 245
white crow analogy, 73
Wingfield, Kate, 102
Winsor, Anna, 111
witches, witchcraft, 19, 34, 56, 75,
    82, 94, 139–40, 234, 239, 243–45
Wundt, Wilhelm, 12, 15, 298, 311
Wyman, Jeffries, 209

X

X, Miss, 59, 72, 102, 167
xenoglossy, 109, 113, 116, 192, 248

www.ingramcontent.com/pod-product-compliance
Lightning Source LLC
Chambersburg PA
CBHW020323170426
43200CB00006B/251